GUIDE TO THE COMMERCIAL AGENTS REGULATIONS

Guide to the Commercial Agents Regulations

FERGUS RANDOLPH
and
JONATHAN DAVEY

with chapters on French
and German Agency Law
Contributed by Séverine Sainter,
Maitrise en droit, LLM, Phd
and Alf Aretz

·HART·
PUBLISHING

OXFORD – PORTLAND, OREGON
2003

Hart Publishing
Oxford and Portland, Oregon

Published in North America (US and Canada) by
Hart Publishing c/o
International Specialized Book Services
5804 NE Hassalo Street
Portland, Oregon
97213-3644
USA

Hart Publishing is a specialist legal publisher based in Oxford, England.
To order further copies of this book or to request a list of other
publications please write to:

Hart Publishing, Salter's Boatyard, Folly Bridge,
Abingdon Road, Oxford OX1 4LB
Telephone: +44 (0)1865 245533 or Fax: +44 (0)1865 794882
e-mail: mail@hartpub.co.uk
WEBSITE: http//www.hartpub.co.uk

British Library Cataloguing in Publication Data
Data Available
ISBN 1–84113–156–3 (paperback)

Typeset by Hope Services (Abingdon) Ltd.
Printed and bound in Great Britain on acid-free paper by
Biddles Ltd, *www.biddles.co.uk*

Contents

Table of Cases

EUROPEAN

European Court of Justice

UNITED KINGDOM

FRANCE

Table of Legislation

EUROPEAN

NATIONAL LEGISLATION

Belgium

Belgian Commercial Agency Law

France

Germany

Statutory Instruments

1

Introduction

1.1 THE NEW RULES

UNTIL THE START of 1994 the relationship between agents and their principals was not subject to any specific legislation in the UK. Other EC countries, notably France, Germany and Italy, have however provided statutory protection to agents for many years. There was a feeling that the different levels of protection afforded to agents by the different systems of law within the EC might disadvantage businesses in some areas of the EC or result in distortions of competition.

For these reasons specific rules in the form of an EC directive were proposed, requiring EC member states to change their systems of law so as to provide a uniform level of protection for commercial agents. These proposals were the subject of lengthy and detailed negotiation and comment within the UK and in other EC member states before Directive 86/653 ('the Directive') was finally adopted in 1986.

It is the Directive, and the Commercial Agents (Council Directive) Regulations 1993 (as amended)[1] ('the Regulations') which implement the Directive into English law, which are the specific subject of this work. A copy of the Regulations as amended, together with the Directive, can be found at Appendix 1 and 2 respectively. There is separate implementing legislation for Northern Ireland.[2]

1.2 WHY ARE THEY IMPORTANT?

The Regulations are important because they mark a fundamental change in English law relating to agents. In particular, the Regulations give the following new rights to agents:

—a right to compensation or to an indemnity payment when the agreement comes to an end (even where this is as a result of the death, disability or retirement of the agent);

---

[1] SI 1993/3053: these regulations have been amended twice: first by the Commercial Agents (Council Directive) (Amendment) Regulations 1993 (SI 1993/3173) and secondly by the Commercial Agents (Council Directive) (Amendment) Regulations 1998 (SI 1998/2868). The latter amended the provisions of the regulations dealing with jurisdictional maters following representations from the European Commission. See further ch 4, para 406.

[2] SR 1993/483.

—a right to be paid commission in certain circumstances even where the principal's contract with the customer has not been concluded;

—a right to commission on certain transactions in circumstances where the existing agency agreement does not give the right to commission;

—a right to commission on transactions concluded after the agency agreement has terminated in some cases;

—a right to a written statement of the terms of the agency contract; and

—a right to extracts from the principal's books of account to check the amounts of commission due.

1.3 IMPLEMENTATION

Because of the extent of change, whilst most other member states were obliged to implement the Directive by 1 January 1990, both the UK and Ireland were granted an extension to 1 January 1994, to implement the Directive. The Regulations duly came into force on 1 January 1994 and implement the Directive into English law from that date.

1.4 OUTLINE OF THIS WORK

Chapter 2 examines the European dimension to the Regulations and Chapter 3 examines the approach and direction taken by the UK Government in implementing the Directive into English law through the making of the Regulations. These chapters are necessary in order to understand fully the Regulations. Chapters 4–9 then examine the provisions of the Regulations in detail. The remainder of this chapter deals with two issues:

—the various strategies (including the appointment of agents) available to a business looking to expand sales, either within the UK or abroad; and

—a brief overview of the English law of agency prior to the coming into force of the Regulations.

This book states the law as at 1 July 2002, unless otherwise stated.

BUSINESS DEVELOPMENT STRATEGIES

1.5 POSSIBLE STRATEGIES

For any business looking to expand operations within the UK or abroad, a variety of business development strategies are available. These choices need to be reviewed at this stage since the Regulations are likely to influence the decision.

Such strategies might include:

—the appointment of one or more distributors or agents, whether on an exclusive or non-exclusive basis;
—the licensing of intellectual property rights, where relevant;
—the establishment of a local branch including manufacturing and/or distribution facilities to be owned by the business itself and the employment of locally based personnel;
—the employment of a local sales person; or
—the acquisition of an undertaking involved in the relevant business in the territory concerned.

1.6 WHAT ARE THE KEY DETERMINING FACTORS?

The above is not an exhaustive list, but in reality several of these potential strategies may not be viable for any particular business for a number of reasons, including the following:

—cost (particularly where the establishment of a branch or the acquisition of another undertaking is proposed);
—the absence of suitable intellectual property rights for licensing;
—a desire to retain control over prices and terms, or conversely a desire to avoid bad debt risk in respect of new customers, particularly where those customers are overseas;
—taxation considerations (including import duties and where appropriate taxation payable by an employer)—a detailed treatment of taxation issues is beyond the scope of this book;
—local and industry customs and customer preferences;
—other local legislation (for example, protective local employment laws): some countries, for example Belgium, grant statutory protection to distributors which may include substantial compensation on termination.

So, for example, a business engaged in the textile industry may find that its customers expect to deal with a local agent rather than a distributor or employee and may therefore be inclined to appoint an agent. Similarly, a business engaged in the provision of high value items of heavy industrial equipment may effectively be forced to appoint agents since no appointee will be prepared to accept bad debt risk, the cost of insurance or the potential liability resulting from customer claims for late delivery or defective goods.

As is explained below, one of the principal differences between an agent and a distributor is that the distributor sells goods for his own account and in his own name. Therefore, any contractual claims will be made by the customer against the distributor. The distributor may be able to claim against the supplier, but the terms of the contract with the supplier may restrict the distributor's ability to do so.

Conversely, a large multi-national undertaking may wish to retain control of local activities and may not find the significant costs involved in establishing a branch or 'green field' operation or effecting a major acquisition prohibitive. For the same reasons, a very small undertaking is likely to favour the licensing of intellectual property, franchising or the appointment of an agent or distributor.

1.7 AGENTS, DISTRIBUTORS AND EMPLOYEES: THE MAIN DISTINCTIONS

For many businesses, the choice referred to above is likely to come down to a choice between three options:

—the appointment of an agent;
—the appointment of a distributor; or
—the employment by the business itself of a salesperson, or dedicated sales force.

1.8 THE APPOINTOR'S PERSPECTIVE

A number of factors will affect this decision and frequently the appointor will identify the appropriate representative before deciding the basis of appointment. For the appointor the key issues are likely to be as follows:

—taxation;
—the absence or otherwise of laws protecting employees in respect of unfair dismissal and redundancy;
—a desire to have direct contact with customers and to decide upon prices and other terms;
—a willingness or otherwise to accept bad debt risk;
—the nature of the products concerned and in particular their value, and the need for servicing, maintenance and support facilities;
—the appointor's knowledge of the customers concerned and their creditworthiness;
—cost, particularly at the outset: an employee is likely to be paid a salary from appointment, whereas an agent will only receive commission upon any sales effected and a distributor will be remunerated by way of the margin which it adds to prices charged by the appointor; and
—competition law: generally restrictive terms in agreements with agents who are an integral part of the appointor's business may be disregarded for the purposes of EC competition law but (in particular) if the parties are considering unusual restrictions or the agent has other businesses then the competition law issues should be considered further. For a more detailed consideration of these issues, see generally the *Flemish Travel Agents*[3] and *Pittsburgh Corning Europe*[4]

---

[3] [1989] 4 CMLR 213.
[4] [1973] CMLR D2.

decisions and the Guidance Note to the new block exemption on vertical restraints.[5] The latter deals in detail with the distinction between an agent who is a mere shadow of his principal and an agent who is an independent economic actor. The Guidance Note states that the determinative factor in assessing whether Article 81(1) of the EC Treaty is applicable to an agency relationship is the financial and commercial risk borne by the agent in relation to the contracts concluded under the agency agreement. Only in the case of an independent economic actor is EC competition law potentially applicable to agency agreements. Competition law issues (and in particular compliance with the relevant EC block exemption on vertical restraints[6]) generally require more detailed consideration in the case of distributors. As regards UK competition law, following the coming into force of the Competition Act 1998 on 1 March 2000, the position in the UK will mirror that at Community level by virtue of the system of 'parallel exemption' and the requirement that UK courts and authorities 'have regard to' decisions of the Commission, including the above-mentioned Guidelines.

1.9 THE APPOINTEE'S PERSPECTIVE

For the appointee, the principal issues will be as follows:

—A distributor determines prices and other terms of business, but bears bad debt risk. The appointor may oblige a distributor to hold stocks and to provide after-sales or maintenance services.
—An agent takes less commercial risk. Generally it is the appointor who bears the bad debt risk , but the agent will not usually have the power to set prices or terms of business.
—An employee will be much more closely bound in to the appointor's business and generally is obliged not to work on behalf of third parties. Although it is possible as a matter of English law to remunerate an employee wholly or partly on a 'commission' basis, an employee who is paid a fixed salary may be better remunerated during the early part of the appointment: employees will generally not be as generously remunerated when a high level of sales is generated.

1.10 HOW HAVE THE REGULATIONS AFFECTED THESE CHOICES?

The Regulations are a new factor which expanding businesses will need to take into account in deciding between the various business development strategies referred to above. For those businesses which are forced by commercial considerations to appoint agents, the Regulations will simply amount to an unavoidable additional burden and the resulting costs will need to be taken into account, for instance, in

---

[5] [1999] OJ C270/42: 24 September 1999.
[6] Regulation 2790/99; [1999] OJ L336/21.

deciding commission rates. For a business which is able to choose between the various options, the Regulations will be a factor dissuading it from utilising agents as opposed to appointing distributors or an employed sales representative, or establishing a local branch.

Prior to their implementation, the Regulations encouraged businesses which already utilised the services of agents to reconsider the terms of appointment, and indeed the utilisation of agents in general. Although no firm data is available on this point, the anecdotal experience of the authors suggests that prior to 1 January 1994 a large number of businesses reconsidered the terms of appointment of agents and either amended those terms so as to reflect best practice in the light of the Regulations, or dismissed agents prior to that date, reverting either to the use of an employed sales force or to the use of distributors. This issue and the question of the alternatives to the appointment of an agent generally are considered in further detail below.

Conversely the potential appointee is likely to find the rights created by the Regulations attractive.

BRIEF INTRODUCTION TO THE ENGLISH LAW OF AGENCY

1.11 GENERAL

A detailed treatment of the English law of agency is beyond the scope of this work. Reference should be made to one of the comprehensive works listed in the bibliography. Readers who are not familiar with this area of the law may find a brief overview of assistance.

1.12 WHAT DOES THE WORD 'AGENT' MEAN?

The term 'agent' can be used to describe two different types of representative as follows:

—a 'sales' agent: a sales agent has authority to bind the appointor to contracts with third parties; thus, if a sales agent agrees prices and terms with a customer, those prices and terms will bind the appointor and a contract will come into place between the appointor and the customer;
—a 'marketing' agent: a marketing agent does not have power to bind the appointor and merely acts as a channel of communication between appointor and customer, feeding enquiries back to the appointor who decides on the price and terms to be quoted, communicating these to the customer through the marketing agent.

Although 'sales' agents are a common feature in some areas of commerce, in general agents are almost always 'marketing' agents (see the Law Commission

Report, p 40, a copy of which is at Appendix 3). As will be seen in chapter 5, this fact gives rise to an immediate difficulty of interpretation when reviewing the Regulations.

It should also be noted that in certain situations, an entity can be called an agent, even appointed as such under a written agreement, and yet actually operate as an independent contractor or distributor. Courts in the UK will have regard to all relevant circumstances when determining the position.[7]

1.13 CAN THE AGENT BIND THE APPOINTOR TO CONTRACTS?

Because the majority of commercial agents are 'marketing' agents, it is normal for the agency contract to stipulate that the agent does not have any power to bind the appointor to contracts.

An agent may have authority to bind the appointor:

—as a result of an agreement between the agent and the appointor; or
—by implication as a result of the nature of the relationship between, or the conduct of, appointor and agent; or
—by way of 'apparent authority' (even if the agent has not actually been given any authority to act) where the appointor has acted in such a way as to represent to third parties dealing with the agent that the agent does have authority to act on the appointor's behalf.

There are other situations in which an agency relationship may arise but these are not frequently relevant in practice (see generally *Bowstead and Reynolds Agency* 17th edn, (London, Sweet & Maxwell, 2001), chapter 2).

The agent may have this 'apparent authority' even where the contract between appointor and agent states that the agent is to have no authority whatsoever: it is a fundamental principle of English law that a contract only creates rights and obligations between the parties to it. Unless the third party is aware that the agent has no authority, the appointor will not be able to rely on that fact against the third party. Thus, even where the contract expressly denies any authority, the appointor must be careful in his dealings with the agent and others not to invest the agent with the appearance of authority. To some extent, it may be impossible to avoid liability for the agent's acts in the appointor's name. In addition, even if there is no authority, the agent will be closely associated with the appointor's products in the minds of customers. For all of these reasons, it is vital that the appointor knows and trusts the agent.

---

[7] For recent authorities on this issue, see *AMB Imballagi Plastici SRL v Pacflex Ltd* [1999] All ER (Comm) 249 and *Mercantile International Group plc v Chuan Soon Huat Industrial Group Limited* [2002] 1 All ER (Comm) 788.

1.14 THE RELATIONSHIP WITH THE CUSTOMER

Another general principle of the English law of agency is that where, through the efforts of the agent, a contract arises between the appointor and the third party (or customer), the agent generally is not a party to that contract. Although there are exceptions to this general rule, the agent normally has no rights under that contract, nor can the agent be sued by the third party in respect of that contract. For exceptions to this general rule, see one of the comprehensive texts on the English law of agency referred to in the bibliography.

The Contracts (Rights of Third Parties) Act 1999 makes it possible to give rights under a contract to a person who is not a party to it. This is unlikely to be of relevance to commercial agency relationships.

1.15 AGENT'S DUTIES AND RIGHTS

Generally, English law has taken the view that the appointor is the person who requires protection against the agent's wrongful acts, rather than vice versa. Thus, the majority of duties which exist as a matter of the common law between the parties to an agency agreement fall on the agent. The appointor however is generally obliged to indemnify the agent against all liabilities reasonably incurred by the agent in acting within the scope of its authority (if any). It is thus normal for agreements appointing commercial agents to stipulate that the agent will pay all the expenses of the agency, or to set out expressly which specific expenses are to be paid by the appointor.

An agent is entitled to a lien (that is, a legal right to retain possession of goods) in respect of all property of the appointor which has come into the possession of the agent in its capacity as agent, until all of the agent's legitimate claims against the appointor are satisfied.

For the reasons mentioned above, the law implies a large number of duties upon the agent towards the appointor. An agent's relationship with the appointor is characterised by common law as a 'fiduciary' relationship, that is a close relationship of trust imposing upon the agent duties to act in the interests of the appointor and in good faith. Thus the agent is bound to act in accordance with the terms of its contract with the appointor and must not exceed its authority. The agent must carry out its duties with reasonable dispatch and must use due skill and care in carrying them out. Because of its fiduciary relationship to the appointor, the agent must not allow itself to remain in a position where its own personal interests and those of the appointor conflict, without disclosing this to the appointor. For the same reason the agent is not entitled to make secret profits when acting as agent.

Prior to the coming into force of the Regulations, an agent had no general legal right to receive commission, nor was an agent entitled to any minimum period of notice prior to termination of the agency agreement. Further, the agent was not entitled to any compensation or any other payment on termination in the absence of breach of contract.

CHOICE OF LAW AND JURISDICTION

1.16 OVERVIEW

It is always advisable to include an express clause dealing with issues of choice of law and jurisdiction in any written agreement, particularly where there is a 'foreign' element. Because they have different legal systems Northern Ireland, Scotland, the Channel Islands and the Isle of Man are 'foreign countries' for this purposes. It should be noted that this work deals only with law as it applies to England and Wales. The Regulations also apply to Scotland and, as mentioned above, a separate implementing instrument (SR 1993/483) implements the directive in respect of Northern Ireland. In so far as Northern Irish or Scottish law or the law of another jurisdiction may apply to the arrangements under consideration, reference should be made to an appropriate work on the law of agency in that jurisdiction, and to any specific guidance available on the implementation of the Directive in that jurisdiction.

Brief comment on choice of law and jurisdiction is set out here; for more detailed treatment, reference should be made to one of the standard works listed in the bibliography. It should be noted that the questions of governing law and applicable jurisdiction are separate; it is quite possible for English law to apply but for the French courts to have jurisdiction and vice versa.

Generally, where the parties are domiciled in EC member states, a bona fide choice of law expressed in the contract will be effective and any express choice of jurisdiction will be deemed to be an exclusive choice. When however one of the parties is not domiciled in the EU, even a *bona fide* choice of non-EU member state law may not be effective, if the effect of such a choice is to deny the commercial agent the protection of Directive 86/653. In a recent decision of the European Court of Justice—Case C–381/98: *Ingmar v Eaton Leonard Technologies Inc.* of 9 November 2000[8]—it was held that provisions in Directive 86/653 relating to a commercial agent's right to post-termination indemnity or compensation were applicable even though the agreement specifically stated that the applicable law was that of California. The European Court of Justice held that a principal in such a situation could not evade his obligations under the Directive by the simple expedient of the choice of law clause in question.

Whether agents or distributors are being appointed, the appointor will normally insist that the law of the state in which it is domiciled will apply and that the courts in that state will have jurisdiction. The logic behind this insistence is that

[8] [2001] 1 CMLR 9

the alternative would be the appointment of agents or distributors in various states in each case on the basis of local law and jurisdiction. This might result in identical provisions in agreements with agents or distributors being interpreted in different ways by the courts of different states and this is clearly undesirable.

Further, where there is a dispute which involves the appointor and more than one agent or distributor, it may be that litigation in more than one state would be necessary in the absence of a single uniform choice of jurisdiction and this is likely to prove expensive and inconvenient for all parties.

The remainder of this work assumes that, having conducted the assessment process referred to above, the business concerned has decided to appoint an agent or agents, and that the arrangement will be governed by English law, with the English courts having jurisdiction to hear any disputes which may arise.

2

The European Dimension

THIS BOOK IS concerned with UK legislation on commercial agents. Why then should three whole chapters (this chapter and chapters 10 (German law) and 11 (French law)) be devoted to Europe and some of its specific legal frameworks? The reason for this is straightforward. The genesis of the UK legislation was and is European legislation in the form of Directive 86/653. In drafting the terms of the Directive, the Commission looked to existing French and (principally) German laws. In recognition of this, the English Courts[1] have shown themselves willing to look to national laws in other member states for assistance in interpretation and application.[2] For this reason, it is essential that the European dimension is examined if the Regulations are to be understood properly. Given the particular importance of French and German laws to the Directive, the authors have secured the assistance of French and German lawyers respectively to set out in two specific chapters in this book an overview of their relevant domestic laws.

Since the first edition of this book, the Maastricht Treaty has been succeeded by the Amsterdam Treaty. This has had a wide impact on the development of the European Union, most of which is outside the scope of this work. However, one result of the Amsterdam Treaty is the renumbering of the EC Treaty provisions. This has provided a boon for publishers and deep depression for many practitioners. Thus, the two EC Treaty articles which form the legal basis for Directive 86/653 have changed from Articles 57 and 100 to Articles 47 and 94 respectively. Future references in this work to these provisions will carry both the old and new numbers.

2.2 THE SCOPE OF THE EUROPEAN DIMENSION

In these days of constantly changing boundaries, one can be forgiven for not being completely sure of what exactly the European dimension comprises.

---

[1] And the Scots courts—*see King v Tunnock* [2000] EuLR 531.
[2] See, for example, *Moore v Piretta*,[1999] 1 All ER 174, a (poor) attempt to apply German law and the judge's earnest attempts to wrestle with the need to follow French law in *Duffen v Frabo* [2000] Lloyds Law Reports 180, 197–8.

At the time of writing, The European Union comprises 15 member states. These are Austria, Belgium, Denmark, Germany, Greece, Spain, Finland, France, Ireland, Italy, Luxembourg, Netherlands, Portugal, Sweden and the UK. However, the 'acquis communautaire' or the established law of the European Community covers more than just the 15 member states. Under terms of the agreement on the European Economic Area, which came into force on 1 January 1994, many of the legislative provisions of the European Community are to be binding upon the parties to the agreement. Aside from the EC member states, Iceland, Liechtenstein, Norway and Switzerland are parties to the agreement; Switzerland however voted against the agreement in December 1992. The effect of the agreement is that many EC provisions will now be applicable in the countries and the Directive is one of them—see Annex VII E of the agreement on the European Economic Area, where the Directive is specifically described as being applicable in the EEA states. It should also be recalled that there are a large number of countries involved in accession talks to join the European Union and it is widely expected that this first wave of successful applicant countries will include Poland, the Czech Republic, Hungary and Slovakia.

2.3 OVERVIEW OF THE COMMUNITY LEGISLATIVE ORDER

There are three forms of binding Community legislation: Regulations, decisions and directives.

2.4 REGULATIONS

Regulations have general application, are binding in their entirety and are directly applicable in all members states: see Article 249 of the EC Treaty (formerly Article 189). They thus become law in the member states without any need for implementation by the national legislatures.

Regulations may be of direct effect. This means that they may confer rights on individuals which the national courts must protect, but this will depend on whether the particular provisions relied upon are sufficiently precise and unconditional.

2.5 DECISIONS

Decisions are binding in their entirety upon those to whom they are addressed: see Article 249 of the EC Treaty. They are not intended to have general application but are directed at specific member states or specific undertakings.

Decisions may be of direct effect if unconditional and sufficiently precise. Those who may take advantage of this will be not only those to whom the decision is addressed but also those affected by the decision: see Case 9/70: *Grad v Finanzamt Traunstein* [1970] ECR 825.[3] Where a decision is addressed to a member state, the same considerations, relevant to directives and set out below, will apply—see ¶2.6.

2.6 DIRECTIVES

Directives are binding as to the result to be achieved, on each member state to which they are addressed, but they leave to the national authorities the choice of form and methods: see Article 249 of the EC Treaty. They therefore do not have to be addressed to every member state, but if they are, they must now be published in the Official Journal: Article 191(2) of the EC Treaty—this provision merely translated what was long-standing practice into a formal duty. Usually member states are given a specified period within which to implement the provisions of any given directive. Thus, the UK and Ireland were given until 1 January 1994 to implement the provisions of the Directive: Article 22(3) Directive 86/653.

The issue of direct effect of directives is more complex than for Regulations, but should be examined because agents and principals may have rights pursuant to the Directive which must be safeguarded by the national courts. The reason for this complexity is that all directives are addressed to member states and therefore at first blush the issue of direct effect does not arise. However, the European Court of Justice has made clear that directives can be relied upon by individuals before the national courts in certain situations and that in any event, domestic legislation must be interpreted in the light of the relevant provisions of a given directive, thereby giving rise to the indirect direct effect of those provisions. Thus, in the present context, agents and principals may have rights arising from the provisions of Directive 86/653 which can be safeguarded in national courts through the mechanism of direct effect.

The general principle is that directives may have direct effect but only in certain respects. In other words, restrictions have been placed on the direct effect of directives, which are not present for Regulations. For example, directives are not capable of being directly effective between individuals (Case 152/84: *Marshall v Southampton South West Hampshire Area Health Authority* [1986] ECR 723). The only rights which may be relied upon are those which an individual has against the member state (or an emanation of that state) in question. The member state in this context can be acting as employer or public authority (Case C–188/89: *Foster & Ors v British Gas plc* [1990] ECR I–3313). Further, in order for an individual to be able to rely on a directive or individual provisions therein, the time-limit for implementation of the directive must have expired without the full and correct implementation of that directive (Case 148/78: *Publico Ministero v Ratti* [1979] ECR 1629). Finally, it should be noted that as with Regulations, the provisions

---

[3] See most recently in this connection, Case T–254/97: *Fruchthandelgesellschaft mbH Chemnitz v Commission*, 28 September 1999.

relied upon in a directive must be sufficiently precise and unconditional if they are to be directly effective.

Even where provisions in a directive are not directly effective or the question of direct effect does not arise, national courts must still interpret the national law implementing the directive in question in conformity with the terms of the directive implemented (Case 14/83: *Von Colson & Kamann v Land Nordrhein-Westfalen* [1984] ECR 1891). This is so even where the national implementing legislation was adopted prior to the directive in question (Case C–106/89: *Marleasing v La Comercial Internacional* [1990] ECR I–4135).

In a recent decision, the House of Lords confirmed that, although the *Marleasing* concept was confined to legislation and could not be extended to cover contracts made between individuals, nonetheless as a matter of English domestic law, national courts were obliged to interpret such agreements in the light of the relevant directive.[4]

2.7 INCORPORATION OF COMMUNITY LAW INTO THE UK LEGAL ORDER

The EEC Treaty, as it was called then, was incorporated into UK domestic law by the European Communities Act 1972. This Act came into force on 1 January 1973. Section 2(1) of the Act provides:

> All such rights, powers, liabilities, obligations and restrictions from time to time created or arising by or under the Treaties, and all such remedies and procedures from time to time provided for by or under the Treaties, as in accordance with the Treaties are without further enactment to be given legal effect or used in the UK shall be recognised and available in law, and be enforced, allowed and followed accordingly; and the expression 'enforceable Community right' and similar expressions shall be read as referring to one to which this sub-section applies.

The above provision should be read together with section 2(4) of the Act which makes it clear that in the event of a conflict between domestic and Community law, the latter should take precedence. Thus, the doctrine of the supremacy of Community law is enshrined in the UK legal order. Practically, this means that if the national provisions implementing the Directive conflict with those of the Directive itself, the national implementing provisions are to be ignored in favour of the Directive's provisions.

2.8 OVERVIEW OF REMEDIES AVAILABLE UNDER COMMUNITY LAW

Although the doctrine of direct effect provides that individuals may rely on Community rights before the national courts, the specific remedies available to

---

[4] See *White v White and the Motor Insurers' Bureau* [2001] 1 WLR 481.

enforce those rights are not prescribed by Community law. This is because the European Court has taken the view generally that the remedies to be available in the national courts are for the laws of the particular member states to determine (Case 33/76: *Rewe-Zentralfinanz eG & Rewe-Zentral A G v Landwirtschaftskammer für das Saarland* [1976] ECR 1989). The European Court has however stressed the need for effective remedies at the national level in order to protect Community law rights (Case C–213/89: *R v Secretary of State for Transport, ex parte Factortame* [1990] ECR 1–2433). It has also held recently that, as a matter of Community law, member states may be required to compensate individuals for damage caused by an infringement of Community law for which the member states are responsible (Cases C–6/90 and C–9/90: *Francovich, Bonifaci & Ors v Italy* [1991] ECR 1–5357).

In so far as the UK is concerned, the position is as follows: a distinction has been drawn by the courts between private and public law remedies.

2.9 PRIVATE LAW REMEDIES

In terms of private law claims, damages are available for breach of a directly effective provision of Community law, the cause of action being breach of statutory duty *(Garden Cottage Foods v Milk Marketing Board* [1984] AC 130).[5] It follows under English procedural law that, where such actions are brought, injunctions may also be sought and granted where damages will not be an adequate remedy *(Cutsforth v Mansfield Inns Ltd* [1986] 1 WLR 558)

2.10 PUBLIC LAW REMEDIES

In so far as concerns remedies for breach of Community law by a member state or an emanation thereof, the European Court of Justice has laid down the following guidelines:

—Liability for loss and damage caused to individuals as a result of breaches of Community law attributable to a national public authority constitutes a principle inherent in the system of the EC Treaty which gives rise to obligations on the part of the member states.
—It is for each member state to ensure that individuals obtain reparation for loss and damage caused to them by non-compliance with Community law, whichever public authority is responsible for the breach and whichever public authority is in principle, under the law of the member state concerned, responsible for making reparation.[6]
—In order for a member state to be required to make reparation for loss and damage caused to individuals as a result of breaches of Community law for which

[5] See the recent judgment of the ECJ in Case C–453/99: *Courage v Creehan* [2001] ECR 1–6297.
[6] See Case C–302/97: *Konle v Austria* [1999] ECR I–3099.

that state can be held responsible, three conditions must be met: the rule of law infringed must have been intended to confer rights on individuals, the breach must have been sufficiently serious and there must be a direct causal link between the breach and the loss or damage sustained.[7]

The House of Lords recently applied these guidelines when finding that the UK was liable in damages to a number of foreign, mainly Spanish fishermen for breaches of their fundamental Community law rights.[8]

2.11 RIGHTS AGAINST THE UK FOR FAILURE TO IMPLEMENT CORRECTLY THE DIRECTIVE

Despite the fact that the *Francovich* case was concerned with the total failure of a member state to implement a directive, it is clear that its findings are relevant to a situation in which a member state has failed to implement correctly a given directive. If an individual can show that the proper implementation of the directive would have led to the granting of rights to individuals, that these rights were identifiable from the provisions of the directive and that the damage suffered by the individual could be linked to the failure of the member state to implement correctly the directive, then that individual should be entitled to damages for the member state's actions. Thus, if the UK has incorrectly implemented the directive and if the conditions set out above are met then damages should be available.

It should be noted that no action has been taken by the Commission to bring legal proceedings against the UK for failure to implement the Directive properly. This does not mean that such action could not arise in the future, especially if the national courts were to interpret exclusion clauses such as those relating to secondary activities in a way which could be considered to be incompatible with the provisions of the Directive. It should also be noted that, following Commission intervention, the domestic legislation implementing the Directive was amended in so far as its scope was concerned.[9]

2.12 THE LEGISLATIVE BACKGROUND TO THE DIRECTIVE

As first sight, the need to analyse the legislative background to the Directive might not seem readily apparent. We are, after all, concerned with the finished Directive. Why is it necessary to look at the early proposals and previous drafts? The need to do so becomes clear once the way in which Community law is interpreted is understood.

---

[7] See Joined Cases C–46/93 and C–48/93: *Brasserie du Pecheur and Factortame* [1996] ECR I–1029.
[8] See *R v Secretary of State for Transport, ex parte Factortame and Others* [2000] EuLR 40.
[9] See ch 4.

Community law is interpreted in a contextual and purposive way, rather than literally. The reason for this is twofold. First, because Community legislation is published and equally authentic in all the official languages of the EC (11 at present), and because translation is not an exact science, variations arise. It is essential in such cases that courts have the possibility to interpret the law freely rather than be tied to the literal interpretation of the text. Secondly, much EC legislation is expressed in less specific terms than would be the case normally with UK legislation.[10] Because of the lack of specificity, it is essential that the courts are able to reach their decisions on particular interpretations using as wide a basis as possible. The European courts defined the way in which EC law should be interpreted as follows:

> ... every provision of Community law must be placed in its context and interpreted in the light of the provisions of Community law as a whole, regard being had to the objectives thereof and to its state of evolution at the date on which the provision in question is to be applied (Case 283/81: *CILFIT v Italian Ministry of Health* [1982] ECR 3415, 3430).

In placing the directive in its context and in order to have regard to its objectives, an examination of *inter alia* the proposals and drafts of the Directive should therefore be undertaken. An in-depth analysis of individual provisions in the proposals and drafts will not be carried out here but rather in the relevant parts of chapters 5–9 inclusive, where they can be analysed in conjunction with the relevant provisions of the directive as adopted.

2.13 THE LEGISLATIVE CHRONOLOGY OF THE DIRECTIVE

The first formal proposal made by the Commission for a directive co-ordinating the laws of the member states relating to self-employed commercial agents was submitted to the Council of Ministers on 17 December 1976. To this proposal was appended a very useful Explanatory Memorandum from the European Commission. Despite the fact that the adopted Directive has changed markedly since this initial first formal proposal, nonetheless the Explanatory Memorandum is still of assistance in interpreting the more general aspects of the present Directive. Thus, for example, the Memorandum contrasts commercial agents with salaried or wage-earning commercial travellers; it makes clear that the eventual Directive should apply to situations not only including two or more member states, but also to those involving only a single member state; it also states that the eventual Directive should be seen in effect as a codification of the law. A copy of this document is at Appendix 3, appearing as an Annex to the Law Commission Report.

This proposal was then submitted by the Council to the Economic and Social Committee on 11 January 1977 for its opinion. This body has advisory status and,

---

[10] In the recent case of *King v Tunnock* [2000] EuLR 531, the Inner House of the Scottish Court of Session described some of the drafting of the Directive to be '. . . in the eyes of UK lawyers . . . at the best somewhat clumsy'.

pursuant to the EC Treaty, the Council must seek its opinion on *inter alia* matters relating to internal market harmonisation measures, of which the Directive is one. The Committee consists of representatives of the various categories of economic and social activity (Article 257 of the EC Treaty—formerly Article 193). In practice, it consists of three groups; employers, workers and others. The Committee issued its opinion on the Commission's proposals on 24 November 1977: [1978] OJ C59/31.

The Commission proposal was also submitted to the European Parliament for its opinion. This opinion was delivered and subsequently published on 9 October 1978: [1978] OJ C239/17. Despite the fact that the Parliament's opinion was also advisory, it has more power to affect proposed legislation than the Economic and Social Committee. This difference in importance can be seen by the fact that the Commission amended its original proposal to take into account more of the Parliament's suggested amendments ([1979] OJ C56/5) than those of the Economic and Social Committee's suggestions. The Commission's amended proposal was submitted to the Council on 29 January 1979. Thus, up to this stage, the legislative process had taken just over two years.

This momentum was then lost, for there was then a wait for nearly eight years before the final text was published as Council Directive 86/653 on 31 December 1986. Although the authors have not had sight of the Council Minutes, it is clear that most of this delay can be attributed to the fact that the member states were not agreed on the draft Directive and that as this period was prior to the Single European Act the differences could not be dealt with by qualified majority voting.

3

Development of the Regulations

3.1 INTRODUCTION—WHY CONSIDER THE DOMESTIC DRAFTING PROCESS?

CHAPTER 2 TRACED the drafting and development of the Directive up to the time of its adoption. This chapter traces ministerial thinking and the drafting of the Regulations following adoption of the Directive and may be of assistance to practitioners and others in understanding why certain provisions are included in the Regulations and why they are phrased as they are. As a note of caution, however, although the courts will look to drafts of the Directive to interpret its spirit and purpose, the English courts are not generally entitled to look at drafts or other documents which form part of the drafting process.

3.2 BEFORE THE DIRECTIVE

The 1977 House of Lords Select Committee Report (Appendix 4)

As will have been noted from the previous chapter, the original Commission proposal for a directive concerning commercial agents was submitted to the Council at the end of 1976. It was thus from that time that the member states, which comprise the Council, first became formally aware of the Commission's proposal. It is therefore not surprising that soon thereafter came the first response from the UK in the form of a House of Lords Select Committee Report dated 27 July 1977—Appendix 4 hereto. The purpose of the Report was to determine whether there was any justification in principle for introducing such a directive at all. The conclusion of the Select Committee was that there was no such justification. In particular, and based on evidence which had been presented to them,[1] the Committee found there was a 'variegated pattern of agencies' in the UK and that there was no justification to impose a single body of inflexible legal rules, such as those contained in the Directive, on such a pattern. The Committee felt that a better solution would be to provide flexibility which would enable the parties to an agency contract to arrange terms which suited their respective needs. The Committee was further of the view that if rules favouring commercial agents were imposed, then principals would find other means of selling. The Committee concluded by stating that it noted with concern a tendency by the Commission to interfere, in ways which were not

---

[1] Whose deponents included one Robert (better now known as Bob) Ayling, then the Solicitor to the DTI.

altogether judicious, with particular segments of the national legal systems. Such systems, or the segments thereof, had not come into existence by accident; rather they had arisen from the local circumstances, habits and sentiments of the people. Changes thereto should, in the Committee's opinion, only be effected with care and where real need was demonstrated.

The 1977 Law Commission Report (Appendix 3)

Following swiftly on from the above-mentioned House of Lords Select Committee Report, the Law Commission reported on the Commission's proposal in October 1977. The Report is not only of interest in so far as it comments on the draft Directive, but also in so far as concerns its annexes, which comprise the draft itself, the Commission's Explanatory Memorandum thereto[2] and a copy of the 1953 German law and the Report provisions which were at the basis of much of the Commission's proposal. These annexes, together with the Report, are reproduced at the end of this book.

As to the Law Commission's views on the Commission's proposal, perhaps unsurprisingly they do not differ markedly from those expressed by the House of Lords Select Committee. However, it does produce a very useful synthesis of German law and its links to the directive. Its main findings were as follows:

—The proposed legislation was intra vires the EC Treaty, in that it was possible to contend that differences in the laws of the member states relating to commercial agents did affect the functioning of the Common Market in that they inhibited the commercial agent's freedom of establishment within the Community and could interfere with the agent's freedom of movement of goods and services between member states.
—The term 'commercial agent' had no precise connotation in English law; it did not represent a category of persons who had a common legal characteristic.
—The provisions of the proposed Directive were clearly based on German commercial law and in particular sections 84 to 92c of the German Commercial Code; those sections related to a special category of agent who had to perform certain functions permanently in commerce and for a principal who had to be a standing client; the same sections made clear that a commercial agent was identifiable as a member of a particular social group with special social and economic needs, he was apparently a quasi-employee who whilst retaining some independence, was substantially dependent on his principal and therefore required protection.
—The goodwill indemnity provisions in the draft Directive reflected similar provisions in the German Commercial Code and were intended to compensate the agent for the fact that as a rule the agent's work increased the goodwill of the

---

[2] Referred to in ch 2, para 2.13.

principal and not that of the agent and that on termination of the agency, the principal derived a benefit from the accrued goodwill whilst the agent suffered a corresponding loss; as to this indemnity payment, the Law Commission stated that 'it is difficult to see why in general the agent should receive a payment, for which he has not bargained, when the contract terminates. This is particularly so where the agency contract is for a fixed period and makes no provision for such a payment.'

—The proposed Directive would not remove the uncertainties that existed over the content of commercial agents' rights; rather, the proposal was likely to create uncertainty whenever there was a conflict between the provisions of the Directive and what the parties had in fact agreed. The recurring theme was that even if the policy behind the proposal was sound, which was doubtful, its provisions were likely to produce great uncertainty across a very wide area.[3]

—The rules which the proposal purported to declare were full of uncertainties, gaps and inconsistencies and in many respects offended against basic principles of the English law of agency; the provisions depended for the operation on a corpus of law which was not stated in the Directive and their introduction would necessitate the distortion of the common law of agency and of other areas of commercial law.

Overall then, it can be seen that the UK establishment was not in favour of the Commission's proposal. However, as with many things, such opposition was not sufficient to block the proposal; all it did was delay it for over ten years.

3.3 AFTER THE DIRECTIVE

After the Directive was published on 31 December 1986, at least two important guidance notes were put out by the Department of Trade and Industry ('DTI') describing the provisions and indicating the UK Government's position to their implementation into domestic law. Although such guidance notes are not binding, they are of interest to practitioners. To that end, the two most important notes—those published in July 1987 and in 1994—appear at the end of this book in Appendix 5. A brief overview of the 1987 guidance notes will be given below. In so far as concerns the 1994 guidance notes, these will be referred to in later chapters when specific provisions are being analysed.

It could have been expected, given the relatively prompt production of the notes, that a draft of the Regulations would have been available in 1988, allowing a substantial period for consultation and redrafting, but a first draft was not available for public comment until May 1990.

No doubt submissions were received following the publication of the notes, but details of those responses have not been published.

---

[3] In this at least, the Law Commission has been proved to be correct, as an increasing number of frustrated practitioners can testify.

3.4 EFFECT OF THE DELAY

As already mentioned, the Directive is unclear in several important respects and the DTI noted the fundamental changes in the English law of agency which would result from implementation of the Directive. Although the DTI subsequently advised against acting on the basis of drafts (*Financial Times*, 15 December 1993), given the effective retrospectivity of the Regulations in various respects, it was inevitable that from the moment the Directive was adopted (or before that time), well-briefed clients and their advisers would be actively considering the terms of the Directive and its likely effect both in making the decisions considered in chapter 1 and in determining the likely costs of termination of agency relationships.

Given this, it is unfortunate that the time between the publication of the 1987 Note and the making of the Regulations themselves—a period of almost six and a half years—was not used to finalise the form of the Regulations and to implement them well in advance of the 1 January 1994 deadline with a long transitional period, so as to give principals and agents ample time to adjust their relations and to take the Regulations into account. It is likely that much of the uncertainty and ensuing litigation which resulted from the late introduction of the Regulations would have been avoided had this course been adopted. In the event, the Regulations were made on 7 December 1993 and laid before Parliament on the following day, a period of only three weeks before the date when they would apply to all new *and* existing agency agreements.

3.5 THE 1987 EXPLANATORY AND CONSULTATIVE NOTE

Much of the 1987 Note consists of a description of the terms of the Directive and this is not repeated here. However, Section C of the Note is of interest as it considers the various options allowed to member states by the Directive, these being as follows:

—Article 2(2) allows members states to exclude from the scope of the Regulations persons whose activities are deemed by national law to be 'secondary'. The DTI noted that there was not yet any such definition in UK law but that it was the government's intention to define and exclude such activities. Paragraph 51 stated that individuals whose activities as commercial agent were not their primary 'business' occupation and also individuals who sell from mail order catalogues were to be excluded. Although the Regulations deal expressly with the latter (see paragraph 5 of the Schedule) the remainder of the Schedule to the Regulations takes a different tack in that it looks at the purpose of the arrangement between agent and principal, rather than business activities as a whole.

—Article 4(3) dealing with the obligation on the principal to communicate with the agent regarding transactions procured by the latter. The Directive did not provide a specific option here, but the DTI noted that the government did not intend to stipulate that the principal must inform the agent of the execution of commercial transactions.

—Article 7(2) (right to commissions where the agent is either entrusted with or has an exclusive right to a specific geographical area or group of customers): the DTI noted that the government's initial preference was for the latter and the Regulations mirror this choice.

—Article 13(2): member stated are entitled pursuant to the Directive to provide that an agency contract is not valid unless evidenced in writing. The DTI invited comments from interested parties, but was clearly not inclined to stipulate that agency contracts must be in writing. In fact, this provision of the Directive is something of an oddity since questions as to the validity of the agency contract are most likely to arise when the agent wishes to claim compensation on termination; given that the purpose of the Directive is to protect agents, it is noteworthy that this provision of the Directive seems likely (where adopted by member states) to operate against the agent's interests.

—Article 15(3) (minimum periods of notice): member states were entitled to provide that in the fourth, fifth and sixth years, the minimum notice period would be four, five and six months respectively. The DTI noted that the government did not propose to take up this option since the three-month notice period would be sufficient. It would be open to the parties to agree longer periods if they wished to do so. Although the sufficiency of the three-month notice period is not questioned, it could be considered that the DTI's logic is somewhat flawed in that the whole purpose of much of the Directive is to override any written agreement on certain matters which might be made between principal and agent.

—Article 15(4) stipulates that where longer notice periods are agreed the notice period for the agent must not be longer than that for the principal. In fact there may be very good commercial reasons why the principal requires longer notice from the agent than he is required to give: for instance, in distant markets or in areas where consents and registrations are necessary for a new agent, the principal may require some time to find a suitable replacement agent and to deal with any necessary formalities. The same logic does not necessarily apply where the principal wishes to dispense with the agent's services: he may already have identified a suitable individual and started the necessary registration processes.

—Article 17 (the choice between the indemnity and compensation routes upon termination of the agency contract): the DTI noted that 'member states are required to include one of these options in their implementing legislation'. The note stated that the government favoured the compensatory route, but the Regulations in fact allow the parties to choose the indemnity route in their agreement and this possibility was only added in the final version of the draft Regulations.

—Article 17(2)(a), indent 2: this entitles member states to provide that the application or otherwise of a restraint of trade clause could be taken into account in deciding whether the payment of an indemnity was equitable. Again, the DTI merely requested views from interested parties. Although the indemnity option was subsequently incorporated in the Regulations, this option was never specifically included. There is however nothing in the Regulations which prevents a court taking this issue into account in deciding what is equitable.

These comments were largely confirmed by a minister in response to a question raised in the House of Commons in 1989 (*Hansard*, 15 March 1989, question answered by Humphrey Atkins, Chancellor of the Duchy of Lancaster). The minister also made it clear that the Regulations would not be made before 1992.

THE DEVELOPMENT OF THE DIRECTIVE AND THE REGULATIONS

3.6 THE FIRST DRAFT (CA.4/22/3/90)

Whilst it is not proposed to go through each provision of each of the drafts, there are interesting differences reflecting changes in thinking and approach between the two drafts and the Regulations and some of these are explored below:

—The draft contained a definition of 'quarter' for the purposes of payment of commission under what is now regulation 10(3), but the final form of the Regulations leaves it to the parties to determine the start and finish dates of quarters.
—There was a lengthy list of individuals who would not be considered to be commercial agents for the purposes of the Regulations. Secondary activities were described briefly in paragraph 2 (compare the tortuous provisions of the Schedule in the Regulations). Bizarrely, the first draft excluded from the definition of commercial agents persons who were wholly involved in other activities!
—The question of the territorial application of the Regulations and its interaction with choice of governing law and jurisdiction is a difficult issue. The first draft merely stated that the Regulations would apply to any agency contract whose applicable law was the law of England and Wales or Scotland and that the Regulations could apply to protect agents not established in a member state if the parties so agreed.[4]
—The draft attempted to recast the duties of principal and agent as set out in Articles 3 and 4 of the Directive.

---

[4] This issue has now been the subject of an amendment to the Regulations and case law—see ch 4, 4.6–4.15 below.

—Paragraph 7 stated that the question of whether there was customary remuneration in the absence of an agreement on commission was to be tested both in the area in which the commercial agent operates and in the area in which his office is situated.

—Transactions on which commission is due: the first draft omitted the wording from Article 7(1)(a) of the Directive regarding 'concluded as a result of his action' and replaced this with the words 'conclusion of the transaction was effectively caused by the act of the commercial agent'.

—The draft omitted the words 'as soon as and to the extent that' in Article 10 of the Directive: those words suggest that, where the contract between principal and third party requires delivery/payment by instalments, commission will also be payable by instalments.

—The draft replaced the word 'executed' which appears in Articles 10 and 11 of the Directive with the words 'carried out', which are no clearer.

—One of the most fascinating elements of the draft is paragraph 14. Chapter 8 deals with the question of the extent to which provisions of Articles 7–10 are mandatory or non-mandatory, but (contrary to the view of most writers on the subject and the DTI's own Guidance Note published in 1994) paragraph 14 stated that a term would be void insofar as it conflicted with paragraphs 11–13 (ie in its entirety)—these are the provisions mirroring Articles 10–12. Neither the Regulations nor the second draft make any reference to this issue.

—Compensation: paragraph 18 of the first draft differs in several important respects from the relevant provisions of Article 17 of the Directive. The problematic expression 'compensation for . . . damage' from the Directive was replaced with the words '[compensation] . . . for losses, liabilities, costs and expenses' which the agent has incurred. The difficulties raised by the former expression are referred to in chapter 9.

—Similarly, as regards the second paragraph and indents in Article 17(3), rather than being stated to be circumstances in which damage will be deemed to have occurred particularly, the draft stated that 'in particular the compensation shall take into account' the matters set out in those indents, but the indented expressions themselves are not faithfully reproduced, these amendments being an attempt to clarify words and expressions in the Directive which were of uncertain meaning.

—The draft did not reproduce faithfully the provisions of Article 18 of the Directive, attempting instead to state the situations in which compensation would be payable.

—The Directive's reference to default justifying immediate termination became a reference to breach entitling the principal to terminate under the general law and rather than merely referring to the death of the agent referred to frustration of the contract including the agent's death.

—Restraint of trade: this was more narrowly defined in the first draft and extended only to a clause in an agreement restricting the right of a commercial agent to act as a commercial agent following termination, whereas the Directive refers to an agreement restricting the business activities of a commercial agent. In addition, paragraph 19(b) of the first draft is not reflected in the Regulations—this stated that a restraint of trade clause would be valid only if it was reasonable from the point of view of the principal and the commercial agent and their common customers—perhaps an (inaccurate) attempt to summarise the English law on restraint of trade generally. In any event, the Directive and the Regulations state that other rules of national law which impose restrictions on the validity of restraint of trade clauses are unaffected. Therefore, even though a two-year covenant may be non-problematic from the point of view of the Directive and the Regulations, if it would be void by reason of the restraint of trade doctrine, then the relevant provisions of the Regulations and the Directive will not save it.

In almost all cases, the Regulations have reverted to the wording from the Directive, leaving it to the courts to determine the meaning of these words at the expense of litigants. This is one of the particular reasons why uncertainty is likely to persist notwithstanding the making of the Regulations and the DTI's Guidance Note.

The authors' view is that the DTI was discouraged from attempting to clarify by the *Francovich* decision referred to in chapter 2. Since it is established that in certain circumstances a failure to implement (and, seemingly, to implement properly) a directive can result in liability upon the member state concerned, the DTI may have decided that the risk of such actions would be reduced as much as possible by merely reflecting the wording of the Directive in the Regulations.

The danger is however that in so far as the English courts determine the meaning of unclear expressions in the Regulations and this diverges from any subsequent interpretation by the European Court of Justice, the government is likely to be held to have failed to implement correctly in any event and will therefore be open, arguably, to actions based upon the *Francovich* principle. The authors suggest that it would have been advisable for the DTI to conduct detailed discussions with the Commission with a view to ascertaining the Commission's view and minimising this risk. Whether such discussions took place is not known.

3.7 THE SECOND DRAFT

This was issued under cover of a letter of 4 June 1993. The covering letter stated that the second draft (CAREGS02.S17), took into account comments received during the initial consultation. The reason for the delay in excess of three years in producing this revised draft is not clear, but whereas the period for consultation on the first draft was in excess of seven months, the consultation period on the second draft was only just over seven weeks.

The principal features of the second draft were as follows:

—The definition of commercial agent expressly alluded to the agent who acted as agent in respect of services, but it was not clear from the draft whether this would exclude agents who acted as agent in respect of any services whatsoever, or would only exclude the services element of the contract.

—Definitions of 'agency contract', 'commission', 'goods', 'quarter' and 'restraint of trade clause' were included. Only definitions of 'commission' and 'restraint of trade clause' have survived to the Regulations. The definition of goods was different from that in the first draft, but the reason for this is not clear.

—Governing law and jurisdiction: paragraph 3 of the first draft was deleted and replaced with a simple statement that the Regulations extend to Great Britain (compare regulations 1(2) and 1(3)). In addition, a new paragraph 23 was added stating that where the agreement did not require the agent to carry on any activity on behalf of his principal within the EC, the Regulations would not apply unless the parties agreed otherwise. This seemed to be a logical compromise between the government's clear antipathy towards the Directive and the aim of harmonising UK laws with the laws of other member states. Paragraph 23 does not appear in the Regulations.

—Derogation: paragraph 5 was new and set out in detail those provisions from which derogation was not permitted. It stated that terms which were inconsistent with paragraph 3 and 4 (duties of principal and agent) would be void and that certain other provisions could not be excluded, varied or restricted to the detriment of the agent. Although the list of such provisions is unsurprising in itself, it provides a pointer to the question (discussed in chapter 8) of the ability to exclude, for instance, the terms of Articles 7 and 8 of the Directive. Certainly, the suggestion in the second draft is that Articles 7 and 8 are capable of exclusion. Article 5 is also relevant to the question of the status of inconsistent terms.

—Paragraph 12 included a definition of 'books and papers' in connection with the agent's rights to review the principal's records.

—Articles 21 and 22 of the second draft were completely new. Paragraph 21 stated that a contract could be entered into before 1 January 'in terms which are in accordance with these regulations' (presumably entitling the parties to incorporate the Regulations into their contract even before the implementation date), stating that nothing in the Regulations would affect the rights and liabilities of an agent or principal which had accrued before 1 January 1994 (but seemingly leaving it open to a court to calculate the notice period by reference to the total duration of the contract and look to the period before 1 January in calculating compensation). Paragraph 21 also stated that the Regulations would apply after 1 January 1994 to a contract made before that date and that accordingly provisions which were less favourable than the mandatory provisions of the second draft were to be read as if they were in accordance with the appropriate regulation or if they could not be so read would be void.

As with the first draft, the Regulations largely forsake the novel provisions of the second draft in favour of tracing the wording from the Directive.

On 17 September 1993, the DTI circulated its Compliance Cost Assessment relating to the Regulations. This procedure is followed for all new legislation and seeks to identify the likely cost to business of seeking advice upon and complying with new legislation.

The covering letter stated that it was likely that the main changes to be made from the second draft would be for reasons of clarity rather than changes of substance. The letter sought comments on likely costs and also included some comments on other aspects of the Regulations in 'question and answer' format. A final form of the Compliance Cost Assessment was produced in December 1993.

The DTI expected that the Regulations would affect up to 1,500 principals and up to 20,000 agency businesses in the UK. The Compliance Cost Assessment indicated that there were three areas of difficulty namely applicable law, activities regarded as secondary and the compensation option. According to the Compliance Cost Assessment, the 1984 Business Statistics Office enquiry into the distributive and service trades recorded turnover for agents of £375 million from 1,399 businesses. The DTI received representations from an organisation representing agents putting the estimate of total turnover figures for agents to be £8 billion. The DTI's conclusion was that commission agency in manufactured goods seemed to represent between one and three per cent of total wholesaling.

On the question of costs, the Compliance Cost Assessment estimated that the average cost to principals per agent in terms of legal fees and staff costs in implementing the Regulations would be between £500 and £9,000 and the 'recurrent costs per year' of compliance would include legal fees and staff costs of between £450 and £1,100 per annum and compensation of between £5,000 and £40,000 per annum.

Although the question of indemnity and compensation is dealt with in detail below, the Compliance Cost Assessment stated that the figures for compensation related to premature termination of fixed-term and open-ended contracts. Surprisingly, it stated that in many instances no compensation would be necessary where the contract was allowed to run its full term. It went on to say that an agency contract for an agent with a large annual commission whose contract was terminated at or near the end of its term was likely to receive compensation in the lower range but conversely an agent with a low commission whose contract was terminated at or near commencement would receive compensation in the higher range.

The authors would question the logic and validity of all these suggestions. Although the Compliance Cost Assessment referred to the introduction of the indemnity option, it gave no clues as to which was likely to be the less expensive.

The DTI stated that it intended to carry out a survey of businesses asking about compliance towards the end of 1994. The Directive provides for a review of the compensation and indemnity provision within eight years of the date of notification of the Directive. This took place and resulted in a Commission Report in 1996.[5] This Report is referred to in detail in chapter 9 below.

---

[5] *Report on the Application of Art 17 of Council Directive on the Co-ordination of the Laws of the Member States Relating to Self-employed Commercial Agents* (Cm 364, 1996; final 23 July 1996).

4

Regulation 1—Commencement and Applicable Law

4.1 OUTLINE

THIS CHAPTER COVERS the crucial issues relating to the application of the Regulations to agency agreements entered into before 1 January 1994, ie before the Regulations themselves came into force, as well as the territorial scope of the Regulations. For example: what is the position of an agent carrying out activities not only in Great Britain but also in other member states of the European Union; do the Regulations apply to agents whose activities are carried on entirely outside the European Union?

4.2 WHEN DID THE REGULATIONS COME INTO FORCE?

Regulation 1(1) states that the Regulations come into force on 1 January 1994. This needs to be read in conjunction with regulation 23 which deals with the position of contracts which were in existence before that date. The important questions are as follows:

—Do the Regulations apply to contracts made before 1 January 1994?
—In calculating the agent's entitlement to notice, to commissions and to compensation, to what extent is the period before 1 January 1994 to be taken into account?
—What is the status of agreements terminated before 1 January 1994?

4.3 DO THE REGULATIONS APPLY TO CONTRACTS MADE BEFORE 1 JANUARY 1994?

Regulation 23(1) makes it clear that the regulations apply after 1 January 1994 to a pre-existing contract and that provisions in any such agreement inconsistent with the Directive will be ineffective. Many agency contracts made before the Regulations came into force stipulate that no compensation will be payable upon termination, largely in an attempt to avoid the application of protective rules in continental jurisdictions. In most if not all cases, this attempt at exclusion was unlikely to be effective before a court in a continental jurisdiction and will now be ineffective before the English courts.

To this extent, the Regulations apply retrospectively: even where a contract was entered into before the UK joined the then EEC, the Regulations will apply to it after 1 January 1994. Since as a matter of English law, contracts cannot be amended unless both parties agree, a principal alarmed at the possible consequences of the Regulations before 1 January 1994 could only encourage the agent to agree an amendment, or terminate. Not all principals will have been aware of the terms of the Directive before the Regulations were made and indeed some principals and agents may still be unaware of the terms of the regulations, although recent publicity given to decisions such as that of *King v Tunnock, Barrett McKenzie v Escala* and *Ingmar v Eaton Leonard Inc.* makes this increasingly unlikely.

4.4 TO WHAT EXTENT IS THE PERIOD BEFORE 1 JANUARY 1994 TO BE TAKEN INTO ACCOUNT?

For pre-existing contracts, does the retrospective effect mentioned above mean that for all purposes the clock starts running only on 1 January, or is it intended that the period before 1 January should count for all purposes? Although regulation 23(2) states that nothing in the Regulations shall affect the rights and liabilities of agent or principal which have accrued before 1 January 1994, the authors' view is that the period before 1 January 1994 should be taken into account in calculating periods of notice, the amount of compensation or indemnity payment due and in ascertaining on which orders commission will be due. This approach has been adopted by the English courts in recent decisions.[1]

Seen in the light of the above conclusions, the Regulations are something of a windfall for an agent. The agent agreed some time in the past to conduct specified duties for a given remuneration. Those duties are altered by the Regulations, but the principal will also be required to pay compensation which he had not taken into account in calculating the cost of conducting business through the agent. It is conceivable that, if the agent is entitled to significant compensation, business which was profitable before the Regulations came into effect may prove to be unprofitable once the cost of compensation is taken into account. Had the principal been aware of this situation earlier in the relationship, he might have terminated or forced renegotiation of the contract.

All of this is in line with the terms of the Directive which stated that the UK should bring into force provisions necessary to comply with the Directive by 1 January 1994 and that from such date the Regulations should apply to contracts in operation. For member states other than the UK and Ireland, there was a two-step process: implementation was required by 1 January 1990 so that the applicable rules would affect agreements concluded after that date, but from 1 January

---

[1] As regards indemnity, see *Moore v Piretta PTA Limited* [1999] 1 All ER 174, 180–18; as regards compensation, see *Ingmar GB Limited v Eaton Leonard Inc* 31 July 2001, judgment of Morland J.

1994 the rules were to apply to all contracts then in force. The extra four years given to the UK and Ireland to implement the Directive effectively wiped out this transitional period and it is suggested that legal certainty has suffered as a result.

4.5 WHAT IS THE STATUS OF AGREEMENTS TERMINATED BEFORE 1 JANUARY 1994?

The answer to the above question lies in Regulation 23(2). If a right or liability accrued before 1 January 1994, then the Regulations will not disturb that position. Thus, if an agency contract was terminable on three months' notice and that notice was given in August 1993 so as to expire in November 1993, then the rights of the parties will be determined solely by reference to the terms of the contract and the Regulations will not apply. The agent would not be entitled to compensation or indemnity and if the agency contract said that there would be no right to any further commissions, then this term would be effective.

4.6 WHAT IS THE TERRITORIAL SCOPE OF THE REGULATIONS?

At first sight, regulation 1(2) seems to be clear and unambiguous. It simply defines the scope of the Regulations as being applicable to the activities of agents in Great Britain—Great Britain is the relevant territory because of the constitutional need to provide separate legislative measures for Northern Ireland. This provision must now be read in conjunction with the amended regulation 1(3)(a), which provides that the parties to a commercial agency contract can agree to be bound by the law of another member state. This possibility can apply even if both parties are in Great Britain. However, certain problems arise, as follows:

—What constitutes activities?
—What is the position of a commercial agent who carries out activities not only in Great Britain but in other member states? Do the Regulations only apply to the activities carried out in Great Britain and not to those carried out elsewhere in the European Union?[2]
—What is the position of an agent who carries out all of its activities outside the territory of the European Union?
—What happens if the agent has activities both within Great Britain and outside the European Union?

---

[2] It should be noted that by amendment to the original Regulations, reference to member states in the Regulations includes Contracting States to the EEA Agreement: the Commercial Agents (Council Directive) (Amendment) Regulations 1998 (SI 1998/2868).

4.7 THE DIRECTIVE

The Directive is of little help on the above issues as, by its very nature, it sets out the co-ordinating measures to be implemented across the European Union and does not (and indeed could not) address the issue of the scope of the individual member states' implementing legislation. That is a matter for the national implementing legislation. However, it raises a problem inherent in the use of directives as a means of harmonising legislation throughout the European Union. All member states must implement directives fully and correctly. This does not mean that they will all implement a particular directive in exactly the same way. Thus, differences may and often do exist between the different national implementing measures for a particular directive. Such differences should eventually be ironed out by the European Court of Justice but this may take some considerable time. In the meantime, different member states may have different views of the same directive. It is interesting to note that earlier versions of the Regulations did not contain a similar provision to that at regulation 1(2). Indeed, it was only in the final draft of the regulation that this provision was brought in. Prior to that, the only clause that had an impact on this issue was contained in paragraph 23 of the second draft. This provided that the Regulations did not apply when an agent's activities would not take place within the European Community. The Regulations are much narrower, applying only where the agent's activities take place within Great Britain.

4.8 THE UK'S POSITION

The UK authorities have taken a standpoint on the problems mentioned above. This is contained in this guidance notes published by the DTI over the past few years referred to in earlier chapters, which can be found at Appendix 5 in this book. The DTI makes it clear that the views expressed in the notes should not be taken as binding authority and that the final arbiter in such matters is the European Court of Justice. The Court of Appeal made it clear that the DTI Notes were not admissible for use by the courts to interpret the Regulations.[3] They nonetheless remain of interest in view of the conclusion reached by the Court in that case.

4.9 THE CARRYING ON OF ACTIVITIES WITHIN GREAT BRITAIN

Given the increasing use of electronic communications between businesses, in particular via the Internet, the question of where an agent's activities are carried out is of some importance. If for example an agent were to be physically situated

---

[3] *Ingmar v Eaton Leonard Technologies Inc.* [1999] EuLR 88, 92A–B.

in France, but sought clients and/or sales of goods in Great Britain through electronic media, there should be no reason why the Regulations could not apply.[4]
However, that contrasts with the position taken by the DTI in its 1994 Guidance
Note to the Regulations, which suggest that a physical presence in Great Britain is
required if the Regulations are to apply. It should be noted that by a 1998 statutory
amendment to the Regulations[5] referred to above, the courts of Great Britain were
given the ability to apply the Regulations to situations in which the agent's activities were outside of Great Britain, so the debate may now be otiose.

It should be noted that in order for the Regulations to apply, it is *not* necessary
for the principal to be established in a different member state to that of the agent.
Although there is specific mention in the Directive of the difficulties posed by
principals and agents being in different member states, the European Court of
Justice has made it clear that the national implementing legislation can (and
indeed should) apply even when both parties to a commercial agency agreement
are within the same member state.[6]

4.10 ACTIVITIES WITHIN THE EU

Where an agent carries out its activities both in Great Britain and in other member states, the view of the DTI is that the Regulations govern the agent's activities
in Great Britain but do not cover the same agent's activities anywhere else in the
European Community. If this is correct, then the practical impact will be considerable. Rather than having one jurisdiction dealing with a particular contractual
relationship between a principal and an agent, there may be 15 (or in the future
more) jurisdictions examining the same contractual relationship. This will clearly
add to the costs of the parties litigating in such circumstances and reduce the value
of each individual claim. If this view is correct it will make it much more difficult
for agents to enforce their rights. However, given the fact that the Directive co-
ordinated rather than harmonised national laws on commercial agents, leaving
different countries with different laws, the situation appears to be inevitable.

4.11 ACTIVITIES OUTSIDE THE EU

If all of the agent's activities take place outside the territory of the European
Economic Area, the DTI's view follows the principle established in the first and
second drafts—that is to say that the Regulations will not apply, even where the
parties to the relevant contract have agreed that the agreement is to be governed

---

[4] For support of the stance taken by the authors, see Lawrence Collins (Gen Ed) Dicey & Morris *The Conflict of Laws* (13th edn), (London, Sweet & Maxwell, 2000) para 33–407.
[5] The Commercial Agents (Council Directive) (Amendment) Regulations 1998 (SI 1998/2868).
[6] See Case C–215/97: *Bellone* [1998] ECR I–2191.

by English law. However, the parties could agree specifically to include in their contract some or all of the provisions contained in the Regulations. This again follows the principles of earlier drafts of the Regulations. It should be noted that the draft paragraph containing the relevant provisions on non-EC activities was not included in the final text. Accordingly, there is no guidance on the issue apart from what was in the previous drafts and the DTI's views on those drafts. However, it is thought that this represents a sensible position, given that one of the stated aims of the Directive is to remedy the impact of differences in national agency laws on the conditions of competition *within* the EU.

4.12 ACTIVITIES BOTH WITHIN AND OUTSIDE THE EU

If the situation where there are activities within and outside the EU is viewed as being analogous to the situation discussed above of an agent operating both in Great Britain and elsewhere in the European Union, then only those activities taking place within the EU should be covered by the Directive. This position appears to have received support from Advocate General Leger in the *Ingmar* case, in which he stated that '[t]he existence of a territorial link—either through the actual presence of one of the economic operators in the territory of a member state, or through the pursuit of an economic activity in that territory—thus imposes Community jurisdiction on the legal relationship in question.'[7] Interestingly, this approach would permit the Directive, and therefore the Regulations, to apply to a situation in which the principal was established in Great Britain with the agent being established and active outside the EU.

4.13 CRITICISM OF THE STANCE TAKEN

The ability to split jurisdiction however would seem to be inconsistent with the English rules of private international law. These provide that normally the same legal system applies to all obligations under a particular contract. The parties are free to 'split' jurisdiction over the contract between different legal systems (the course advocated by the DTI), but this should only occur where the parties have clearly agreed that this should be done. The mere fact that the parties have to perform their obligations in different countries has been held not to be such an indication: see *Zivnostenska Banka v Frankman*.[8] The path taken by the DTI is that favoured by certain continental countries, in that it adheres to the doctrine of *lex loci solutionis* (the law of the place of performance). This has not been traditionally the way in which English law has developed. English law prefers the principle whereby the system of law applicable to any given contract follows the intentions

---

[7] AG Leger's Opinion in Case C–381/98: *Ingmar* of 11 May 2000 at para 37, [2001] 1 CMLR 9.
[8] [1950] AC 57.

of the parties or where no intention is expressed or inferred, then the applicable proper law of the contract will be that with which the contract has its closest and most real connection.

4.14 WHAT ARE THE RULES AS TO CHOICE OF LAW?

Regulations 1(2) and 1(3) as amended make clear the position as regards applicable law, where there is choice of law clause and that choice is an EU law.

If the parties chose English or Scottish law, then the Regulations will apply irrespective of where in the EU the agent carries out its activities. This follows regulation 1(3)(b) as amended which provides:

> A Court or tribunal shall (whether or not it would otherwise be required to do so) apply these regulations where the law of another member State corresponding to these regulations enables parties to agree that the agency contract is to be governed by the law of a different member State and the parties have agreed that it is to be governed by the law of England and Wales or Scotland.

Thus, as long as the EU law of the place of performance allows for another applicable law to be chosen by the parties, then the Regulations will apply in such a situation.

If, on the other hand, the parties chose a law of another member state, then the Regulations will not apply and the implementing provisions of the Directive in that other member state will apply instead. This arises from regulation 1(3)(a) which provides:

> A Court or tribunal shall apply the law of the other member State concerned in place of regulations 3 to 22 where the parties have agreed that the agency contract is to be governed by the law of that member State.

Both situations outlined above are based on the overriding importance given to the ability of parties to chose the law applicable to contracts into which they enter or wish to enter, which importance is reflected, both in English conflicts law and in the Rome Convention of 19 June 1980 on the Law Applicable to Contractual Obligations. The amendment under regulation 1(3)(b) reflects the concern of the European Commission with the original wording of the Regulations, which caused a lacuna to arise in situations in which English law was the parties' choice of law, but where the agent's activities were outside the UK. In such situations, there was a possibility that the agent would not receive the benefit of any domestic EU law implementing the Directive.

4.15 THE NON-EXPRESS CHOICE OF LAW

If, contrary to what is described above, there is no express choice of law, then the Rome Convention states that the contract in question shall be governed by the law of the country with which it is most closely connected (Article 4). Thus, in a situation in which an agent's activities in Great Britain comprised 20 per cent of the total with the remaining 80 per cent being taken up by activities in France and where no express choice of law was made by the parties, it could be argued that instead of the Regulations applying to the contract, the French law implementing the Directive should be the relevant law.[9]

4.16 THE NON-EXCLUSION OF REGULATIONS 1, 2 AND 23

It should be noted that regulation 1(3)(a), as amended, only relates to regulations 3 to 22. Thus, where the law of another member state applies, regulations 1 and 2 and 23 may continue to apply. These provisions are not lacking in importance. For example, regulation 2 determines which commercial agents shall be covered by the Regulations and which shall not. It is thus crucial to any situation affected or potentially affected by the Regulations.

It must follow (and indeed the DTI take this view) that the deliberate exclusion of regulations 1, 2 and 23 in regulation 1(3)(a) means that the question of the scope of the regulations is still to be determined pursuant to the regulations and in particular regulation 2, even though another law has been chosen as the law governing the contract. As the DTI points out in its 1993 Guidance Notes, this approach assumes that the other member state in question, whose law has been chosen to govern a particular contract, has properly implemented the Directive.

---

[9] As to the position where a non EU law is chosen, see Case C–381/98: *Ingmar GB v Eaton Leonard Technologies* [2001] I CMLR 9 and above at ch 1, 1.16.

5

Regulation 2(1)—Commercial Agents

5.1 OUTLINE

THIS CHAPTER DEALS with the central question of which agents are covered by the Regulations including the issue of whether the Regulations apply to commercial agents dealing in both goods and services.

5.2 WHAT IS A COMMERCIAL AGENT?

The definition of a commercial agent is of central importance to the interpretation and understanding of the rest of the Regulations. As noted in Chapter 3, it has been the subject of considerable thought by the DTI, although the Regulations in fact largely replicate the terms of the Directive.

Regulation 2(1) defines a commercial agent, but as will be seen in the next chapter, regulation 2(2) then excludes certain categories of agent from the Regulations.

5.3 DEFINITION

A commercial agent is defined as a self-employed intermediary who has continuing authority to negotiate or to negotiate and conclude the sale or purchase of goods[1] on behalf of and in the name of another person. Each of the elements of this definition merits separate consideration.

5.4 'SELF-EMPLOYED INTERMEDIARY'

Some writers have been misled by the words 'self-employed' to conclude that the Regulations do not apply to companies—see, for example, T. Brennan and C. Jones 'Compensatory Measures' *The Gazette*, 6 January, 1994. This is incorrect. These words are taken from Article 43 of the EC Treaty (and specifically Article 47), which relate to the adoption of directives for the co-ordination of laws in member states concerning the taking up and pursuit of activities as self-employed persons by EC nationals. The distinction is not, however, between natural and

---

[1] Although buying agents are rare, note that the agent in *Page v Combined Shipping and Trading* [1997] All ER 656 (see ch 7, para 7.12) was both a buying and selling agent.

legal persons. Indeed the draft Directive which was the subject of the Commission's Explanatory Memorandum of 14 December 1976, appended to the Law Commission Report, expressly allowed the exclusion of certain of the agent's rights where the paid-up share capital of the agent exceeded a given figure clearly indicating that corporate entities will fall within the definition of commercial agent. It is unclear whether the word 'intermediary' adds anything—its presence in the Directive is probably merely a reflection of the fact that these words are a term of art in other member states.

5.5 'CONTINUING AUTHORITY'

Clearly, what is contemplated is something more than authority to act on a single occasion for a particular principal. The DTI's 1994 Guidance Notes suggest that if an agent is appointed on a temporary basis or for a specified number of transactions, then the Regulations would not apply. Is this correct? Does 'continuing authority' mean the authority to conclude an unlimited number of transactions? It would be a strange result if it were possible to avoid the Regulations by appointing the agent to conclude a specified but large number of transactions.

Further, regulation 7(2) contemplates the agent being granted exclusive rights to a specific group of customers. Why should an agent who is granted exclusive rights in respect of a handful of customers be covered by the Regulations when an agent who is granted authority for a limited number of transactions is not? Further, suppose that an agent is given an exclusive right to ten named customers pursuant to an agency agreement entered into for a period of three years and the agent successfully negotiates a long-term supply contract in excess of three years with each of those customers, should the question of whether the Regulations apply depend upon whether the contract stated that the agent would only have authority to act in respect of ten transactions?

The authors believe that the better view is that where an agent has authority for more than one transaction this authority should be seen as 'continuing'. The authority *continues* up to the point when the second transaction is concluded and that authority is (in the absence of other provisions) of indefinite duration even if of limited scope. The authors do not believe that it is safe to assume that limiting authority to a specified number of transactions will take the arrangement outside the Regulations.

5.6 PRECEDENT CLAUSES

The precedent clause set out at A below might be utilised where there is to be authority for only one transaction. The precedent set out at B below is a provision which might be incorporated for the avoidance of doubt in arrangements which are in reality distribution agreements or other relationships and where there is to be no agency relationship. By way of caution, it should be noted that the court will look at the factual question of whether there is continuing authority or not: the mere inclusion of such a provision will not change the facts and advisers should be careful in counselling clients on this fact.[2] The authors also believe that it is unlikely that the effect of the Regulations can be avoided by entering into a series of contracts each of which relates to a single transaction: the courts are likely to look through such a relationship and to find that there is in fact continuing authority, the agent reasonably assuming that he will be granted authority for a further transaction when he has concluded one transaction. In *Moore v Piretta PTA Limited*,[3] the court construed the phrase 'the agency contract' in regulation 17 as referring to the entirety of the agency relationship between principal and agent and not merely to the latest in a chain of contracts between them.

The suggested precedent clauses are as follows:

A   The Parties agree that the Agent has been appointed solely for the purpose of concluding a single transaction between the Principal and the Customer and that accordingly the Agent shall not have nor be deemed to have any continuing or other authority to negotiate or to negotiate and conclude any other transaction on behalf of the Principal.

B   The parties agree that the Distributor is acting as an independent trader in purchasing the goods from the Manufacturer and selling those goods to its own customers at prices and upon terms determined solely by the Distributor. Accordingly, it is agreed that the Distributor shall not have nor be deemed to have any continuing or other authority to negotiate or to negotiate and conclude any transaction for the sale of goods or otherwise for or on behalf of the Manufacturer nor to pledge the credit of or bind the Manufacturer in any other way.

5.7   WHAT IS THE POSITION OF SUB-AGENTS?

What is the position of a sub-agent via-à-vis his principal? The position of sub-agents is not fully worked out in English law, and the Regulations are likely to add a confusing additional factor into this equation.

Where a sub-agent is properly appointed, his acts bind the principal as if they had been performed by the agent. Does this mean that the sub-agent has continuing authority to negotiate or negotiate and conclude on behalf of the principal? If so, the Regulations apply as between the principal and the sub-agent. Do they also apply as between the agent and the sub-agent?

There is no privity of contract (that is, no contractual link) between a principal and a sub-agent as a matter of course. Contractually, therefore, in the absence of an agreement between principal and sub-agent, the common law provides the sub-agent with rights against the agent but not against the principal. The definition of

---

[2]   See, for example *AMB Imballaggi Plastici SRL v Pacflex Limited,*[1999] All ER (Comm) 249, see footnote 11 below.

[3]   [1999] 1 ALL ER 174, 180.

'commercial agent' in regulation 2(1) talks of 'continuing authority' but does not state that that authority has to be the result of a contract between principal and sub-agent.

This question was the subject of a reference to the European Court by the English High Court in *Pace Airline Services Limited v Aerotrans Luftfahrtagentur GmbH*,[4] but it is understood that the case settled before the European Court considered it. The authors' view is that the sub-agent's claim should be made against the principal: the sub-agent has no continuing authority to act on behalf of the agent.

It has also been suggested that a sub-agent is not covered by the Regulations because the goods in relation to which the sub-agent's authority subsists are not the agent's goods (ie are not owned by the person with whom the sub-agent has contracted). Presumably this assertion springs from the fact that the Regulations talk of 'continuing authority to negotiate . . . the sale . . . of goods *on behalf of and in the name of another person*' (authors' emphasis). Given that a sub-agent has authority to bind the *principal* (not the agent), the Regulations clearly assume that the goods belong to the principal and do not contemplate any role for the (intermediate) agent. Given that authority comes from the principal and that, usually, the goods are owned by the principal, there should be no issue here.

If the agent is dismissed by the principal, then his claim for compensation should not include any compensation which may be payable to the sub-agent. However, if the agent utilises the services of a third party on the 'advice' of the principal then his claim for compensation may include any sums which he has thereby incurred and has not been able to amortise for the purposes of regulation 17(7)(b).

Similarly, under the indemnity head, the sub-agent should claim separately on the basis of the goodwill which it has brought to the principal's business.

For this reason principals will certainly wish to ensure that they are happy with the terms of appointment for any sub-agent before the sub-agent is appointed. They may also wish to reach agreement direct on the excludeable elements of the Regulations and on the question of indemnity or compensation.

The position of sub-agents may be a prime situation in which the Contracts (Rights of Third Parties) Act 1999 may be of use.

Will the Regulations otherwise give rights to sub-agents against the principal even if there is no contract? Seemingly the answer is yes.

5.8 'GOODS'

The first and second drafts contained definitions of goods by reference to other statutes. There is no definition in the Regulations, but the DTI's Guidance Note suggests that these words should be interpreted in accordance with EC law gener-

---

[4] Case C–64/99, [1999] OJ C121/123.

ally. The DTI believes that the definition in section 61 of the Sale of Goods Act 1979—excluding land and money—would be a reasonable guide. It is reported[5] that the High Court judge in the unreported *Pace* case[6] considered that cargo space on aircraft could be 'goods' for this purpose. It seems to the authors that this argument is difficult to sustain.

In *Tamarind and others v Eastern Natural Gas and Eastern Energy*[7] it was accepted that gas was goods and there seems to have been a suggestion from the judge that he also considered electricity to be goods.[8] There have been rumours that the Commission may at some stage publish a draft directive extending protection to agents who deal in the supply or purchase of pure services. No draft has yet emerged. It might be questioned whether such a measure would affect any significant number of agents in the EC.

5.9   ARE AGENTS WHO DEAL IN GOODS AND SERVICES PROTECTED BY THE REGULATIONS?

The second draft included the words 'but not services' but these words have not been included in the Regulations. The interesting question which this raises is the status of an agent who deals in both goods and services. If, for instance, the agent is seeking orders for major items of capital equipment on behalf of a principal, it is likely that the principal will agree to provide consultancy services, or to install and commission the equipment, or to provide guarantee or maintenance services, through the agent. This issue may have some bearing on the question of whether the agent's activities are 'secondary' (see paragraph 6.3 below) but also raises the question of the status of the services element of such an arrangement. If the agent has been paid commission on the consultancy/installation and commissioning/servicing and maintenance aspects of the transaction with the customer (which may be a substantial part of the price):

—Do the rules regarding the payment of commission apply to these elements?
—Are these elements of commission to be taken into account for the purpose of calculating compensation or an indemnity payment?
—If not, what happens if, because the principal quotes a single global price for all the services provided, it is not possible to ascertain what element relates to the goods and what element to the services?

The DTI did not address the issue in its Guidance Notes, but the authors' view is that the reference to goods is merely a matter of defining the status of the commercial agent and that, unless his activities in relation to services render his activities as an agent in respect of the sale of goods secondary, the Regulations will apply.

---

[5] S Sidkin, *Commercial Lawyer* February 1999, p 101.
[6] Which was referred to, as regards as Art 234 reference, in footnote 4 above.
[7] Commercial Court, [2000] EuLR 708.
[8] The judge referred to 'selling electricity or other products'.

But do the Regulations apply in respect of the whole of the sum due to him by way of commission and will the whole amount payable be taken into account in calculating compensation or the indemnity payment? If the answer is that the whole consideration is taken into account then this raises an interesting drafting question. If the draftsman is faced with a situation where the agent is likely to act in respect of both goods and services, what is the effect of drafting two separate agreements—these could be tied together through cross-default provisions to ensure that for certain purposes they would work as if one single agreement. If the relationship is to be viewed as one of commercial agency since the goods element outweighs the services element, then separating the two may mean that the compensation/indemnity payment is lower and may mean that the principal escapes some of the other mandatory provisions of the Regulations in relation to the services element. However, if the inclusion of services within the agreement would render the agent's activities in relation to the sale of goods secondary, then the effect of separation would be to ensure that the Regulations applied to part of the relationship when combining the two would have taken the whole of the relationship outside the regulations.[9]

This points to an interesting inconsistency. If an agent earns 55 per cent of his commission in relation to services, then his activities as an agent in respect of the sale of goods may be viewed as secondary, whereas if the proportions were reversed the Regulations might apply with their full weight to the whole of his commission payments.

If the proportion changed during the course of the contract, then an agent could be within the terms of the Regulations for part of the duration of the contract and outside the Regulations for the remainder. The parties may be unaware that the relationship has ceased to be subject to the Regulations or has become subject to them. In such circumstances, should the court apply the Regulations only if and for so long as the Regulations apply in calculating compensation or indemnity and should it discount the period during which the agent's activities in relation to the sale of the goods are secondary? This is not as fanciful a set of circumstances as might first appear: if an agent is seeking to procure orders for major items of equipment from customers at the outset and is successful, then in the latter part of the term of the contract it may well be that the bulk of income[10] ceases to be earned from equipment sales, but relates principally to maintenance or guarantee services, training and so forth. This is an issue which neither the Directive nor the Regulations address. The Schedule to the Regulations is ill-suited to resolving this question, but see paragraph 6.3 below.

The best answer to the above problems is a practical one. By careful drafting and ensuring that commission is calculated on the goods element only, the principal

---

[9] Given the view expressed by the court in *Moore v Piretta PTA Limited* (see para 5.6 above), it may be that the court would ignore form and view this as a single agency even if it consisted of two separate contracts.

[10] Indeed, it is unclear whether any such balance would be struck on the basis of volume or value of transactions effected; in this example, value would likely point in one direction, volume in the other!

should avoid claims to commission based on the value of services. If this is done, then (at least if the compensation route applies) the value of services should not form part of the compensation calculation. This might, however, operate as a disincentive to the agent to effect sales of services.

5.10 'ON BEHALF OF ANOTHER PERSON'/'IN THE NAME OF THAT PRINCIPAL'

Because other aspects of the definition comprehend the fact that the agent will be acting to some extent on behalf of another, the words 'on behalf of another person'/'in the name of that principal' add little. Interestingly, although these words relate to the word 'negotiate' in the definition, the words 'on behalf of and in the name of that principal' are applied to the words 'negotiate and conclude', the extra words assumedly being tagged on to the latter to exclude agents who either act on a completely undisclosed basis (that is, in circumstances where the third party thinks that it is dealing with the agent rather than the principal) or on the basis that (although the third party knows that it is dealing with another through the agent) the identity of that other is not disclosed. Why in principle such an agent should be excluded from the scope of the Regulations (if this is the effect of these words) is not clear, nor is it clear whether this effect was intended.

It is clear that, where the court concludes that the agent is negotiating for itself rather than the principal, it will conclude that the relationship is not an agency for the purposes of the Regulations.[11]

5.11 'NEGOTIATE'/'NEGOTIATE AND CONCLUDE'

'Negotiate and conclude' is less problematic than 'negotiate'—an agent who has continuing authority to negotiate and conclude transactions is clearly the type of agent referred to in chapter 1, who actually has power to bind the principal to transactions. Unfortunately, at least in the UK, this type of agent is very much rarer than his counterpart, the agent who funnels orders and business back to the principal but does not have or purport to have any authority to bind the principal to contracts. Is this type of agent (referred to in chapter 1 as a 'marketing agent') within the scope of the Regulations at all? What is the meaning of the word 'negotiate' when used on its own?

---

[11] A rather thin distinction to this effect was entered in *AMB Imballaggi Plastici SRL v Pacflex Limited* [1999] All ER (Comm) 249. The court had no difficulty in concluding that the relationship in that case was not one of commercial agency; although the contract allowed for agency dealings, dealings were in fact conducted on a sale and re-sale (distributorship) basis with the agent determining resale prices. The above-mentioned case was reviewed recently in *Mercantile International Group plc v Industrial Group* [2002] 1 All ER (Comm) 788, a judgment of Andrew Smith J in the Commercial Court, in which it was held that an arrangement for renumerating by way of 'mark-up' rather than by commission was not inconsistent with agency. The judgment has been upheld on appeal.

5.12 DO THE REGULATIONS APPLY TO MARKETING AGENTS?

If 'negotiate and conclude' comprehends the power to bind the principal to transactions, then 'negotiate' must mean something less than actual or apparent authority to bind the principal. But how far need the agent be authorised in order to be 'negotiating'? In what sense can someone be said to have power to negotiate when he does not have power to conclude? Where the 'agent' does not have 'authority' to take any part in the process leading up to contract formation, the agent cannot be said to be 'negotiating'—so, an 'agent' who merely circulates literature or samples does not in the authors' view 'negotiate'. However, if the agent has a greater role—for instance it presents price lists or standard terms of trading, liaises with the principal and so forth—it is negotiating and therefore falls within the scope of the Regulations. The test is not a difficult one to satisfy.

It is the authors' view that this expression includes most if not all 'marketing agents'. The reality is that the agent is likely to act as the point of contact between principal and customer, at least at the outset. It will be the agent who (either directly by visiting the customer's premises, or through advertisements and the general creation of product image for the principal's goods in the territory) acts as the catalyst to orders for the principal in most cases. Normally the agent will visit the customer alone and present product brochures, specifications, the principal's price list. The agent will ascertain the customer's requirements and advise the principal of these, even if it is doing so with a view to asking whether a particular modification can be made or a particular discount can be granted. It is often the agent who communicates the principal's response to the customer, but even if principal and customer enter a dialogue direct, the catalyst for this will have been the agent. In the broader sense, the agent is surely 'negotiating'. Certainly, he is doing all that he could do on behalf of the principal without actually 'concluding'.

The Law Commission Report notes that 'by far the majority of commercial agents in the member states are at the present time authorised only to negotiate on behalf of their principals, the conclusion of the actual agreement for the transaction being a matter for the principal himself. The Directive reflects this situation.'

This specific issue has been considered by the English courts in at least two cases relating to petrol station attendants and in one other case. In the earlier, unreported case of *Elf Oil UK Limited v Pilkington* (1994), the court held that the crucial issue was whether the 'agent' negotiated or merely managed: only in the former case would he be a commercial agent for the purposes of the Regulations.

In the other case, *Parks v Esso Petroleum Company Limited*,[12] the Court of Appeal considered a number of grounds of appeal by Mr Parks against the decision of the Vice Chancellor. The Court of Appeal had to consider whether he was a commercial agent for the purposes of the Regulations and whether his activities as a commercial agent were secondary so as to take him outside the scope of the

---

[12] [2000] Eu LR 25.

Regulations. It decided that he was not a commercial agent on the basis that he did not negotiate. Whilst not questioning this decision on its facts, the authors believe that the approach taken by the Court of Appeal is flawed and may lead to incorrect decisions if followed in other cases. In asking whether Mr Parks negotiated, the court was directing itself to the wrong question; what it should have asked was whether Mr Parks had *authority* to negotiate.[13] The reality in many mature commercial agencies is that the agent does little negotiating day to day. Long-established customers secured for the principal by the agent use fax, phone or e-mail to communicate repeat orders on the basis of a published price list. There is no ongoing *negotiation* here in any meaningful sense. But the agent undeniably has *authority* to negotiate.

The third case, also unreported, is *Hunter v Zenith Windows*,[14] in which the court decided that an agent whose role was principally to train and co-ordinate the activities of other agents[15] was nevertheless to be viewed as having authority to negotiate. The agent's claim failed, however, on the basis that his activities as agent were secondary.[16] It seems that the judge's reasoning revolved in part around a view that the agent was negotiating even though he was doing so through the medium of sub-agents.[17]

5.13 SPECIFIC EXCLUSIONS

Regulation 2(1) goes on to exclude three types of persons specifically from the definition of 'commercial agent', namely:

—company officers;
—partners; and
—insolvency practitioners (the earlier drafts referred to receivers, liquidators and others).

The first of these is presumably only of potential relevance in so far as the company officer is not an employee.

5.14 OTHER DEFINITIONS

Regulation 2(1) also defines 'commission' and 'restraint of trade clause', and these definitions are dealt with in the sections to which they relate.

---

[13] For other criticisms of the *Parkes* case, in particular in comparison to similar cases in Germany with different results, see an article by Sellhorst and O'Brien in *International Business Lawyer* July/August 2000, p 320.

[14] Unreported, Norwich County Court 13 June 1997.

[15] Described in para 6.2 as a 'super-agent'.

[16] See ch 6, para 6.3 below.

[17] Contrast this with the views expressed in para 5.7 above regarding sub-agents.

6

Regulations 2(2)–2(5)—Commercial Agents Outside the Scope of the Regulations

6.1 OUTLINE

T HIS CHAPTER EXAMINES the types of commercial agents which are excluded specifically from the scope of the Regulations. It also covers those situations where the activities of commercial agents are secondary to other activities and which then cause the agents concerned to fall outside the ambit of the Regulations.

6.2 WHICH TYPES OF COMMERCIAL AGENT ARE SPECIFICALLY EXCLUDED FROM THE REGULATIONS?

Regulation 2(2) stipulates that certain persons who would otherwise fall within the definition of 'commercial agent' will nevertheless remain outside the scope of the Regulations. These include:

—agents whose activities are unpaid;
—agents when they operate on commodity exchanges or in the commodity market (note that the definition of 'commodity market' from the first draft has not been reproduced in the Regulations); and
—Crown agents.

None of these is surprising, but it is important to note that certain persons will be viewed as commercial agents, as follows:

—Agents appointed on a 'trial basis'. Comparison will be made below between the position of employees on the one hand and commercial agents on the other. In UK law, an employee has no right to an unfair dismissal or redundancy payment for a period of one year following commencement of employment and no right to redundancy payments for a period of two years following commencement of employment. There is no such 'honeymoon' period with agents and the Regulations apply with their full force from the first day of the relationship;
—Agents who do not have a written agreement with the principal. Regulation 13 gives each party a right to receive from the other a signed written document

setting out the terms of the agency contract. Clearly then, agents without written agreements are nevertheless within the terms of the Regulations.

—Non-exclusive agency contracts as well as exclusive agency contracts, the only difference being in relation to the payment of commission (see below).

Another type of relationship merits some comment here. Sometimes principals appoint a number of agents, but utilise one of these agents as a 'super-agent' (sometimes referred to as a 'sales manager' or—more dangerously—'sales director') whose role—often in addition to his role in acting as agent in a particular territory—is to supervise the other agents and provide them with assistance.[1] This is another situation in which the principal may wish to consider dividing the relationship into two separate agreements. Provided that suitable cross-default provisions are incorporated, there is the possibility that compensation/indemnity payments will be calculated only by reference to the agency commission and not to the remuneration paid for acting as 'sales manager', even if this is based on the amounts of commission earned by the agents for the territory concerned.[2]

6.3 WHICH TYPES OF ACTIVITIES ARE DEEMED TO BE SECONDARY?

Regulation 2(3) together with the Schedule is important in that it helps to define the scope of the Regulations as a whole. Clearly if a person's activities as a commercial agent are secondary, then the Regulations will not be applicable. However, there are very few types of agency contracts which are specifically excluded from the Regulations. Apart from those set out in regulation 2(2), the Schedule only specifically deals with two types of contract, preventing them from coming within the scope of the Regulations, namely those involving mail order catalogues for consumer goods and those involving consumer credit agreements (paragraph 5 of the Schedule). It should be noted that even for these types of contract, the reference to them in the Schedule amounts only to a rebuttable presumption that they fall outside the Regulations as they will be secondary to other activities. The Schedule is poorly worded, unclear and usually unhelpful.[3] Regard should also be had to the judgment of Morrison J in *Tamarind International Ltd. and Others v Eastern Natural Gas (Retail) Ltd. and Others*,[4] in which the court held that the concept of a commercial agent whose activities are secondary under the Schedule was not one which had any meaning in English law and it was not a term of art com-

---

[1] For an example of such a situation, see the comments on *Hunter v Zenith Windows* (unreported) in ch 5, para 5.12.

[2] This may not be effective if the Court follows the approach taken in *Moore v Piretta PTA Limited* (see ch 5, para 5.6). Both the compensation and indemnity basis refers to 'commission', although the one year cap of indemnity is defined using the broader expression 'remuneration'.

[3] See the *obiter* remarks on the Schedule's lack of clarity by Lord Justices Waller and Peter Gibson in *AMB Imballagi Plastici SRL v Pacflex Ltd* (see ch 5, footnote 11).

[4] [2000] EuLR 709.

mon throughout mainland Europe. The court continued, stating that there was therefore no yardstick in the common law which measured and defined those agents whose activities were secondary and those whose activities were not. Given this lack of specificity it is important to examine the various early drafts of Directive 86/653, the Directive itself and the early drafts of the Regulations to see whether any help can be gained from such provisions.

6.4 THE COMMISSION PROPOSAL FOR THE DIRECTIVE

Article 3 of the Commission's proposal of 17 December 1976 excluded four specific types of intermediary from the scope of the Directive:

—those who were employed;
—those who acted in their own name;
—those who were appointed to act for a specified transaction or a specified number of transactions;
—those who acted in the insurance or credit fields.

Further, Article 4(1) of the Commission's proposal of 17 December 1976 gave member states the right not to apply provisions relating to remuneration and compensation to persons acting as commercial agents but by way of secondary activity only. The draft made it clear that the question of whether an activity was secondary or not was one which was to be determined in accordance with the commercial usage of the relevant member state. It also provided that member states could apply, if they so wished, the provisions of the Directive to persons who were not commercial agents, but who could be assimilated by them.

6.5 THE OPINION OF THE ECONOMIC AND SOCIAL COMMITTEE

In its opinion on the Commission's proposal, the Economic and Social Committee suggested with regard to the scope of the Directive that the list of the specified types of intermediary excluded from the Regulations should be amended to read '[those] who carry out their activities in the insurance field or on behalf of credit institutions'—see paragraph 2.3.2 of the Opinion. Further, the Committee suggested that another type be added to the list those who work for firms engaged in mail-order or doorstep selling. The opinion also made the following comments which should be noted:

(1) 'The explanatory memorandum states that the Commission intends to submit a draft Directive coordinating the laws of the member states on agents working in the field of insurance and on behalf of credit institutions . . . (paragraph 2.3.3 of the Opinion).

(2) Article 4 gives member states the right not to apply certain legal provisions of the agency contract to persons who act as commercial agents 'by way of secondary

activity only'. It also empowers member states to apply the Directive to other persons who can 'be assimilated to commercial agents' (eg women who collect bulk orders for mail-order establishments or who organise collective sales in their own homes) (paragraph 2.3.4 of the Opinion).

(3) The Committee considers that Article 4 gives member states too much latitude and this might make it difficult to define the scope of the Directive precisely.

(4) Article 4 should, therefore, be deleted. The proposed fifth indent to Article 3 reinforces the case for deletion. Mail order agents account for the bulk of the category referred to in Article 4(1) (paragraph 2.3.5 of the Opinion).

As to the draft Directive on insurance intermediaries and credit institutions, instructive reference can be made to Directive 64/224 concerning the attainment of freedom of establishment and freedom to provide services in respect of activities of intermediaries in commerce, industry and small craft industries OJ 1964 L69/64. The second recital to that Directive provides that:

(5) Whereas certain activities of intermediaries are not covered by this Directive, either because they belong to branches of activity for which separate Directives are to be adopted or because, in accordance with the General Programmes, they are to be liberalised at a later date.

Thus, at Article 4 of Directive 64/224, the following types of intermediaries' activities are excluded from the scope of the Directive:

—insurance of all kinds (in particular insurance agents, brokers and assessors);
—banks and other financial establishments (in particular foreign exchange dealers, stockbrokers, mortgage brokers and the like);
—matters concerning immoveable property (in particular estate agents and brokers);
—transport undertakings (in particular shipbrokers, forwarding agents, customs agents and travel agencies).

Reference to Directive 64/224 is useful in that it demonstrates why certain activities of commercial agents are outside its own scope. Can the same reasoning not be applied to Directive 86/653? Commentators have followed this approach as far as exclusions are concerned. Further, Directive 86/653 specifically refers to Directive 64/224 in its opening recital.

6.6 THE OPINION OF THE EUROPEAN PARLIAMENT

In its opinion on the Commission's proposal, the European Parliament suggested two additions to the specified types of intermediaries excluded from the scope of the draft Directive. The first addition was to cover part-time agents involved primarily in mail-order sales to consumers from catalogues published periodically, at least twice a year, offering a wide range of goods for sale by cash or hire purchase. It can be seen that this is similar to the amendment suggested by the Economic and Social Committee. The second addition was to cover intermediaries who carried out their activities in the aviation sector.

6.7 THE COMMISSION'S AMENDED PROPOSAL

The Commission amended Articles 3 and 4 of its original proposal without taking into account the suggestions of the Economic and Social Committee and the European Parliament. The Commission's amendment added a further category of intermediaries to be exempt from the Directive. The amendment was in the following terms:

> . . . to intermediaries who, accordingly to the practice prevailing in the State in which they habitually carry on their activities, are regarded as doing so by way of secondary activity only.

In its amended proposal, the Commission also deleted Article 4(1) but kept Article 4(2).

6.8 THE DIRECTIVE AS ADOPTED

In the text of the Directive as adopted, the Council reshaped the original Article 3 fundamentally. The original specified types of intermediaries to be excluded were deleted and the following were inserted:

—commercial agents whose activities are unpaid;
—commercial agents when they operate on commodity exchanges or in a commodity market;
—Crown agents for Overseas Governments and Administrations;
—Article 2(2) of the Directive.

As to the issue of secondary activity, the Council followed the amended proposal of the Commission and extended the original proposal so that the whole of the Directive was excluded for those persons whose activities as commercial agents were considered secondary by the law of the member state in question: Article 2(3) of the Directive.

It will be noted that, despite the fact that the proposals from the Economic and Social Committee and the European Parliament were not taken up by either the Commission or the Council, the UK legislative authorities made use of the suggestions with regard to mail order agents and included them in paragraph 5 of the Schedule. This is a good example of why draft European legislation should be examined when conducting an exercise such as the present one. Such drafts may also indicated a position to take on a given point, which position is not clear from the wording of the final text itself.

6.9 THE DRAFT REGULATIONS

The first draft of the Regulations was published in 1990. Regulation 2(2) listed those persons who should not be deemed to be a commercial agent. The list included many more categories than set out in the Directive including those persons wholly or mainly engaged in a business of selling or buying goods on their own behalf, those persons engaged in selling goods from mail order catalogues and those persons who were wholly or mainly engaged in activities other than those of a commercial agent. The Directive, it will be recalled, set out a finite number of types of commercial agent to which the Directive did not apply. It can thus be seen that there was a fundamental difference existing between the first draft of the Regulations which set out certain persons not deemed to be commercial agents and who were not therefore affected by the Regulations—and the Directive— which listed those activities of commercial agents deemed not to be covered by the provisions of the Directive. It was this dichotomy which led, it is presumed, to a re-drafting of the proposed Regulations. Thus, the second draft carefully followed the text of the Directive as to which types of commercial agent were not to be covered by the Regulations. It also removed the categories which were not provided for in the Directive (referred to above) and placed them in a new section dealing with secondary activities. The list of commercial agents' activities deemed to be secondary appeared to be exhaustive. From the perspective of correct implementation of a directive, it appeared that as far as these latter provisions were concerned, the UK authorities had carried out their task correctly. However the position changed dramatically between the second draft and the Regulations as adopted.

6.10   THE REGULATIONS AS ADOPTED

The Regulations kept the position the same with regard to the three types of commercial agents who were excluded from the scope of the Regulations. However, with regard to the provisions on secondary activities, the previous draft provisions were rejected in favour of an extensive schedule. It is assumed that this was done in order to give more flexibility to the concept of secondary activities and to get away from the exhaustive list that it replaced. The result is however rather nebulous, which may widen the opportunities for agreements to be categorised as falling outside the scope of the Regulations, but which has a rather negative effect on legal certainty.[5] It should be noted that consumer credit agents are deemed by the Schedule to fall outside the scope of the Regulations. This category of agent did not appear in the any of the earlier drafts but it will be recalled that the proposals by the Commission sought to exclude agents who carried out activities in credit fields.

---

[5] See, by way of example, the different conclusions reached by the Court in the cases of *Hunter v Zenith* and *Tamarind v Eastern National Gas* (see para 6.3 above) on the specific question of whether procuring one transaction was likely to lead to further transactions.

6.11 PROBLEMS ARISING FROM THE SCHEDULE

—What is the determining factor of 'secondary' or is there none?
—What happens if an individual starts off in a contract with his or her principal in which activities as commercial agent are secondary but then during the course of the contract his or her commercial agent's activities become primary: does the contract start by falling outside the scope of the Regulations and then come within their scope at some point in time, thereby setting in train the operation of the Regulations?[6]
—The inclusion of two provisions in the Schedule seems to make little or no commercial sense. An agent has to use his own resources when devoting effort, skill and expenditure to developing markets to be deemed to be acting as a commercial agent. Under the other provision, the contract goods have to be specifically identified with the principal rather than with another person.

6.12 THE DETERMINING FACTOR

According to the DTI's 1994 Guidance Notes, the determining factor in deciding whether activities are secondary, and therefore whether a given agency contract comes within the provisions of the Regulations, is whether the agent is required to keep, as his own property, a considerable stock of the product. This test is taken from the Commission Notice on Exclusive Dealing Contracts with Commercial Agents: OJ 1962/139. The notice deals with the application of the EC competition rules to agents. In the notice, the Commission states that Article 81(1) of the EC Treaty (formerly Article 85(1)) does not apply to situations in which an agent is not acting as an independent trader with regard to the principal. The Commission states that if an agent is required to keep as his own property a considerable stock of the product then that agent is likely to be treated as an independent trader rather than a commercial agent.[7]

It is thought that the choice of such a determining factor is misleading for the following reasons:

—The test used in the Commission notice is to determine matters relating to competition law. The Regulations have nothing to do with competition law.
—The test was used by the Commission to determine whether an agent was an independent trader. The issue at stake in the Schedule to the Regulations is what constitutes secondary activity. The two are not the same or even similar.

---

[6] The court in *Tamarind* seems to have decided that the test should be applied solely at the outset as opposed to an analysis of the situation post-termination. Whilst it seems correct not to analyse the post-termination situation, the court did not address the question of whether the test might be applied more than once during the life of the contract.

[7] See also Commission Notice 2000/L291/01: *Guidelines on Vertical Restraints*, where the relevant determining factor is that of financial or commercial risk borne by the appointee.

—The test as used by the Commission was not the only criterion set out in the notice. There were two other alternatives—first whether the agent was required to organise, maintain or ensure at his own expense a substantial service to customers free of charge and secondly whether the agent could or did in fact determine prices or terms of business. Neither of these two further alternatives were relied on by the DTI.

—The reliance on the single test marks an obvious move away from the DTI's position as set out in the 1993 Guidelines. There, the DTI stated that the existence of any one of the criteria set out in the Commission notice would not in itself be inconsistent with an agent's commercial activities being secondary—see paragraph 23.

In the authors' opinion, the DTI would have done better to keep to its statement in the 1993 Guidelines that there existed '. . . *no readily apparent test or tests to apply in order to determine the matter of secondary activity*'—see paragraph 24. This broader approach seems to have been endorsed in the *Tamarind* case referred to above, in which it was held that the court's obligation when examining the issue as to whether a particular agent was primarily a commercial agent for the purposes of the Regulations, was to look at the nature of the commercial bargain between the parties. Was it in the principal's commercial interests that an agent should have been appointed to develop the market in particular goods by the expenditure of agents' time, money and own resources?

6.13 A CHANGE DURING THE CONTRACT TOWARDS SECONDARY ACTIVITIES

It is not clear when the condition relating to secondary activities must be satisfied. If activities of an agent are deemed to be secondary at the start of a contract does that mean that if the relevant activities become more important then this factor is not taken into account? It would seem from a common sense point of view that the test should be a continuing one even though this may lead to the Regulations being applied to a particular contract which was clearly outside their scope when it began operating.

6.14 THE IRRELEVANCE OF CERTAIN CRITERIA

With regard to the need for an agent to use his own resources when devoting effort, skill and expenditure to developing markets in order to be deemed to be acting within a commercial agency arrangement, it is not understood why the agent's own resources have to be used to demonstrate that the activities are not secondary.

With regard to the need for the contract goods to be specifically identified with the principal rather than with another person, again it is not understood why the existence of branded goods as opposed to unbranded ones should affect the way in which the agent is treated.

Ultimately, the practical question is whether the Schedule works to exclude relationships in which logic suggests that any agency activity is secondary.

6.15 SECONDARY ACTIVITIES IN PRACTICE—THE CASE LAW TO DATE

Unsurprisingly, judges have struggled with the Schedule.

In the *Tamarind* case[8] the question was whether agency activities relating to the sale of gas and electricity were or were not secondary. The judge concluded as follows:

—There was no need to find or define the opposite of 'secondary'.

—The question is a 'vertical', not a 'horizontal' one: that is, it is a matter of looking at the relationship between the principal and the agent, rather than at the whole of the appointee's business.

—The Regulations are essentially asking 'whether this agent has been engaged in such circumstances as he can be said to have been engaged to develop goodwill in the principal's business'.

The authors believe that the first two points set out above are correct. The difficulty with the third is that it is also true of distributorships, franchises and no doubt other relationships. This attempted gloss on the wording of the Schedule does not seem to be determinative and merely complicates matters further. What is needed is a wholesale review of the Schedule.

The judge in *Tamarind* did helpfully run through each of the elements of the Schedule, answering each in turn. He answered as follows, adopting the numbering in the Schedule:

2(a)   Yes. The gas was 'goods of a particular kind' because it was being branded by Eastern even if it was the same as gas sold by BG or others.

(b)(i)   Yes.

(b)(ii) Yes. Even though customers secured were likely to stay loyal and there would therefore not be further contracts with them, contracts with other customers in the same street/area were likely—indeed customers were asked to identify neighbours who might switch suppliers.

Additionally, the 'further transactions' referred to in 2 (b) (ii) did not have to be negotiated by the agent.

3(a)   Yes, Eastern distributed this product.

(b)   Gas was identified with Eastern.

(c)   Yes.

(d)   Most sales were through the agents.

(e)   Neutral—contracts described as 'service agreements'.

---

[8] [2000] EuLR 709.

4(a)   No. Though some material was sent direct.
 (b)   No. Exclusivity was, the judge thought, implicit.
 (c)   The agents had actively sold Eastern's product to potential customers.

There is no complete report on which to analyse *Hunter v Zenith Windows*, which in any event is only a County Court decision. In that case it is reported that someone who might be described as a 'super-agent',[9] whilst otherwise being a commercial agent for the purposes of the Regulations, was not entitled to compensation because his actions were unlikely to lead to further transactions. If the report is correct, the court applied only paragraph 2(b)(ii) of the Schedule.

Even on that point, it is submitted that the reasoning in *Tamarind* is to be preferred: paragraph 2(b)(ii) refers not only to this customer but to others, and does not rely on the agent securing the further business concerned.

6.16   WHAT IS THE POSITION AS REGARDS NORTHERN IRELAND?

As mentioned above, the Regulations do not apply to Northern Ireland, for which there is a separate implementing regulation: SR 1993/483. They were made on 17 December 1993 and came into force on 13 January 1994, a little after the due implementation date. Detailed reference should be made to that regulation, but it largely mirrors SI 1993/3053. The comment above regarding regulations 1(2) and (3) (see 4.14 and 4.15) is of relevance in determining whether an agent who operates for the whole of the UK need make two separate claims for compensation/indemnity or only one claim, in circumstances where his or her agreement with the principal is governed by English law.

---

[9] See 5.12 and 6.2 above.

7

Regulations 3, 4 and 5—Rights and Obligations of Agent and Principal

7.1 OUTLINE

THIS CHAPTER DEALS with the duties of a commercial agent to his principal and the duties of a principal to his commercial agent.

7.2 STRUCTURE

This part of the Regulations (Part II) consists of regulations 3, 4 and 5. Regulation 5 states that it is not permissible to derogate from regulations 3 and 4 and that the law applicable to the contract shall govern the consequence of breach of the obligations set out therein. In English law, this issue comes down to the question of whether the Regulations operate to imply contractual terms into the agreement between principal and agent, or operate at a different level from contractual obligations and are the subject of other (possibly tortious) remedies.

Regulation 3 sets out the agent's duties to the principal and regulation 4 sets out the principal's duties to the agent.

7.3 WHAT ARE THE AGENT'S DUTIES?

Regulation 3 requires the agent:

—to look after the interests of his principal and act dutifully and in good faith;
—to make proper efforts to negotiate and, where appropriate, conclude the transactions he is instructed to take care of;
—to communicate to his principal all the necessary information available to him;
—to comply with reasonable instructions given by his principal.

As was mentioned in chapter 1, an agent has certain fiduciary duties to the principal and the first of the above duties therefore adds little to the existing law. Indeed, generally, the above duties add little if anything to English law as regards the agent's duties but serve to codify obligations which already existed at common law.

Consider the position of an agent who acts as agent for more than one principal in the same geographical market. It is likely to be selling complementary ranges of products. How does the agent resolve its conflicting duties to the various principals, in particular the duty to look after their respective interests? This problem has always existed, but the agent now has a statutory duty in addition to any common law duty.

By way of an example, suppose that agent X acts for manufacturer M who manufactures coffee-making machinery for restaurants. Agent X also acts for manufacturer P who produces ground coffee suitable for use in M's present machines. If M develops a new type of coffee-making machine which requires coffee prepared on a different basis than that supplied by P, how does X resolve the conflict between its duty to sell M's new machine (which perhaps earns greater profits for M than the sale of the existing machinery) and X's duty to P? Certainly (presumably subject to any confidentiality obligations) X will be obliged to inform P of the new development and the impending introduction of M's new machine. X is however in an even more difficult position if it is bound by an obligation of confidence to M and cannot supply this information to P in circumstances where, perhaps, it could have done so had it discovered M's plans and had it not been acting as M's agent. Perhaps the disclosure of information in these circumstances comes within the exception set out in regulation 21— nothing in the Regulations requires the disclosure of information where to disclose would be contrary to public policy.

As was noted in chapter 1, English law has traditionally viewed the principal as the person requiring protection and the common law therefore developed very few rules for the protection of the agent.

Regulation 4 imposes duties upon the principal as follows:

—to act dutifully and in good faith;
—to provide the commercial agent with the necessary documentation relating to the goods concerned;
—to obtain necessary information for the agent;
—to notify the agent within a reasonable period once the principal anticipates the volume of transactions will be significantly lower than that which the agent could normally have expected;
—to inform the agent within a reasonable period of the principal's acceptance or refusal or non-execution of a commercial transaction procured by the commercial agent for the principal.

As will be seen below, though they may appear bland, these duties may give explosive remedies to the agent.[1]

7.6 NECESSARY DOCUMENTATION

What is 'necessary documentation relating to the goods concerned'? Is this a reference to technical specifications, promotional material, price lists or otherwise? The answer is likely to vary on a case-by-case basis.

7.7 NECESSARY INFORMATION

It is interesting to compare the duty of the principal to obtain for the agent 'information necessary for the performance of the agency contract' and the agent's duty to communicate to the principal 'all the necessary information available to him'. The principal's duty seemingly extends to securing information which the principal does not have available. In addition to the 'information necessary', to what could this duty extend? As a matter of principle why should it extend, for instance, to lists of potential customers or to details of potential new legislation in the territory which could affect the products? If the duty extends to this sort of information, is that not material which the principal could legitimately expect the agent to secure, rather than vice versa?

7.8 DUTY TO INFORM—LOWER VOLUME OF TRANSACTIONS

On an allied point, why should it be the duty of the principal to inform the agent when the volume of transactions may be significantly lower? The principal may well have engaged the services of the agent in large part because the agent understands the territory better than the principal. Will it not, therefore be the agent who is better placed to advise the principal in this regard? At the very least, should the Directive not have imposed a similar duty upon the agent? If an agent is employed in a distant market unknown to the principal and conditions in the territory change because of the imposition of exchange control restrictions, or the enactment of new legislation on health and safety, or new consumer protection legislation, should it not be the agent's duty to communicate this information to the principal? Some of this may fall within the agent's general duty to look after the principal's interests and to act in good faith.

---

[1] See para 7.12.

7.9 DUTY TO INFORM—TRANSACTIONS PROCURED BY AGENT

As regards the final duty to inform, there is some overlap here with regulation 12 which requires the principal to supply the agent with a statement of commission due and the main components used in calculating the amount of commission. It is difficult to see how the principal could comply with the latter obligation if it did not tell the agent which transactions had gone forward and which would not be proceeding.

7.10 ARE THE DUTIES OF AGENT AND PRINCIPAL CONTRACTUAL OR STATUTORY IN NATURE?

Are the duties set out in regulations 3 and 4 (and indeed the other obligations imposed upon principal and agent by the Regulations) terms which are to be implied into every contract, or do they form part of a statutory scheme which overlies the contractual position?

To illustrate this point, consider the difference between the Sale of Goods Act 1979 as amended and employment protection legislation—in particular the Employment Protection (Consolidation) Act 1978.

The 1979 Act states that certain provisions will be implied into every contract for the sale of goods. The Act states that those terms will be conditions (that is, major terms) of the contract and it is accordingly clear that a breach of those terms gives rise to contractual remedies and that these include a right in favour of the innocent party to terminate the contract as a result of that breach.

In contrast, the 1978 Act overlies the contractual position. So, therefore, an employee who is dismissed wrongfully and without notice has two claims:

—one claim is a claim for breach of contract and is remedied by the award of damages; and

—the other remedy (which is provided by an industrial tribunal) is for non-contractual compensation based upon the terms of the 1978 Act.

This may seem like an academic question, but it has some serious consequences for the operation and enforcement of the terms of the regulations.

If the Regulations are intended to imply terms into contracts (as in the 1979 Act):

—The Regulations do not state this and do not state whether those terms will be conditions of the contract (allowing the innocent party to terminate) or will be lesser terms (giving rise to a right in damages, but not to a right of termination).

—There would be little need to spell out the basis upon which damages are to be calculated since there is a wealth of material at common law on this subject.

If however the Regulations are to operate in a non-contractual manner (as with the 1978 Act):

—None of the necessary mechanics are included in the Regulations (with some exceptions—see below) to enable the court to operate those provisions effectively. If, for instance, regulations 3 and 4 are statutory obligations, is there a remedy in damages for their breach?

—Are damages to be calculated on a contractual or a tortious basis, or on some other basis?

—Without specific provision, if the regulations provide statutory non-contractual remedies, then there is presumably no question of an ability to terminate the contract for breach of them.

7.11 RIGHTS UNDER REGULATION 17

It is clear from the regulations that the rights set out in regulation 17 are statutory non-contractual remedies—or at least this is clear as a result of regulation 17(5) in the case of the indemnity. The authors suggest that the same is true of the compensatory option. Any remedies under regulation 17 are in addition to and not in substitution for contractual remedies.[2] Indeed, many of the circumstances in which compensation or an indemnity is payable are not circumstances which amount to a breach of contract by either party. This mirrors to a great extent the position regarding wrongful and unfair dismissal at common law and in the 1978 Act.

It would be even more strange, therefore, if other elements of the Regulations were intended to operate on a contractual basis, since there is no provision in the Regulations which enables the reader to make the distinction between the 'contractual' obligations and the 'statutory' obligations.

The conclusion, therefore, is that the Regulations do not operate by way of implying terms into contracts but rather from part of a statutory scheme overlying the contractual position. They do however have effects on agency contracts, so that if for instance a provision of the contract contradicts regulation 10(2), the contractual provision will be of no effect and regulation 10(2) will apply. If, however, regulation 10(2) is a term to be implied into contracts, then the status of the two conflicting terms is resolved by regulation 10(4) which states that any agreement to derogate from regulation 10(2) is void. If the principal then purports to operate the void provision, is this a serious breach of a term implied into the

---

[2] This view of the Regulations as creating extra-contractual remedies seems to be reinforced by the case law to date, such as *Moore v Piretta PTA Limited*—see para 5.6. The Court of Justice was asked to consider an associated issue in *SPRL Arcado v SA Haviland* [1988] ECR 1539. In that case, it was held that a claim for commission and compensation under national legislation implementing the Directive arose from 'matters relating to a contract' for the purposes of the Brussels Convention on Jurisdiction. This view, that rights under legislation implementing the Directive arise in contract rather than, for instance, in tort, does not disturb the reasoning in this para. However, see the recent decision of the French Court de Cassation in *Figot v Leithauser GmbH and Co* [2000] I.L.Pr. 28 for a finding that a claim for an indemnity by a commercial agent on termination was a claim independent of the contract between the parties. See also most recently the judgment of Elias J in *Bell Electric Ltd v Aweco Appliance Systems GMbH* [2002] EWHC 872 (QB): 8 May 2002.

contract, or is it merely a wrongful act in respect of which the agent could claim damages and/or injunctive relief?

7.12 AGENT'S AND PRINCIPAL'S DUTIES IN PRACTICE

In what was possibly the first reported decision applying the Regulations, the Court of Appeal had the opportunity to look at the duties of agent and principal in *Page v Combined Shipping and Trading Co Ltd*.[3] This is an interlocutory decision—Mr Page was appealing against refusal by the lower court to award him a prior restraint order (formerly a Mareva injunction)—but the court had to decide as part of its consideration whether he had a good arguable case under the Regulations entitling him to substantial compensation.

Mr Page had entered into a four-year agency agreement with CST in January 1995. His role was to buy and sell commodities as agent for CST. However, by June, CST's parent company had decided to close the CST business. Mr Page claimed that this was a repudiation and started proceedings. However, his difficulty was that the agreement left a lot of latitude to CST—it could decide from day to day how much business it wanted to do through Mr Page. As a matter of common law,[4] the Court would assume that a defendant such as CST would, where it had discretion, have acted so as to minimise its liability. If it had done so, its liability to him might be nil.

The court decided, on the basis of CST's duty of good faith under regulation 4, that CST could not rely on the common law rule. Combining the duty of good faith with the wording of regulation 17 ('commission which proper performance of the agency contract would have procured for him') and seemingly swayed by the fact that in other language versions of the Directive, the word 'normal' appeared in place of the word 'proper', Millett LJ concluded that compensation should be calculated on the basis of normal future performance and not abnormal (even if lawful) performance.

The court seems here to be stretching the phrase 'good faith' to its limits. By logical extension, had the contract continued in force but CST *had* reduced trade to zero, the Court of Appeal would presumably have upheld a claim by Mr Page for damages based on the good faith principle!

'Good faith' here seems to comprehend something more than merely fair and honest dealing and extends to a positive obligation to consider the agent's business interests ahead of one's own. It is suggested that this is broader than the common law duty on agents and is tantamount to imposing fiduciary obligations on the principal in favour of the agent.[5]

---

[3] [1997] 3All ER 656.

[4] *Laverack v Woods* [1967] 1 QB 278.

[5] It has even been suggested that to understand the Court of Appeal's judgment in *Page* necessitates a review of French law on the subject (S Saintier, *The Company Lawyer* (19) 8, p 248, 249).

Page makes an interesting contrast with the traditional English approach taken in *Airconsult Ltd v British Aerospace Regional Aircraft Ltd*[6] a case in which, bafflingly, the Regulations were not referred to or applied. In that case, A was entitled to commission on a sale or lease of aircraft by BARA to certain nominated third parties. A procured a lessee and started to earn commission. BARA then sold the aircraft, subject to the leases, to a third party outside the nominated group of third parties. The judge in the Queen's Bench Division concluded that:

> Unless ... there is an implied term that [BARA] ... will not terminate the operating lease ... [A] cannot be entitled to the fee.

The judge also said that:

> There is no question here of denying the defendants [BARA] freedom to deal with their property as they choose [or] ... denying them freedom to [either] their business or not to continue it as they wish.

---

[6] Unreported; QBD 13 February 1998.

8

Regulations 6 to 12—Remuneration of the Agent

8.1 OUTLINE

THIS CHAPTER DEALS with the key issues relating to the remuneration of a commercial agent, including when commission is payable and the circumstances which can extinguish the agent's right to commission.

8.2 STRUCTURE

Regulation 6 deals with remuneration in the absence of agreement and states that regulations 7 to 12 inclusive do not apply unless the agent is remunerated wholly or in part by commission. It should be noted that compensation or an indemnity payment is due on termination even when the agent is not remunerated by way of commission.

The Court of Appeal has held, unsurprisingly[1] that the concept of 'remuneration' for the purposes of the Regulations does not extend to circumstances in which the representative earns a 'turn' on the difference between purchase and resale price, where the representative buys and later resells, the mark-up being determined by the representative. To conclude otherwise would have brought all distributorships within the scope of the Regulations.

Regulation 7 deals with entitlement to commission during the term of the contract, regulation 8 deals with entitlement to commission on transactions concluded after termination and regulation 9 deals with apportionment of commissions between an incoming and an outgoing agent following termination.

Regulation 10 deals with the circumstances in which commission becomes due and the date upon which commission is payable, regulation 11 deals with the extinction of the right to commission in certain circumstances and regulation 12 deals with supply of information by the principal and the agent.

---

[1] In *AMB Imballagi Plastici SRL v Pacflex Limited* (CA) [1999] 2 All ER (Comm) 249. See also in this connection the recent judgment of Andrew Smith J in the Commercial Court in *Mercantile Industrial Group plc v Chuan Soon Huat Industrial Group plc* [2002] 1 All ER (Comm) 788 in which the fact that the agent received a 'turn' between the purchase and resale prices did not mean that the Regulations were not applicable. It simply meant that the agent was not remunerated by way of commission. The matter is now subject to an appeal.

Regulation 6(1) states that in the absence of agreement as to remuneration between the parties, the agent will be entitled to:

—the remuneration that agents appointed for the goods which are the subject of the agency contract are customarily allowed in the place where the agent carries on his activities;
—(if there is no such customary practice) reasonable remuneration taking into account all the aspects of the transaction.

This regulation is likely to be of relevance only in a very few cases, since even in the briefest of oral agreements, commission is likely to be an issue on which there is express agreement.

It should be noted that there is nothing which requires the parties to agree an objectively reasonable level of commission, although given that the reason for the Directive was the perceived inequality of bargaining power, it might have been expected that the Directive would tackle this issue. Indeed, the fact that the commission rate agreed is lower than average or lower than some objective standard is not even stated to be a factor to be taken into account in calculating compensation or an indemnity payment.

Customary remuneration

The relevant custom is that of the place where the agent carried on his activities (compare earlier drafts of the Regulations which took a slightly different stance). It is conceivable, therefore, that agents in different territories performing the same obligations might receive differential rates of commission (or other remuneration) as a result of the operation of this provision. Rather than harmonising, therefore, in this respect the Directive perpetuates existing inequalities.

If there is no custom on which to rely, the agent is entitled to reasonable remuneration (presumably whether this reasonable remuneration takes the form of commission or not) taking into account 'all the aspects of the transaction': is this a reference to the agreement between principal and agent, or between principal and third party? If the latter, it would require a separate consideration of the issues in respect of each transaction on which the agent was entitled to commission. It is an almost inescapable conclusion of the wording used that the reference is to each individual transaction between principal and third party, particularly since the same word is used in regulations 7 and 10 to refer to the contract between principal and third party, but if this is correct then it engenders uncertainty in so far as the parties will find it difficult to determine whether the right amount of commission has been paid. Would it not have been more logical to have used the duties which the agent has expected to perform as the touchstone for this calculation?

Regulation 6(2) states that it is without prejudice to the application of any enactment or rule of law concerning the level of remuneration. There are no such enactments in England and Wales.

Regulation 7 sets out three circumstances in which the agent is entitled to commission on transactions concluded during the term of the contract, as follows:

—where the transaction is concluded as a result of the agent's action;
—where the transaction is concluded with a third party whom the agent has previously acquired as a customer for transactions of the same kind; or
—where the agent has an exclusive right to a specified geographical area or to a specific group of customers and the transaction is entered into with a customer belonging to that area or group.

Each of these limbs is considered separately below. It should be noted that the preamble to regulation 7 uses the word 'concluded', perhaps an unintentional echo of the words 'negotiate and conclude' as used in the definition of 'commercial agent' itself. The authors' view is that this word can only refer, in both contexts, to the conclusion of a binding contract between principal and third party. To this extent, it can be contrasted with the word 'executed' which is utilised in regulation 10 and which refers to the performance by a party of its obligations under the contract which has been concluded.

The first limb of regulation 7 refers to transactions concluded as a result of the agent's action. At common law, the question was whether the agent was the effective cause of the transaction and there is much case law in this area, concerning in particular the role of estate agents. It is not sufficient for the agent's act to be the *causa sine qua non* of the transaction. In case of conflicting claims to commission, the courts at common law would determine which of the competing agents was the effective cause of the transaction (compare with the issue discussed below at paragraph 8.7).

Could two agents both state that a single transaction had been entered into as a result of their respective actions? In this sense, it may be that the standard set by the Regulations is more lax and entails greater danger for the principal than the common law rule.

The second limb of regulation refers to the conclusion of a contract with a third party whom the agent has previously acquired as a customer for transactions of the same kind. It should be noted that there is no reference to obtaining this customer as a customer for the same principal, nor is there a reference to goods of the same kind as the goods in question. Is it enough that, in a previous incarnation as agent (or perhaps distributor or employee) of the present principal's main competitor, the agent secured this customer as a customer for similar goods? If so, then the principal may be in a worse position (from the point of view of the Regulations, at least) in engaging an experienced agent known in the market than he would otherwise be.

Assuming, however, that the agent has received some compensation or indemnity upon termination of its relationship with the competitor (if that relationship was that of principal and agent) why should the agent effectively receive a second payment even though, by definition, it has not satisfied the first limb of regulation 7 and the transaction has not resulted from its action? In fact, the perverse conclusion is that the customer concerned could have come direct to the present principal precisely because he or she was dissatisfied with the agent's former principal or even with the agent itself! It seems an odd conclusion that the principal should be obliged to pay commission in such circumstances.

8.7 THE THIRD LIMB

The third limb of regulation contemplates a degree of exclusivity, either in respect of a geographical area or group of customers. It should be noted that it is not necessary for this exclusivity to have been agreed on the face of the contract and there must be a danger for principals that the fact of merely having one agent for a particular area or group of customers will give rise to claims under this limb. Confusingly, both the Directive and the Regulations use the words 'concluded' and 'entered into' to refer to the same transaction, but the different wording is presumably not intended to import any difference of meaning.

What does 'exclusive' mean in this context? Does it mean strict exclusivity, with neither the principal nor any other party having the right to seek customers in the territory concerned, or does it cover 'sole' agencies where in effect the agent is in competition with the principal for orders? Particularly given the fact where the agent is only 'negotiating' (and not 'negotiating and concluding') that the principal will be involved in contract formation, it may be that the intention is that 'sole' agencies will be covered as well as 'exclusive' agencies.

It should be noted that both the second and third limbs of regulation 7 operate where the agent has not been the cause of the transaction concerned.[2] It is a frequent complaint of principals with mature agency networks that, in fact, sales volumes stagnate as agents who originally worked hard for relatively modest remuneration at the outset rest on their laurels when earning significant commissions as a result of

---

[2] As regards Regulation 7(2), this was confirmed by the Court of Justice in Case C–104/95: *Kontogeorgas v Kartonpak AE* [1996] ECR I–6643.

repeat orders from long-term customers. The Regulations do nothing to address this situation.

In *Kontogeorgas v Kartonpak AE* [3] the Court of Justice stated that the expression 'customer belonging to that area' in Article 7(2) of the Directive (and therefore regulation 7 (2)) means that, where the agent is a legal person, one looks for the location of that person's commercial activities.

It recognised, however, that this alone could result in a single transaction being regarded as attaching to the territories of two different agents. Accordingly, it stated that, where customer or agent operated in several places, one must consider other factors to determine the centre of gravity of the transaction, including where negotiations took place (or should have taken place in the normal course), the place of delivery and the location from which the order was placed.

8.8 DOUBLE AND TRIPLE TROUBLE—MULTIPLE CLAIMS

A particular difficulty may arise with a multi-location customer and competing claims to commission. Suppose that a principal is represented in territories A, B and C by agents X, Y and Z. Each of the agents has been appointed on an exclusive basis. Q Plc places an order with the principal through its branch in territory A, but does not go through agent X. Agent X is nevertheless entitled to a commission under the third limb since he has an exclusive right to territory A. However, the order concerned resulted from work carried out by agent Y, who has persuaded the finance director of Q Plc, at a trade fair recently held in territory B, to purchase the principal's products. Y is entitled to a commission under the first limb. Agent Z had nothing to do with the present order, but has previously acquired Q Plc as a customer for this principal, perhaps at a time when he was the exclusive agent of the whole of the territory now divided up between X, Y and Z. Z seems to be entitled to commission under the second limb.

How are these competing claims to be handled? Although regulations 8 and 9 are considered below, it will be noted that regulation 9 provides a way of dealing with competing claims as between an incoming and outgoing agent. Why is there no such provision to deal with competing claims during the term of agency contracts?

This difficulty is compounded in practice since the principal may, at the time when the order referred to above is received, pay commission to agent X. It may be some months or years since agent Z acquired business for Q Plc and the principal may not even know at this stage that agent Y has attempted to sell the products to Q Plc. This 'double' or 'triple' trouble ideally should be resolved by amendment to the Regulations. But what is the position in the meantime?

There are two answers to this question. First of all, it is to be hoped that the courts will take a sensible approach to this issue, allowing the principal to divide commission on an equitable basis between the three agents. This does not, however, obviate the risk that the basis of such division is subsequently challenged,

---

[3] See footnote 2.

even assuming that the principal is aware of all claims on deciding how to divide commission.

The reality is that agents are unlikely to litigate this point during the term of the contract and that this issue may therefore only arise once the agency contract has determined. Suppose that, at the time concerned, the principal merely paid the whole of the commission due to agent X. It is only on termination of agent Y's contract that, in addition to claiming compensation or indemnity under Part IV of the Regulations, agent Y also claims commissions on a large number of orders including that which we are considering. Would the court entitle the principal subsequently to set off any sums actually paid to agent Y against sums subsequently due to agent X? Even if the court would allow this, this set-off is only available to the principal if agent X is still in existence and if there is still an entitlement to commissions. If agent X has died or (if a company) has been liquidated, then this option is not available to the principal.

The second answer to this question is that the principal should take care in drafting agency contracts with a view to providing for the payment of differential commission rates in such circumstances. It should be noted that there is nothing in regulation 6 or regulation 7 to prevent the payment of differential commission rates depending upon the circumstances and indeed regulation 9, which is considered below, effectively sanctions the payment of a lower rate of commission in certain circumstances.

Taking the drafting issue a stage further, is it possible to provide that the rate of commission will be zero, or that no commission will be due, on contracts concluded outside the given area? There seems no reason in principle why this should not be done unless the court would be prepared to state under regulation 6 that there had been no agreement as to remuneration between the parties.

A broader issue here is the question of whether regulations 7–9 are excludeable by express agreement in any event and that issue is considered below. The DTI's only comment on this issue in the 1994 Guidance Notes is the following rather delphic comment:

> The provisions of [7](2) include so-called 'House Accounts' held by the principal ie, where the principal deals directly with the third party although the agent has the rights to that area.

The assumption behind this provision is that exclusivity is an 'all or nothing' concept: either the agent has an exclusive right to a particular area, in which case the DTI is suggesting that the principal cannot carve out specific named customers from that exclusivity, or the area is not exclusive to the agent at all. In practice, the principal will frequently want to remove house accounts from the agent's entitlement to commission: where there is an agent of a large multi-national group in the territory and there are intra-group sales between the principal and an associated company in that territory, it could be disastrous for the principal if it were obliged to pay commissions on those intra-group sales as well as on sales to third parties. If this is the effect of the Regulations as the DTI suggests, why should this be the case? The agent is unlikely to have done any work to procure those intra-group sales and whether there is such a sale or not depends merely on the manner in which the principal has organised its business: if the local operation were merely a branch of the principal's business, then there would be no sale at all—just an intra-company transfer.

8.9 POSITION OF DEL CREDERE AGENTS

A del credere agent is an agent who accepts responsibility towards the principal in the event that customers fail to pay. As such, a del credere agent is an exception to the normal situation which is that following the formation of a contract between principal and customer the agent has no liability on the contract. Are del credere agents in a different position as a result of the introduction of the Regulations?

In recognition of the extra liability which he takes on, the del credere agent receives an extra commission, known as the 'del credere commission' and one important question is whether these commissions will also be the subject of the rules set out in Part III of the Regulations. The del credere commission would seem to satisfy the definition of 'commission' in regulation 2 but is the del credere agent not being remunerated for a separate service which he provides which is not of the type which the Directive intended to cover?

This point is not dealt with in the Directive or the Regulations and will not be resolved until there is litigation on the question. Del credere agency is, in any event, fairly rare and the point is unlikely to be a significant one in the context of the bulk of commercial agency relationships. In contrast, the draft of the Directive considered by the Law Commission Report contained specific provisions regarding del credere agents. The Law Commission asked the interesting question whether a del credere agent is due the normal commission in circumstances where he pays upon failure by the customer to pay. This question remains unanswered.

8.10 ENTITLEMENT TO COMMISSIONS ON TRANSACTIONS CONCLUDED AFTER TERMINATION

Regulation 8 states that the agent will be entitled to commission on transactions concluded after termination if:

—the transaction is 'mainly attributable' to the agent's efforts during the term of the contract and the transaction is entered into within a 'reasonable period' after termination; or
—the third party's order reached the principal or the agent before termination.

Why have the words 'mainly attributable' been used in regulation 8 when the words 'as a result of his action' are used in regulation 7? With reference to the comments at paragraph 8.5 above regarding regulation 7(1)(a), it is presumably possible for only one agent to say that the transaction is 'mainly attributable' to his efforts. Was the test intended to be more severe under regulation 8 than it is under regulation 7?

What is a 'reasonable period'? This will be determined by reference to the facts of each case, but the duration of the agency contract and in particular the notice period to be given under it are factors which should be taken into account. The nature of the principal's business should also be considered—for instance, if the goods are heavy plant, it may take many months to turn an enquiry into an order.[4]

8.11 SHARING COMMISSIONS—INCOMING AND OUTGOING AGENT

Under regulation 9 the basic rule is that the incoming agent is not entitled to commission unless it is equitable for the commission to be shared. Regulation 9 does not contemplate any circumstances in which the outgoing agent would receive no commission—seemingly the outgoing agent gets everything or a share of the commission due. Will this always be appropriate?

Regulation 9 is likely to create further difficulties for the principal: by definition, the principal is parting company with one agent, who probably has a right to compensation or indemnity. The principal has to decide which of the incoming and outgoing agents is entitled to commission, or (if it would be 'equitable' to divide the commission) the ratio of sharing. Although regulation 9(2) states that sums wrongfully paid by the principal to one of the parties shall be refunded, it is likely to be very difficult in practice for the principal to recover the sum due and the principal can presumably not set up the inability to gain recovery of commission from one of the agents as a reason to refuse to pay the other.

In effect, the principal has to make a judgment at the time as to the basis of division of the commission, even though he or she may not be in possession of all the facts. There is an effective 'right of appeal' from this decision to the court, which may decide that the principal's basis of division was completely wrong and require the principal to pay a further sum to the disgruntled agent. There is again the danger here of 'double trouble'. Although this is not likely to be a significant issue in most cases, if the order which gives rise to the dispute is a very substantial order with commission running to hundreds of thousands of pounds, this issue may for the principal be a question of commercial survival, not merely of the discomfort of paying twice. In such circumstances, principals would be well advised to ensure that both agents give a detailed summary of the circumstances surrounding the receipt of the order in support of their competing applications for commission: whether the court will allow the principal to plead that the agent is estopped from claiming a greater share of the commission on the basis that it is now presenting to the court information which it did not present to the principal is questionable.

---

[4] This point was specifically examined in the High Court judgment of *Ingmar GB limited v Eaton Leonard Inc:* 31 July 2001.

Another possibility which has been considered by the authors in these circumstances is that the new agent could agree expressly as a term of his agency contract not to claim any commissions pursuant to regulation 9 from the principal. This issue is considered in the following paragraph, as part of the general discussion of the ability to exclude regulations 7–9.

8.12 ARE REGULATIONS 7, 8 AND 9 CAPABLE OF EXCLUSION?

Many of the provisions of the Directive state that they are not capable of exclusion, or are not to be varied to the detriment of the agent. These declarations are repeated in the Regulations. So, for instance, regulation 19 states that regulations 17–18 (relating to indemnity and compensation) are not capable of exclusion. Similarly, regulation 10(4) states that any agreement to derogate from regulation 10(2) and 10(3) to the detriment of the agent shall be void.

There is no such statement in connection with regulations 7–9. If these provisions are capable of exclusion, then this is of great importance to the principal who can hopefully avoid the prospect of 'double' or 'triple trouble', by providing:

—that the agent will not be entitled to commissions unless it has been the effective cause of the transaction (rather than the fact that it is a result of the agent's action or mainly attributable to its efforts—regulations 7 and 8 respectively). Such a provision could be included even where the agent has an exclusive area;
—that the second limb of regulation 7 would not apply at all;
—that the new agent would not be entitled to any commissions in respect of orders received before its contract commenced (even if it had carried out some work in ensuring that the contract was finally concluded) or on orders which are mainly attributable to the outgoing agent's efforts; and/or
—that the outgoing agent could agree that it would not be entitled to any commission save on transactions concluded during the term of the agency contract.

If exclusion is possible, then regulations 7–9 are in reality only providing a framework to cover the situation where these issues are not addressed at all in the agency contract. This highlights the importance of concluding a suitable written agreement.

The DTI has not commented on this issue at all, save for the odd provision which appeared at paragraph 14 of the first draft. There is no clear pointer on this issue in the wording of the Directive or the Regulations and it seems that the DTI has decided to sit on the fence on purpose. For instance, the parties are clearly entitled to derogate from regulation 6 and this is re-enforced by the opening words 'In the absence of any agreement as to remuneration between the parties . . .' . As mentioned above, areas where derogation is clearly not possible, or is not possible to the agent's disbenefit are similarly highlighted in the Directive and the Tegulations.

Conversely, the wording of regulations 7–9 is not permissive but is absolute. Regulation 10 sets out some general rules, but then provides for a mandatory backstop although there are no such provisions in regulations 7–9.

As mentioned above, the agent is unlikely to raise these issues during the term of the contract and the danger for principals is that, if they continue to operate upon the terms of their pre–1994 agreement and do not pay commission in the new circumstances contemplated by regulations 7–9, the agent is unlikely to claim commission until he rolls all of these claims up with his claim for compensation and any claim for damages for breach of contract upon termination.

It should also be noted that, although the agent must notify the principal within one year from termination if it wishes to claim compensation or indemnity, there is no limitation period set out in the Regulations for any claim to commissions owed. Further, although regulation 19 can be read so as to allow the parties to agree upon a settlement figure post-termination, if regulations 7–9 are mandatory then there is no express provision allowing the parties to agree a compromise.

The authors' view is that regulations 7–9 are capable of exclusion and that it is therefore open to the parties to lay down their own rules as to the transactions upon which commission will be payable both during and after the termination of the agency contract. Given the uncertainty, however, the best advice which can be given to principals is to proceed on the basis that commission may be capable of exclusive in the circumstances set out in regulations 7–9 but to be aware of the possibility of a successful claim in this regard in due course.[5]

Given the government's obvious dislike for the Directive, it is strange that (if the DTI shares this view) it did not set out in the Regulations a clear statement to this effect. This is another example of an area in which the government was perhaps worried by the prospect of *Francovich* actions, and chose merely to mirror the wording of the Directive. This indecision is damaging to business certainty and in any event, if the English courts determine that regulations 7–9 are not mandatory, but the European Court of Justice takes the view that they are, then the government will be held to have improperly implemented the Directive and may be open to *Francovich* actions in any event. Would it not have been preferable for the DTI to have clarified the position in this regard before making the Regulations with a view both to defending itself from *Francovich* actions and (more importantly) fostering legal certainty?

8.13   WHEN IS COMMISSION DUE AND WHEN IS IT PAYABLE?

Regulation 10 deals when the commission is due and when it is payable and regulation 11 deals with the extinction of the right to commission. It should be noted that the questions in the above heading are different questions: the first asks in what circumstances commission is due and the second deals with the date upon which payment should be made.

---

[5] Such uncertainty is further evidenced by regulation 11—as to which see para 8.15 below.

Here, the question of ability to exclude is clearer: regulation 10(1) sets out three tests as to the circumstances in which commission becomes due, but regulation 10(2) (which is expressly stated to be mandatory) sets out a 'backstop' last stage at which commission is due.

The three circumstances set out in regulation 10(1) are that:

—the principal has 'executed' the transaction;
—the principal should have 'executed' the transaction according to the agreement with the customer; or
—the customer has 'executed' the transaction.

What does the word 'execute' mean? This word is taken from the French language version of the Directive. The Regulations lazily mirror the Directive in using a plethora of different expressions to describe the formation and carrying into effect of the contract between principal and customer. There was an attempt, particularly in the first draft, to clarify, but (no doubt on the *Francovich* ground once again) the DTI has stepped back from the brink. This is unfortunate.

'Execute' must, however, mean something different from 'conclude', and in this context the normal meaning of the word 'execution' for English lawyers is something of a false friend. 'Execution' must mean performance, but does it mean 'starting to perform', or 'finishing performance'? The principal's obligations under the contract are most likely to involve delivery of goods and the customer's main (if not sole) obligation is to pay the price. But in a complex transaction, what if the principal carries out the design work agreed but the transaction proceeds no further? Or, what happens if the third party pays the first instalment of the price but not the remainder, or (even more confusing) pays for the goods element of the transaction but not the services element? The wording suggests that payment may be due only at the conclusion of all performance, but the courts may well take a different view. The DTI's view is that all commission is due upon delivery of the first instalment.

Although regulation 10(1) is seemingly capable of exclusion, regulation 10(2) is not. It states that commission becomes due at the latest when the customer has 'executed' his or her part of the transaction or should have done so if the principal had 'executed' its part of the transaction as it should have. This mandatory backstop will mean that in the majority of cases commission does not become due, seemingly, until the customer has paid. However, if the customer does not pay, or pays late, as a result of some failure or inability to perform on the part of the principal, then commission will become due when the customer would—if it had not been for that failure to perform—have paid. Thus, for instance, if the principal is in breach of its obligations to the customer or supplies defective goods and as a result the customer does not pay, then the principal still has to pay commission. Although this is logical and reasonable, it runs contrary to the provision generally found in agency contracts before implementation of the Regulations, stating that commission would only become due when the principal had received payment in cleared funds from the customer.

8.14 TIME FOR PAYMENT

Having established when the commission is due, regulation 10(3) goes on to deal with the time for payment. Again, the provision operates as a 'backstop' since if the parties have agreed an earlier date for payment, that agreement will prevail.

The rule is that commission is to be paid not later that the last day of the month following the quarter in which it became due. Regulation 10(3) lays down a basis for determining the start date of quarters, in the absence of agreement. This is more favourable to the principal than the position generally laid down in agency contracts, which will typically require payment by the end of the month following that in which commission became due, or payment within 30 days. If the principal takes full advantage of the period allowed by regulation10(3), then (if a quarter ends at the beginning of a calendar month) commission on an order received at the start of the quarter can be postponed for almost five months. The wording 'last day of the month following the quarter' is obscure, but presumably means the end of the calendar month following the calendar month in which the last day of the quarter falls.

8.15 EXTINCTION OF RIGHT TO COMMISSION

Regulation 11 is mandatory. The right to commission can be extinguished only if and to the extent that it is established that the contract between principal and the customer will not be 'executed' (see above) and that fact is 'due to a reason' for which the principal is 'not to blame'. Regulation 11(2) states that any commission which the agent has already received shall be refunded if the right to it is extinguished.

Several elements of Regulation11(1) merit further comment as follows:

—It could be argued that the 'right to commission' to which regulation 11 refers is the right created by regulations 7–10 (inclusive). If so, this would suggest that regulations 7–9 are not capable of exclusion because of the prohibition on excluding regulation 11(1) created by regulation 11(5).

—'. . . It is established' that the contract will not be executed: who is to establish this? There could presumably be substantial periods during which principal and customer are arguing as to the responsibility for delays or problems and it is unclear what will happen. If the contract provides for the reference of a matter to an expert, for instance, and the resolution of that dispute takes several years, then seemingly the principal will have to pay commission and will only have a right to a refund of it at some time in the future if the matter is resolved in his favour. Thus, the principal could have paid substantial sums to the agent long before the principal receives any payment from the customer.

—'The contract . . . will not be executed': the word 'executed' has been the subject of detailed comment above (paragraph 8.13) and there is no reason to believe that it will have a different meaning here. However, the word has previously always been related to performance by either the principal or the agent. Here the reference is merely to execution. Presumably this has to be read as a reference to performance by both parties. The first reaction might be to assume that, if the principal has not executed, this will always be for a reason for which the principal is to blame and that therefore the point is not an important one. However, as noted at paragraph 8.16 and paragraph 8.17 in relation to *force majeure* and frustration this is not necessarily the case.

—The fact of non-execution is 'due to' a reason for which the principal is 'not to blame': why use the words 'due to' when the words 'as a result of' are used in Regulation 7 and are clearer? Is a different level of causation intended? It appears that this wording is merely a lazy use of inelegant language from the Directive. The more difficult question is what reasons are reasons for which the principal is 'not to blame'. Clearly this encompasses breach of contract by the customer, and customer insolvency. But does it apply to the full range of events or actions which could have caused the principal to fail to perform? In particular does it apply to all breaches of contract by the principal, *force majeure* situations; or frustration?

Taking each of these in turn, if goods are not delivered by the due date then the principal may be in breach of contract. However, if this is the fault of a transport contractor, for instance, then (although the principal is in breach) is it appropriate to say that the principal is 'to blame'?

In cases of *force majeure* (such as strikes, power failures and acts of God) should the question of whether the principal is to blame or not depend upon whether its contract with the customer includes a *force majeure* provision excusing it from liability for breach of contract? Presumably, in the case of frustrated contracts, there is no question of the principal being 'to blame' at all.

These words do not sit happily with English law concepts of negligence or breach of contract, nor is there any attempt in the regulations to clarify their meanings. The authors' view is that the words should properly be viewed as relating to breach of contract, and not 'blame' in a moral or causative sense. The underlying principle seems to be the idea that the principal should not be entitled to use its failure to perform as a ground upon which to refuse payment of commission.

The DTI's 1994 Guidance Notes suggest (following a comment in the Explanatory and Consultative Note) that the principal will still be liable to pay commission if (although not paid by the customer) he obtains payment in some other way, for instance through an insurance policy. It is unclear where the DTI finds the basis for this statement within the Regulations. Should the principal be obliged to pay if he has borne the cost of an insurance policy?

8.16 FRUSTRATED CONTRACTS AND FORCE MAJEURE

If the above interpretation is correct, a suitably-worded *force majeure* provision in the principal's contract with the customer should protect the principal and entitle the principal to reclaim commission paid in the event that the contract does not proceed by reason of a force majeure event. Comment has been made in several places above regarding the desirability of a suitably worded agency contract for the protection of the principal: on this point, it is the wording of the principal's contract with the customer which needs to be considered carefully.

8.17 FRUSTRATION

The Regulations do not consider frustration. When the Regulations talk of the principal executing his part of the transaction 'as he should have', what happens if the contract has been frustrated?

It should seem logical that in so far as the customer has paid the principal and commission has been paid, the principal will by definition not bear any 'blame' and that accordingly the commission should be recoverable under regulation 11 (see paragraph 8.15).

As an aside, at least where an agent is negotiating and concluding on behalf of the principal, it is ironic to note that the question of whether commission is repayable by the agent to the principal under regulation 11 could depend upon whether the agent successfully ensured that the principal's conditions of trading became part of the contract between the principal and the customer. If the principal's conditions contain a *force majeure* clause, then the agent's failure to ensure that those conditions become part of the contract may perversely have the effect of ensuring that the commission is not repayable by the agent. If the agency contract is properly worded, however, then a sales agent who fails to contract on the principal's standard terms may be in breach of contract in any event and perhaps commission which is not recoverable from the agent could form part of a claim for damages against the agent. But in such circumstances would such a claim, and therefore the provision requiring the incorporation of the principal's terms in the first place, amount to a derogation of the type prohibited by regulation 11(3)?

As a final point, can the principal set off sums recoverable under regulation 11 against either commission due or any compensation or indemnity payment? There seems to be no reason why such a provision in an agency contract should not be effective.

8.18 SUPPLY OF INFORMATION AND RIGHT OF INSPECTION OF PRINCIPAL'S BOOKS

Regulation 12 requires the principal to supply the agent with a statement of commission due not later than the last day of the month following the quarter in which the commission became due (that is, the date which is the latest date for payment of commission under regulation10(3)). Such statement must set out the 'main components used' in calculating the amount of commission. The main components are, presumably, the commission rate and the value of the contract upon which commission is payable. Reading this with regulation10(2), this will be a statement as to the relevant value of transactions which have been executed by the customer, or which the customer would have executed if the principal had executed its obligations on time.

Regulation 12(2) goes on to state that the agent is entitled to demand that it be provided with all information which is available to the principal and which the agent needs to check the amount of commission due. This is stated in particular to include an extract from the principal's books, although (unlike earlier drafts of the Regulations) there is no definition of 'books'.

Both of these provisions are mandatory. Regulation 12(4) preserves any rule of law which recognises the right of an agent to inspect the principal's books, although the only such circumstance in English law would be the obligation of disclosure as part of the litigation process.

8.19 LACK OF REMEDIES

No specific remedy is provided in the event of a failure by the principal to comply with either of the main obligations under regulation 12. This issue relates to the question of whether the rights of the parties under the Regulations are contractual obligations or otherwise which was considered earlier.

There is a serious deficiency in so far as the regulations do not lay down any penalties in the event of breach. Compare this with the position in employment law where there is a failure to provide a statement of the terms of the contract pursuant to section 1 of the Employment Protection (Consolidation) Act 1978, for which there is no sanction and the penalties for failure to consult unions in advance of redundancies. This may be an area in which the DTI's failure to clarify could lead to claims based on the *Francovich* principle.

Regulation 12 does not impose any obligation of confidentiality on the agent as regards information it obtains from the principal's books. Such an obligation may be implied by the common law and/or as part of the duties imposed upon the agent under regulation 3 (see above). This point can be covered by the inclusion of an express confidentiality provision in the agency contract. Even if there is no such provision, it is probably the case that a stipulation by the principal as to the confidentiality of information so supplied at the time of supplying it would either impose an obligation of confidentiality at common law or would amount to a reasonable instruction given by the principal for the purposes of regulation 3(2)(c).

9

Regulations 13 to 20—Conclusion and Termination of the Agency Contract

9.1 OUTLINE

THIS CHAPTER COVERS the rights of agents to compensation or indemnity payments on termination of their agreements even when such termination is lawfully carried out. One preliminary issue which should be mentioned relates to the scope of the word 'termination'. This issue is important as rights to certain types of commission and indemnity or compensation payments are predicated on the agency contract being terminated. On its face, the matter appears straightforward—termination arises when the agreement between the parties comes to an end. But, does termination within the meaning of the Regulations arise on expiry of a fixed-term contract? English commentators appear strongly to support the approach that it does.[1] However, it is clear that at least in so far as compensation is concerned, the relevant provisions in the Directive were based on a 1958 French law, which specifically excluded compensation on expiry of a fixed-term contract amount to a termination for this purpose.[2] The question which remains to be resolved is the impact of that fact on the issue in question.[3]

9.2 DO THE PARTIES TO AN AGENCY CONTRACT HAVE THE RIGHT TO A WRITTEN STATEMENT OF TERMS?

The short answer to the above question is yes. Regulation 13 sets out almost verbatim what appears in the Directive at Article 13(1).

The only change between the provision as it was originally proposed by the Commission and the final text from the Council are the words 'on request', which suggestion was put forward by the European Parliament in its opinion. This means that the agent or the principal must request the statement of terms.

---

[1] See for example, H Beale (Gen Ed) *Chitty on Contracts* (28th edn), (London, Sweet & Maxwell, 1999), para 32–147.

[2] See *Bowstead and Reynolds on Agency* (17th edn), (London, Sweet & Maxwell, 2001), para 11–046, footnote 24.

[3] The issue was decided at first instance in the case of *Whitehead v Jenks & Cattell* at Birmingham Mercantile Court on 2 February 2001 in favour of the argument that 'termination' includes circumstances in which a fixed term contract expires and is not renewed.

It should be noted that the Directive contains the following provision:

Notwithstanding paragraph 1 a member state may provide that an agency contract shall not be valid unless evidenced in writing.[4]

The UK decided not to take up this option, which decision follows the practice under English law. It has been suggested—see the 1987 DTI Explanatory and Consultative Note—that it is sensible to retain the flexibility, especially in cases where agreements cover minor transactions for which written contracts will not be worthwhile. Nevertheless, it is thought that the vast majority of agency contracts will now be written, given the increased obligations on principals.

The regulation is self-explanatory. The right to receive on request a signed written document setting out the terms of the contract is wide-ranging; it will apply even if the parties agreed originally that a written contract was not required—see the 1987 Explanatory and Consultative Note, paragraph 25.

What is the sanction for non-compliance? Given that the UK has not taken up the possibility under Article 13(2) of the Directive to provide that an unwritten agency contract will not be valid, it is clear that invalidity will not arise on non-compliance. Indeed, in the original Explanatory Memorandum of the Commission—COM(76)670 final of 14 December 1976—attached to its original proposal, it was made clear that the automatic nullity of a contract was one particular reason for not making this provision mandatory. One remedy which might be available if for example one party refuses a relevant request, is a mandatory injunction, since the English courts must as a matter of Community law provide an adequate remedy. However, it is not clear whether this should be the case given that, as the Law Commission Report suggests, the provision might be interpreted as being merely exhortatory (The Law Commission Report, p. 25).

Finally, it should be noted that apart from restraint of trade clauses (regulation 20(1)(a)) there is no obligation that particular clauses must be in writing if they are to be enforced.

It is often assumed by both principals and agents that if there is no written agreement there is no contract and clearly this is not true. Particularly given Part III of the Regulations, principals should view the conclusion of a suitable written agreement with the agent as of paramount importance. This is always good practice, but is now more important because of the effects of the Regulations.

9.3 WHAT HAPPENS TO A FIXED-TERM CONTRACT ONCE THE FIXED TERM HAS EXPIRED?

Regulation 14 provides that if the parties to a fixed-term contract continue to perform it after its expiry date, then the contract will be deemed to have been converted into a contract of indefinite duration.

---

[4] Art 13(2) of the Directive. Note that national rules requiring any other formalities to be observed as a condition of validity of agency contacts are precluded by the Directive: see the judgment of the Court of Justice in *Barbara Bellone v Yokohama SPA* [1998] ECR I–2191.

This provision, like regulation 13, follows almost verbatim the original Commission proposal. The only difference is that the original proposed version was preceded by the words 'unless otherwise agreed'. These were deleted in the amended Commission proposal and it is therefore clear that the parties cannot derogate from the provisions of this regulation. Once this provision has come into operation in a given situation, and the contract has been converted into one for an indefinite period, the rules as to notice set out in regulation 15 will apply. Needless to say, those contracts for a fixed or determinable period, which are not continued thereafter, will end on the expiration of the period for which they were made. This statement formed part of the original proposal for what became regulation 14. However, it was removed by the Council in its adopted text. Its removal does not signify its non-application; merely that such matters did not need to be spelt out in the Directive. It should be noted however that where there is a fixed-term contract which expires and is replaced with another fixed-term contract, it may be argued that the parties would not be bound by the notice period laid down in regulation 15. Compensation or indemnity will not, however, be calculated only by reference to the latest fixed term—the court will adopt a broad definition of the term 'agency contract' and take earlier fixed terms into account.[5]

9.4 WHAT ARE THE MINIMUM PERIODS OF NOTICE FOR TERMINATION OF THE AGENCY CONTRACT?

The minimum notice periods are set out in regulation 15. Unlike the two preceding regulations, this regulation has undergone certain important changes from the time when it was first proposed by the Commission. However, the regulation mirrors the final version of the Directive almost exactly.

9.5 THE COMMISSION PROPOSAL

The initial proposal differed in three important respects from the final adopted Directive. First, it was proposed that only notice in writing would be valid, secondly, that the period of notice should be the same for both parties and thirdly, that member states were entitled to prescribe a maximum period of notice but that the period in question could not be less than 12 months.

The first proposal was deleted by the Council. It is to be assumed that the reason for this is that in some member states, valid notice could be given orally. The second proposal was also deleted by the Council. There has been criticism of this provision—see for example the Law Commission report at p 25—stating that such a rigid rule would not always be appropriate and that confusion could arise where parties made different arrangements in breach of this paragraph. The third

---

[5] See *Moore v Piretta PTA Limited* [1999] 1 ALL ER 174, 180.

proposal changed as a result of amendments put forward by the European Parliament, which suggested that the longest minimum limit of maximum notice period should be three months. The Commission amended its proposal in the light of this to six months. However, in the end, this became otiose. The Commission's proposal as amended had suggested that there should be minimum periods for certain lengths of contract and the longest minimum limit on the maximum notice period which could be set by member states was based on this voluntary concept. However, when the Council moved away from this concept towards mandatory notice periods, the minimum limits were no longer relevant.

9.6 THE PROPOSALS FOR THE REGULATION

The drafts of regulation 15 followed the wording of the Directive on this point fairly closely. Up until the second draft, it had been stated that the provisions of the regulation could not be excluded, varied or restricted to the detriment of the commercial agent. This statement does not appear in the regulations as adopted. However, regulation 15(2) provides that parties may not agree on any shorter periods of notice.

9.7 THE REGULATION

Regulation 15 itself is clear. The minimum periods of notice are one month for the first year of the contract, two months for the second year commenced and three months for the third year commenced and for subsequent years.

The UK did not take up the possibility given to it by the Directive to fix notice periods for the fourth, fifth and sixth years of the contract (Article 15(3) of the Directive). As the DTI stated in the 1987 Explanatory and Consultative Note, the government felt that the three-month notice period was sufficient and that if the parties wished to fix longer notice periods, they were entitled to do so pursuant to regulation 15(3). Regulation 15(3) also provides that in the event that the parties choose longer periods, the notice periods to be observed by the principal must not be shorter than those observed by the agent.

9.8 CRITICISMS OF THE REGULATION

Various criticisms have been raised against regulation 15, largely on the ground that it is too restrictive.

For example, there is no provision for parties to be able to terminate with immediate effect except as provided for by regulation 16 (see paragraph 9.9 below). Does this mean that even if parties agree to do so, they will not be entitled to rely upon such an agreement? There is also no provision for payment in lieu of notice, which is a well-known feature of agency law in the UK. There is also no provision for reasonable notice. However, it could be suggested that the regulation simply codifies what was good practice and should thus be deemed to include the concept of reasonableness. It is also unclear what happens if the proper periods of notice are not observed. The better view would be that the notice would be ineffective. However, in the early drafts of the Directive, remedies for unlawful termination were set out and one of the examples given of unlawful termination was where the proper period of notice had not been observed—see, for example, Article 28(1) of the Commission's original proposal to the Council:[1977] OJ C13/2. It has also been suggested that the notice periods, which are more generous than those existing under the current UK employment legislation, will force principals to acknowledge that agents will become their quasi-employees.[6]

9.9 DO THE PARTIES HAVE ANY RIGHTS TO TERMINATE WITH IMMEDIATE EFFECT?

Regulation 16 makes it clear that the Regulations as a whole do not affect the rights of parties to terminate with immediate effect either because of the failure by one of the parties to carry out all or part of his obligations under the contract or where exceptional circumstances arise.

Again this regulation faithfully reproduces Article 16 of the Directive. However, the relevant provision has changed quite markedly from the early Commission drafts. It is not only instructive to see what was left in, but also what was left out.

9.10 THE DRAFTS OF THE DIRECTIVE

In the original Commission proposal, the emphasis in the first limb was placed on the fault of one of the parties. The doctrine of fault in a contractual setting is known in certain continental law systems but not in the UK where the emphasis is on breach by the relevant party. The Law Commission Report predicted that difficulties would arise if the concept of fault were allowed to remain.

With regard to the second limb, the proposal spelt out what has since become 'exceptional circumstances'. Article 27(1)(b) of the Commission proposal ([1977] OJ C13/2) provided that termination may take place 'where some circumstance arises which makes it impossible to perform the contract, or which seriously prejudices its performance, or which substantially undermines the commercial basis of the contract . . .'. Such details may be helpful when seeking to interpret 'exceptional circumstances'.

One provision in the early drafts which has since been omitted from the Directive and thus from the Regulations is that where the contract was terminated in the relevant manner, the party 'at fault' was liable in damages to the other. The fact that it

---

[6] R. Lister 'Time to Re-think UK Agency Agreement' *International Financial Law Review*, July 1992.

was omitted by the Council does not mean that damages are not capable of being awarded in such situations, rather that it was felt that this was something which should be dealt with by national law rather than harmonised by EC law.

The opinions from the Economic and Social Committee and from the European Parliament attempted to put a gloss on the provisions, especially with regard to the first limb. These attempts worked to the extent that in the Commission's amended proposal, it was provided that termination should only arise where a party to the contract had 'conducted himself in a manner which [was] seriously inconsistent with his obligations, or [has] in relation to the contract committed a serious fault'. Wisely, it is thought, these new emphases were not adopted by the Council.

9.11 THE DRAFT REGULATION

The early drafts were almost identical to the Regulations, save for later drafts which stated that the rules of the common law relating to this issue should apply to the contract. The question could therefore be asked as to the position in equity, say for misrepresentation.

9.12 THE REGULATION

Regulation 16 preserves the rules in English law (and it is thought in other continental legal systems as well) whereby parties may terminate a contract without notice.

The first limb clearly covers rescission for failure to perform and should also cover termination in cases of anticipatory breach. It should be noted that in both cases, damages are available under English law. It should also be noted that despite the general rule in English law that rescission of a contract for failure to perform requires a minimum degree of default, because regulation 16(a) includes failure to carry out part of the obligations due under the contract, a party may terminate and seek damages even though that party has suffered little or no prejudice. The DTI's 1993 Guidance Notes stated that the provisions of the regulation have the effect of preventing disputes as to whether there has been a failure to perform such as to justify rescission (the DTI 1993 Guidance Notes, paragraph 63).

As to the second limb, the first explanatory note from the DTI in 1987 states that it would include *force majeure* or unforeseeable, uncontrollable events—see the DTI Explanatory and Consultative Note, paragraph. 29. It should be noted that as a general rule of English law, payments which are outstanding at the time when frustration (which may not have the same ambit as 'exceptional circumstances') occurs would cease to be payable except in so far as the court in its discretion sees fit, taking into account the facts of the situation. In the Commission's Explanatory Memorandum of its original proposal, the example of a commercial agent finding it impossible to continue in business for reasons of health, old age or serious and unforeseeable family circumstances is given as illustrating the type of situation to fall within the term of exceptional circumstances (see the Commission's Explanatory Memorandum, p. 49). It is interesting to note that this example does not differ markedly from regulation 18(b)(ii) which sets out some of the circumstances under which indemnity or compensation payments will be payable despite the fact that the agent terminated the agreement. It should also be noted that the example only mentions the circumstances of the commercial agent. It is to be assumed that the same rationale would arise if the position of the principal was the same.

9.13 WHAT RIGHTS DO AGENTS HAVE TO INDEMNITY OR COMPENSATION
ON TERMINATION?

Regulation 17, which answers the above question, is at the heart of the Regulations. The rights of agents to claim an indemnity or compensation at the end of a contractual agreement irrespective of whether a breach of contract has occurred, and thus imposing a form of strict liability on the principal, are entirely novel in the English law of agency and thus have caused much comment. Regulation 17 also has the most potential effect on the finances of the parties involved and thus is of more immediate concern to individuals than certain other provisions.

Such rights are however well known in continental legal systems where it is felt that the agent should be protected in its dealings with the principal. It has been pointed out that the agent's entitlement to such indemnity under German law is 'intended to compensate him for the fact that as a rule the agent's work increases the goodwill of the principal and not that of the agent and that on termination of the agency the principal thus derives a benefit from this accrued goodwill, while the agent suffers a corresponding loss'. (E J Cohn, *An introduction to the German Law on Agents and Sole Distributors*, British Institute of International and Comparative Law: Special Publication No 3 1964 p 17.) Indeed, it is interesting to note that under German law, a commercial agent appears to be some sort of quasi-employee rather than the independent agent more familiar to English lawyers.

In terms of compensation, which is the default provision under regulation 17, the initial approach of the courts in the UK was to follow the French law rationale for post-termination compensation, as being the representation of the cost of purchasing the agency to the agent's successor or being a representation of the time it would take to reconstitute the client base of which the agent had been forcibly deprived. However, recent judgments of the English courts have moved away from a rigid adherence to French law.[7]

---

[7] See for example the judgments in *Frabo v Duffen; Barrett McKenzie v Escada* and *Ingmar v Eaton Leonard Inc* referred to in more detail below.

9.14 COMPLIANCE WITH THE DIRECTIVE

The question of compliance by regulation 17 with the relevant provisions in the Directive arises because of a last-minute change by the UK Government based, it is said, on late advice from the European Commission (see the DTI Compliance Cost Assessment, December 1993, p. 3). Before this advice, the UK had taken the view that Article 17 of the Directive required member states to choose between indemnity and compensation payments for agents. Article 17(1) of the Directive provides:

> member states shall take the measures necessary to ensure that the commercial agent is, after termination of the agency contract, indemnified in accordance with paragraph 2 or compensated for damage in accordance with paragraph 3.

Most member states have opted for the indemnity system. The UK authorities had originally chosen the compensation system, with which they were more familiar. At the last moment, there was a radical change allowing the parties to individual contracts to make the choice themselves as between compensation or indemnity. The question which arises is whether a member state, in this case the UK, is entitled to do this. The DTI does not shirk from explaining what this might mean in practice. In its 1993 Guidance Note, the DTI states that the system as chosen by the UK will enable the parties to a particular contract to choose one provision for inclusion in one contract and the other in another contract. That in itself is not surprising, although such a course of action will no doubt lead to prolonged negotiations every time a new contract is entered into. However, in its most recent 1994 Guidance Note, the DTI goes further and states that the regulation as it stands does not preclude the parties from using the compensation provisions in some cases and indemnity ones in others *when terminating a particular contract.* This seems remarkable. The provisions with regard to indemnity or compensation relate to termination of an agency contract. It would seem that the DTI envisages partial termination of a contract giving rise to these rights, which is not at all the same.

It could be argued that the UK has failed to implement the Directive correctly by failing to choose which system should operate within its jurisdiction. Despite the fact that the UK's decision was apparently based on advice from the Commission, the ultimate arbiter will be the European Court of Justice. It is to be remembered that if the UK were found to have failed to implement the Directive correctly, then it could be liable in damages to disgruntled agents or principals.

Aside from this difference, the regulation follows the relevant provisions of the Directive very closely. However, it is worth briefly examining the drafts of the Directive.

There are two main differences between the adopted text of the Directive and the previous drafts. First, in the early drafts, there was only provision for payment of a goodwill indemnity; there was no provision made for compensation for damage suffered. It is assumed that this was because the German system upon which much of the original proposal was based only knew of the goodwill indemnity concept. Secondly, the amount of goodwill indemnity payable was limited to one tenth of the annual remuneration calculated on the basis of the average remuneration during the previous five years. This would yield a rather low sum normally. However, the text as adopted increased the claimable amount so that it was not to exceed one year's remuneration based on the agent's average remuneration over the preceding five years, ie 10 times the former amount. It is interesting to note that this is similar to the measure of quantum set down in the original draft of the Directive for lump-sum indemnities payable when *unlawful* termination had taken place.

9.16 TERMINATION

It will be noted that indemnity or compensation payments are only available once a contract is terminated. The question thus arises as to what constitutes termination.

The DTI, in the 1987 Explanatory and Consultative Note, sets out the following as examples of termination under regulation 17. It should be noted that the list is not exhaustive:

—the principal's breach of the agency agreement with the agent's acceptance of the repudiation; this might include service of a notice shorter than that provided for in regulation 15;
—the frustration of the agency agreement, which would include the agent's death (regulation 17(8)), or the agent's retirement or illness (regulation 18(b)(ii)); it is not thought that this provision can be taken to include the liquidation of a company;
—the principal giving notice under regulation 15 or under an express term for early termination of a fixed-term agency contract;
—the expiry by passage of time of a fixed-term agency contract.[8]

Termination leading to the entitlement of the agent to indemnity or compensation will *not* arise in the following circumstances:

—where the principal has terminated because of a breach by the agent which justifies immediate termination (regulation 18(a): the DTI's view in the Note was that this wording in the Directive is a reference to repudiatory breach, but the

---

[8] As to this, see above at para 9.1 above.

authors would query whether this is correct; regulation 18 refers back to regulation 16 which talks of immediate termination because of the failure of one party to carry out all or part of his obligations under that contract);

—where the agent has terminated the agency contract, unless the termination was justified by circumstances attributable to the principal or on grounds of age, infirmity or illness of the agent due to which it cannot reasonably be required to continue its activities (regulation 18 (b): DTI referred to termination by the agent on notice, but both the Directive and the Regulations are silent on this point);

—where the agent has assigned his rights and duties to another person (regulation 18(c)).

Unfortunately, the DTI only sets out the uncontroversial occasions when termination leading to indemnity or compensation will occur. The following examples show the extent of the agent's new rights under the Regulations.

An agent will be entitled to be indemnified or compensated when:

—the agent retires or dies;
—the principal assigns the contract, say on the sale of the business;
—the agent has breached the contract but not so that it would justify the immediate termination of the contract;
—the contract is terminated on grounds of *force majeure.*

It should be noted that with regard to this last point, it has been said that the agent should not be entitled to indemnity or compensation because of the operation of Article 16 of the Directive. It will be recalled that Article 16 provides that nothing in the Directive shall affect the application of the law of the member states where the latter provides for the immediate termination of the contract where, inter alia, exceptional circumstances arise. In the draft Regulations, it was provided that the agent was not entitled to payment where inter alia such exceptional circumstances arose. *Force majeure* will generally fall within the term 'exceptional circumstances' in so far as it will lead to the immediate termination of a contract. However in the Regulations as they were adopted, the exceptional circumstances were dropped from the explicit reasons for which an agent would not be entitled to claim indemnity or compensation. It must follow that where a contract is terminated on grounds of *force majeure,* such termination will entitle the agent to be indemnified or compensated.

9.17 DISTINCTION BETWEEN INDEMNITY AND COMPENSATION

An indemnity payment will only be due to an agent where there has been an agreement to that effect between the parties;[9] failing such an agreement, the default post-termination remuneration under regulation 17 will be by way of compensation.

---

[9] Regulation 17(2).

As has been seen above, indemnity payments under the Directive (and therefore under the Regulations) are modelled on German law. Chapter 10 sets out a detailed analysis of that law. A further analysis of that law in so far as it specifically applies to the question of indemnity payments is set out in the 1996 Commission Report on the application of Article 17 of the Directive, a copy of which can be found at Appendix 6. The Report not only sets out the law, but the steps taken by the German courts to calculate how an indemnity should be paid and in what amount.

One critical distinction between indemnity and compensation payments is that an upper limit is set on indemnity payments whilst there is no limit on compensation payments. Regulation 17(4) makes it clear that the upper limit shall be an indemnity for one year based on the agent's average remuneration over the preceding five years. Despite this limit on the indemnity available, it should not be forgotten that the agent is entitled to make a further claim for damages. The 1993 DTI Guidance Notes give the following example of when such a situation might arise. If the principal dismisses the agent by giving one month's notice instead of three months, then the agent will be able to claim indemnity for the commission on orders obtained in the first month and will also be able to claim damages for being deprived of the opportunity to earn commission during the two other months—see the 1993 DTI Guidance Notes, p 35.

Why do the Regulations provide an alternative? As noted above, initially and indeed up until and including the final 1993 draft, the UK authorities took the view that only compensation would be available on termination of contract. However, interested parties, especially those representing the interests of principals, were very unhappy about this because of the lack of a maximum limit. Because of this pressure and using the late advice from the European Commission, the Regulations were amended to allow parties to agency contracts to choose either indemnity or compensation.

9.18 INDEMNITY PROVISIONS UNDER THE REGULATIONS

An agent will only be entitled to an indemnity if the following conditions are met:

—new customers have been brought to the principal by the agent; or
—the volume of business with existing customers has been significantly increased by the agent; and
—the principal continues to derive substantial benefits from such business; and
—the payment of the indemnity is equitable having regard to all the circumstances and in particular the commission lost by the commercial agent on the business transacted with such customers.

Thus, without one of the two first conditions, the agent will have no right to an indemnity payment. There must also be proof that the principal has continued to derive benefits from either new or existing business. Even if these conditions are fulfilled, the agent will have to convince a court that the indemnity payment is equitable.

The DTI usefully sets out in its 1993 Guidance Notes at pp 33 and 34 the background to the indemnity provisions in the Directive. It points out that under German law, which provided the model for the Directive generally and for the indemnity provisions in particular, three considerations arise with regard to the payment of indemnities to agents:

—that the termination of the agency contract involves an enrichment for the principal in that the latter will still be doing business with clients introduced by the agent, but without now having to pay commission to that agent;
—that the agent suffers a loss because it would have earned commission on the transactions had the agency agreement continued;
—that the indemnity payment has to be equitable in all the circumstances.

On the basis of the above, it is clear that as there has to be a benefit for the principal, the agent is less likely to get such a payment where the agency contract is terminated because the principal is unable to carry on the business. It is also clear that it is for the agent to prove its loss. If, therefore, the agent soon after termination, secures a comparable position selling into the same market then there may be no loss and therefore no indemnity to be paid. Finally, the issue of equity will take into account, according to the DTI, such circumstances as the parties' respective financial situations and how actively the agent worked.

The Commission Report, referred to above, makes clear that the indemnity provisions in the Directive, which have been carried through intact into UK law by operation of the Regulations, were modelled on Article 89b of the German Commercial Code, which has provided for the payment of a goodwill indemnity since 1953. Chapter 10 of this book provides an overview of the relevant German legislation and case law, in so far as they relate to the operation and availability of post-termination indemnities.

The following points of interest arise from the Commission Report:

—An agent is only entitled to an indemnity payment if and to the extent that it has brought new customers to the principal or has significantly increased the volume of business with existing customers and the principal continues to derive substantial benefits from such customers after the cessation of the agreement. This is in contrast to the compensation payment system, which as will be seen below, requires no such pre-requisite facts.
—The payment of an indemnity must be equitable having regard to all the circumstances and in particular the commission lost by the agent on the business transacted.

—There is a maximum level of indemnity, limited to one year's average annual remuneration.

—The indemnity represents the continuing benefits to the principal due to the agent's efforts.

—With regard to the criterion of the principal continuing to derive substantial benefits with its customers post-termination, it will be met even if the principal sells its business or client list, if it can be shown that the purchaser would use the client base.

As to the actual calculation of any indemnity due, the Commission Report sets out three stages.

The first stage is to ascertain the number of new customers and/or the increased volume of business with existing customers. The gross commission related to such customers over the last 12 months of the agreement can then be calculated. It is then necessary to estimate the likely length of time the business with these customers will last. In order to make such an estimation, it will be necessary to consider the market situation at the time of termination. A level of migration then has to be determined, as it will be natural that some customers will naturally move away. This figure comprising the above is then reduced to take into account the accelerated receipt of income.

The second stage investigates the issue of equity and its impact on the indemnity calculation. The following points are taken into account when making this investigation:

—whether the agent is retained by other principals;
—any fault of the agent;
—the level of remuneration of the agent;
—any decrease in the principal's turnover;
—the extent of any advantage to the principal;
—any payment of pensions contirbutions by the principal;
—the existence of any restraint of trade clause; if such a clause exists, then the indemnity will be higher.

The third stage takes the figures calculated above and compares them with the maximum remuneration permitted. On this latter point, it is interesting to note that the Report states that it is rare for the maximum to be reached unless the agent has procured all or most of the customers.

However, the courts will no doubt be made aware of the philosophy behind the Regulations—the protection of the agent—and therefore it is likely that this provision will be widely interpreted with this aim in mind. The decision in the High Court in the case of *Moore v Piretta*[10] supports this analysis; it should nonetheless be noted that in so far as the equity of the indemnity payment was concerned, one factor taken into account led to a reduction in the indemnity—that factor was that

---

[10] [1999] 1 All ER 174.

the agent would receive the moneys more quickly overall than would have been the case had the contract between the parties continued. The court reduced the award by eight per cent because of the accelerated payment factor.

9.21 INDEMNITY—THE CASE LAW

At the time of writing, there is only one UK decided case on the indemnity provision in *Moore v Piretta*.[11] This is unsurprising because of the way the Regulations deal with the choice between indemnity and compensation: the parties must choose the indemnity route in their agreement if it is to apply[12] and therefore the compensation regime will apply to all pre-1994 agency agreements which have not been amended to reflect the Regulations.

Moore v Piretta is a disappointing and unsatisfactory case for the following reasons:

—the judge decided to look to German law for help in ascertaining how the Directive should be construed,[13] but seems completely to have misapplied German law, in particular by using as the base for the calculation of indemnity, not the *commissions* earned on business with customers obtained by the agent, but the *total value* of the business done by the principal with those customers.[14] Unsurprisingly, the resulting figure (even after various deductions) exceeded the capped figure of one year's commission and the agent was accordingly awarded the maximum indemnity allowed by the Regulations! This error would have been avoided had the court applied the principles set out in the Commission's 1996 Report which is all the more mystifying given that the judgment was given in 1998.

—Having purported to follow German law, the court then departed from it in making deduction from the potential award for the agent's costs in performing his agency duties. The authors believe that such a deduction is not made under German law. The court declined to apply the principle of mitigation because it interpreted the indemnity payment as a payment in respect of goodwill.[15]

—The judge did not assume any 'migration'—that is, gradual loss by the principal of the new customers won by the agent, although the Commission's 1996 Report states that this is part of the calculation under German law.

—Although the German system envisages consideration of the period for which the principal will continue to derive benefit from agency customers introduced

---

[11] [1999] 1 All ER 174.

[12] Regulation 17(2).

[13] As to the appropriateness of and consequences of doing this, see above para 21.2.

[14] Although the Commission's 1996 Report is admittedly vague, it is clear from the illustrative example set out on page 4 of the Report that the appropriate base is *commission* not *total turnover*. The authors believe that the approach adopted by the 1996 Report accords with German law, which the judge said he was seeking to follow.

[15] Page 182 at c.

by the agent and the Commission's 1996 Report suggests[16] that a period of two to three years is usual, the judge gave no reason for choosing a period of 2.75 years—it appears he did so simply for convenience, this being the period elapsed between termination and trial and accordingly the period for which counsel supplied figures.[17] Would an earlier or later trial have resulted in a different figure?

—Although we do not know the agent's age or other business or many other facts, it must be highly doubtful whether a case involving an agency which had subsisted less than 7.5 years merited the maximum award—even after the calculation error referred to above, the court should have carried out a common sense check on the resulting award and revisited its conclusion.

Lessons for principals from *Moore v Piretta* are as follows:

—Beware of the indemnity route until it is clear the courts have a settled approach to calculating indemnities.
—If the Court is to refer to 'foreign' law, ensure clear expert evidence is used and applied in any dispute.
—Consider whether delays to the trial date will work for or against you.
—Do not assume that future awards will be net of costs or will apply common law principles of accelerated receipt of mitigation.
—If mitigation cannot be argued, even an agent who has immediately gained a new agency or employment, or compensated for the loss of one agency by devoting more energy to his other agencies, will receive a full award.

Finally, it is worth mentioning the *Tamarind* case again.[18] The agreement in this case provided for an indemnity payment, and a reference in the judgment suggests that the sum at issue was £105 million![19] However, it is understood that this case has settled.

9.22 COMPENSATION PROVISIONS UNDER THE REGULATIONS

In order to be entitled to compensation, an agent must show damage suffered as result of termination of relations with the principal. The Regulations give three non-exhaustive [20] examples of when such damage will arise:

—when the termination of relations with the principal has deprived the agent of commission which would have arisen with the proper performance of the contract whilst providing the principal with substantial benefits due to the agent's activities;

---

[16] Page 3, para (b).
[17] The judge was probably not assisted by the fact that the figures were supplied to him at 'the 59th minute of the 11th hour of the case' (page 184).
[18] See above paras 5.8 and 6.3.
[19] At para 46 of the judgment.
[20] The fact that they are non-exhaustive was confirmed in *King v Tunnock* [2000] EuLR 531 at paras 41 and 42 of the judgment.

—when the termination of relations with the principal has meant that the agent
   has been unable to amortise costs and expenses incurred in the performance of
   the agency contract on the principal's 'advice';
—when the termination of relations with the principal has arisen because of the
   agent's death.

As to the word 'damage', it is interesting to note that in the first draft of the
Regulations, it was substituted by 'losses, liabilities, costs and expenses'.
Particularly because of the inclusion of the latter, it is clear that something other
than merely contractual loss is covered.

As has been noted above, the compensation provisions of the Directive are
taken from French law. The present position of the case law in the UK is split
between two schools of thought as to the impact that French law should have on
the calculation of compensation by courts in the UK. On the one hand, cases such
as *King v Tunnock* take the view that UK law should imitate French law. On the
other hand, recent cases such as *Frabo v Duffen, Barrett McKenzie v Escada* and
Ingmar show a willingness of English courts to move away from second guessing
what French law might or might not do in a given situation, and instead seek to
use common law principles, such as the duty to mitigate one's loss and the need to
avoid windfall payments, to justify departing from the strict French law approach.
A good example of this less hidebound approach can be seen in the recent High
Court judgment in *Ingmar*, in which the Court stated that two years' gross average
commission (the norm under French law) would have given a windfall to the
claimant and therefore three years' net average commission should be used instead
as the measure for compensation.

It will be noted that compensation is payable for damage suffered as result of the
termination of relations with the principal. It has been argued by certain commentators—see for example Scholes and Blane, 'Agency Agreements—New
Protection for Commercial Agents', *PLC* November 1993, p 43—that this phrase
encompasses more than simply the terms of the agency contract, ie that it is different from termination of the contract. However, although it is true that different words are used, it is clear from both the Regulations and the Directive that
compensation will be paid on termination of the agency contract—regulation
17(1) and Article 17(1) respectively. These provisions govern generally the granting of compensation, inter alia, to agents and thus all subsequent subordinate provisions should be read in the light of these general provisions. It is thus thought
that the better view is that the phrase 'relations with the principal' should be read
as comprising the terms of the agency contract.

As to the first of the examples given above, it is clear that difficulties may arise with
the quantification of the phrase 'substantial benefits'. It is not known how the courts
will deal with this provision, although as stated above, they will no doubt be aware of
the aim of the Directive (and therefore the Regulations) to protect agents. It may be
argued that the use of the word 'particularly' in regulation 17(7) can be construed to
mean that an agent may be entitled to compensation even if the principal has not

been provided with substantial benefits. This was the approach adopted by the Scottish Court of Session in *King v Tunnock*.

One of the key issues which is still unclear (at the time of writing) is the correct approach to be taken by the UK courts when determining amounts of compensation to be paid under the Regulations. As has been seen above, at least two cases in England have decided not to follow French law to the letter. If French or German law were to be followed, it would raise a large number of questions, including:

—Which version of national law should be considered? French law changed after the Directive was adopted—has the Directive breathed new life into the old, superseded, French law?

—Does following French law entail also following French practice as regards quantum or on issues such as mitigation, accelerated payment and net (as opposed to gross) commission? The Commission's 1996 Notice states, as regards the French system and the typical two-year payout that 'It is difficult to see how the UK courts will reach this figure', and also refers to concepts such as mitigation, without commenting on this.

9.23 COMPENSATION—THE DTI GUIDANCE NOTES

Surprisingly, given that compensation is the default option under the Regulations, the DTI Guidance Notes are silent on the manner in which compensation is to be calculated.

9.24 COMPENSATION—THE COMMISSION REPORT

The Report makes it clear that the compensation provisions in the Directive, which, as with their indemnity counterparts, have been carried through intact into the Regulations, were based on a 1958 French law, whose aim was to compensate an agent for loss suffered as a result of the termination of the agency contract. According to the Report, the French case law arising out of the operation of this law seeks to justify the payment of compensation on the ground either that it represents the cost to the agent's successor of purchasing the agency or that it represented the time it took for the agent to reconstitute the client base which has been removed through termination.

In contrast to indemnity and the German law on which it was modelled, the principle of compensation is not dependent on future developments. Indeed, French law pays no regard to the future, and therefore issues familiar to an English lawyer such as mitigation of loss play no part in the calculation of compensation under French law. One interesting question is whether this approach should be copied by the UK courts, or whether more familiar principles should be allowed to encroach in this area—see above paragraph 9.22 for a discussion on the recent developments in this area.

According to the Report, judicial custom in France has fixed a benchmark of two years' annual gross remuneration for the calculation of post-termination compensation, although this benchmark may move depending on the factual circumstances of the case.

As with indemnity payments, the 1996 Commission Report mentioned above usefully sets out the French law background to this provision. Chapter 11 of this book contains a detailed analysis of the relevant French law provisions and the manner in which they have been interpreted by the domestic courts in France. As to the weight to be attached to such decisions, and indeed the law which underpins such decisions, it is clear that English courts are not bound by such law or such decisions. Nonetheless, it is permissible when seeking to interpret domestic provisions implementing EC legislation to have regard to the laws which led to the creation of the relevant EC legislation. Although it would appear to be uncontested that courts in the UK can have regard to relevant 'foreign' laws in such situations, differences remain as to the weight to be attached thereto. In *Moore v Piretta* and *King v Tunnock*, the English High Court and Scottish Court of Session effectively followed the relevant 'foreign' laws very closely. By contrast, in the case of *Duffen v Frabo*,[21] Judge Hallgarten QC cautioned against slavishly following French or German law and against making awards as a matter of routine that which would have been made by the domestic courts in those countries. In taking such an approach, the court relied on the statement in the Commission's 1996 Report in which it was said that it was difficult to see how UK courts could reach the figure of two years' gross commission, which was the benchmark under French law for post-termination compensation. The matter remains unclear. This position in *Frabo* was essentially followed in *Barrett McKenzie* and *Ingmar*. However, as a matter of practice, if reliance is to be placed on either French or German law in litigation before the UK courts, then expert evidence should be adduced and if possible, such evidence should be in the form of a joint report.[22]

9.25 COMPENSATION—THE CASE LAW

In contrast to the position on indemnity, there are a number of cases in which a judgment has been given for compensation. Even this is the tip of the iceberg—the authors' experience is that most cases settle before trial. The continued uncertainty surrounding calculation of compensation is one of the prime factors motivating early settlement.

The unreported case of *Skingsley v KJC Carpets*[23] should, the authors believe, be ignored by anyone reviewing the case law. The court looked to German rather than French law for assistance even though this was a compensation case, and some commentators have suggested that the judge was motivated by pity for the claimant. An appeal was started but discontinued.

---

[21] [2000] Lloyds LRep 180.
[22] See *King v Tunnock* [2000] EuLR 531 at para 44.
[23] Unreported, Bristol County Court, 4 June 1996.

Amongst the remaining cases are a reported decision of the Scottish Court of Session case,[24] an English County Court decision[25] and two English High Court decisions.[26] Clearly, the Scottish case will have the greater persuasive weight and should for the moment be viewed as the leading case on compensation[27].

There are also a number of other decisions which, while not including a final award, are of value. These include:

—*Page v Combined Shipping and Trading*[28]—an interlocutory application, but the Court of Appeal concluded that the claimant 'has a good arguable case to recover a substantial sum';[29]

—*Roy v MR Pearlman*[30]—a Scottish Court of Session case, approving the idea of reference to French law for guidance in calculating indemnity and doubting the need for expert evidence on French law.[31]

As to the levels of compensation available, neither the Regulations nor the Directive make this clear. As set out above, there would appear to a difference of opinion as to whether the French law benchmark of two years' average commission should be followed without more, or whether a more tailored approach should be taken on the facts, to avoid what was described in the *Duffen v Frabo* case as giving agents windfalls, rather than the compensation to which they were entitled. The only point which is clear is that compensation is to be based on (but not necessarily confined to) actual damage to the agent by the termination. But then various imponderables must be taken into account. For example, the length of the agreement (assuming it is not a fixed term contract) during which commission would have been earned; also the progress of the contractual relationship—would business have increased, stayed the same or reduced. This last issue would need research into the relevant market. The question of whether the agent needs to mitigate his damage also needs to be addressed. It is thought that he should, and the absence of any indication to the contrary reinforces this view. This view has been reinforced in the light of the recent decisions of the English courts referred to above which deviate from the strict line of French law.

9.26 FIXED-TERM CONTRACTS AND COMPENSATION

In the 1987 Explanatory and Consultative Note, the DTI doubted whether there could be any damage for which compensation would be due in the event of

---

[24] *King v Tunnock* [1999] 1All ER 1946.
[25] *Duffen v Frabo* [2000] 1 Lloyds LR 180.
[26] *Barrett McKenzie v Escada: The Times* 15 May 2001, *Ingmar v Eaton Leonard Inc:* 31 July 2001.
[27] For a description of these cases, see above at 9.22.
[28] [1997] 3 All ER 656.
[29] At 660.
[30] [1999] 2 CMLR 1155.
[31] At p 1170, para 39.

termination by the principal in accordance with the terms of the contract, or the expiry of a fixed term. The DTI's basis for this assertion was that 'termination here would not be premature' but there is no use of the word 'premature' in the Directive and it is unclear what is the basis for this assertion.[32] Could termination of the agency contract as a result of the agent's retirement be called 'premature'? After all, principal and agent could have been aware at the time they entered into the agency contract that the agent intended to retire at a particular date, or the agency contract could specifically stipulate that the agent would be entitled to terminate forthwith upon notice in the event of illness. The DTI wrongly stated that no payment would arise where the agent was guilty of repudiatory breach. In fact there would be no question of termination let alone compensation if the principal did not accept the repudiation.

It should be noted that the DTI produced a compliance cost estimate with regard to the provisions relating to inter alia compensation. The low range was put at £5,000 and the high range at £80,000. Interestingly, under a more recent cost compliance estimate dated December 1993, this low range has stayed the same but the high range has dropped to £40,000. Many cases settle prior to trial and therefore the actual sums paid out under the Regulations are not known. However, it is thought that the DTI figures are a serious underestimate of sums actually received by agents for post-termination compensation.

When termination arises when the agent has enjoyed proper performance of the contract, ie when the contract has been terminated lawfully, there is an argument for suggesting that the only compensation that should be made available to the agent is that relating to unamortised costs and expenses, as apart from these items, the agent will not have suffered any damage. On the basis that the correct test to be applied by the UK courts is that set out in French law, then this argument appears not to have much support, as under French law, the relevant damage will arise at the moment of termination when the value of the agency is removed from the agent.

Finally, the issue of liquidated damages arises. Can the parties to an agency agreement agree in advance a limit on the monies to be paid to the agent in the event of termination? As mentioned below, regulation 19 prevents derogation to the agent's detriment before termination, so that in so far as any such agreement limited the agent's rights, it would be unenforceable. The discussion above regarding the nature of the rights created by the Regulations is also relevant. At least if the Regulations create contractual rights, the ordinary rules of English law would apply, so that in order to be effective, the sum would have to be a genuine pre-estimate of the monies to be paid. This generally arises in the context when the sum has been fixed at such a level as to act as a deterrent to ensure that the contract in question is performed. In the situation of a principal and an agent, it is much more likely that the sum of money agreed will be below any estimated losses. In this case, regard will have to be paid to regulation 19.

---

[32] See also above at para 9.1. As seen above, this view is not shared by the leading commentators nor as at present by the Courts.

Precedent clause

If the indemnity route is chosen, the precedent clause below is suggested:

C If the Commercial Agents (Council Directive) Regulations 1993 (as amended) apply
   to this Agreement, then upon determination of this Agreement (howsoever effected),
   the Agent shall be entitled to be indemnified and not compensated.

9.27 INDEMNITY OR COMPENSATION?

As to which is the preferred option, the authors remain agnostic. It will depend on
the particular circumstances of each case as to which option may be preferable.
The fact that indemnity payments have a fixed limit will appeal to many principals.
However, it is not to be forgotten that the agent may claim damages as well under
the indemnity provisions.

In so far as compensation is concerned, although there is no limit fixed it must
be based on actual damage and a sizeable part of it may be attributed to unamortised costs and expenses, in which case potential liability can be reduced by not
advising that such costs and expenses be incurred. In addition, the recent English
case law shows that the courts are much less willing to give what they describe as
windfall payments in the form of compensation to agents.

9.28 IN WHAT CIRCUMSTANCES ARE THE RIGHTS TO INDEMNITY OR COMPENSATION UNDER REGULATION 17 INAPPLICABLE?

Regulation 18 provides that the agent does not have a right to indemnity or compensation where:

—the principal has terminated the agency contract due to breach by the agent,
  such breach justifying immediate termination; or
—the agent has terminated the contract himself, unless such termination is justified by circumstances attributable to the principal or is justified on grounds of
  age, infirmity or illness of the agent due to which he cannot reasonably be
  expected to carry out his activities;
—the agent assigns his rights and duties under the contract, with the consent of
  the principal, to another person.

This regulation has been dealt with above when examining the scope of regulation 17 (see paragraph 9.16). It is, in refreshing contrast to many of the other regulations, very clear. The regulation is important in that it sets limits to the rights
of agents to claim an indemnity payment or compensation. Only one point need
be made. Under English law, a default justifying immediate termination would
include a serious breach or a breach of a fundamental term in the contract.

Regulation 19 provides that neither the principal nor the commercial agent may derogate from the terms of regulations 17 and 18 to the detriment of the commercial agent before the agency contract expires[33]. This regulation follows verbatim the relevant provision in the Directive. As mentioned above, this may impact on the opportunity to use liquidated damages clauses in agency contracts in order to try to limit the amount of compensation which could be payable to an agent.

Regulation 17 (9) states that an agent's entitlement to indemnity or compensation will be lost if the agent has not 'notified his principal that he intends pursuing his entitlement' within one year following termination.

The required notice was considered in the unreported High Court case of *Hackett v Advanced Medical Computer Systems Limited.*[34] The court apparently stated that notice was sufficient if it gave notice of an intention to pursue claims even if it was not stated whether compensation or indemnity was being claimed.

Regulation 20 provides that restraint of trade clauses are only valid if they are concluded in writing and they relate to the geographical area or group of customers and geographical area entrusted to the commercial agents and to the kind of goods covered by their agencies. It also provides that such clauses will not be valid for more than two years after termination.

The regulation implements Article 20 of the Directive almost verbatim. However, it is interesting to examine the previous drafts of the Directive on this issue as certain changes have taken place which may affect parties to an agency agreement.

In all of the drafts of the Directive up to and including the amended Commission proposal, there were provisions for the payment of a suitable indemnity by the principal to the agent during the time when the restraint of trade was in force. The only exception to this entitlement was when the principal had terminated the contract because of default attributable to the agent which justified immediate termination. This provision was not carried through to the Directive as adopted by the Council,

---

[33] The fact that Regulation 17 is mandatory was confirmed by the European Court of Justice in Case C–381/98: *Ingmar GB v Eaton Leonard Technologies* [2001] 1 CMLR 9.

[34] 24 September 1998: see *PLC* Magazine, Jan/Feb 1999, p 57.

but there would appear to be nothing in the Directive nor the Regulations to prohibit the agent from forcing the principal to take into account in the calculation of the indemnity or compensation the time during which a restraint of trade clause was operational.

In terms of English law, it is worth noting that prior to the implementation of the Directive, unwritten restraints of trade were valid. Thus this is a change of which principals should be aware. Also under English law, restraints of trade for periods of less than two years have been held to be invalid. It is the DTI's view that the restraint of trade doctrine does not apply to the extent that it is overridden by regulation 20. It remains to be seen whether this is a correct interpretation of regulation 20(2). It is thought that if a restraint of trade clause is set at say four years, the last two years could be severed leaving the clause valid for two years: the first draft of the Regulations stipulated that a restraint of trade clause would be valid only if it was limited to a period of not more than two years after termination. The Directive and the Regulations both state that a restraint of trade clause '*shall be* valid for not more than two years after termination' (authors' emphasis).

Finally, if such clauses are to be valid, they will still have to be reasonable as between the parties as well as not being against the public interest in keeping with the English common law doctrine.

10

Commercial Agency Law in Germany

IN THE LAST 10 years the law on commercial agency in Germany has been changed and amended quite significantly—the most recent changes having been made pursuant to Council Directive 86/653

10.1 GENERAL REMARKS ON COMMERCIAL AGENCY AGREEMENTS

German law on commercial agency is regulated by both voluntary and compulsory provisions pursuant to sections 84 et seq of the German Commercial Code.

When there is no mandatory provision applicable, it is possible to deviate from any voluntary provisions which could otherwise apply, by virtue of section 84 of the German Commercial Code when making a commercial agency agreement. Commercial agency agreements may be concluded orally, except for 'Del Credere' agreements (s 86 b) I 1 German Commercial Code) and for non-competition agreements (s 90 a) I, 1 German Commercial Code). Section 85 German Commercial Code contains an exception regarding the form of the contract, which states that either party may demand that the terms of the contract be set out in a document signed by the other party. When using the standard form for commercial agency agreements, the German Act of General Terms and Conditions ('AGBG') is applicable. In those circumstances, section 9 thereof will apply, which prohibits contractual provisions which might disadvantage the contractual partner, as for example by reducing the limitation period for claims (according to section 88 German Commercial Code) from four years to six months.

The commercial agent may be a legal person (limited liability company, stock corporation, registered association, registered cooperative, limited partnership, general commercial partnership, however not in civil law partnership, and not an association having legal capacity) or may be a natural person. The commercial agent is considered to be a merchant pursuant to sections 1, 1 and 2 of the German Commercial Code, as long as the person is a commercially organised business operation. The commercial agent is also required to have a commercial firm name according to section 17 of the German Commercial Code.

10.2 CONSTITUENT ELEMENTS OF A COMMERCIAL AGENT

A person soliciting business on behalf of another ('Vermittler') is a commercial agent, if all of the constituent elements contained in section 84 of the German Commercial Code are met.

An independent person engaged in business is a Vermittler according to section 84 of the German Commercial Code if he is essentially free to structure his activities and is free to determine his hours of work. Where these facts are not present, the person is considered to be an employee according to section 84 II of the German Commercial Code. However, the limits are not fixed. According to the prevailing view of the courts and of the literature, the matter has to be determined pursuant to an assessment of the contractual arrangement and the work of the person involved. Formal criteria of self-employment include, for example, membership in the International Chamber of Commerce ('IHK'), commission payments or taking over several agencies. Substantive indications for self-employment include, for example, the ability to structure one's own activities and whether instructions are given by another on how to operate the business in question.

According to section 84 I of the German Commercial Code, a commercial agent has to solicit business or actually enter into business transactions on behalf of another. 'Soliciting' means that the commercial agent will directly or indirectly, eg through subagents, assist the business transactions through negotiations with third parties. Commercial agents who are authorised actually to enter into transactions are rather rare in practice. Where a commercial agent transacts business, section 91 (a) of the German Commercial Code deals with the particular situation of an agent acting without authority, when the third party in question did not know about the lack of that authority. However, section 91 (a) of the German Commercial Code is not applicable in cases when the authority is misused or in cases of authority by estoppel ('Anscheinsvollmacht'). The general provisions of sections 177–9 of the German Civil Code ('BGB') remain unaffected.

Acting within the scope of his regular authorisation to solicit business for the principal, the commercial agent solicits business in the name of and on account of the principal. The so-called 'ständige Betrauung' (the normal authority to solicit business for the principal) refers to a certain time period during which the commercial agent's relationship is in force and during which the commercial agent tries to enter into a number of business transactions on behalf of his principal.

10.3 TYPES OF COMMERCIAL AGENT

There are several types of commercial agent defined in section 87 II of the German Commercial Code. There is the commercial agent who has been assigned to a specific district ('Bezirksvertreter'), who has the right to commission for business transactions entered into in this specific district; then there is the commercial agent who is assigned to a particular group within a specific district ('Alleinvertreter') and who in addition has the right of customer protection against the principal. Furthermore the main commercial agent may entrust third persons, subagents ('Untervertreter'), with the power of representation. Subagents, however, as auxiliary staff do not take over the obligation owed by the commercial agent to the principal. It is not necessary to seek the principal's permission to work with subagents.

Another form of commercial agent are the insurance, building and loan association agents pursuant to section 92 German Commercial Code. Given that an insurance agent generally solicits long term contracts, which in principle do not lead to additional orders, the general provisions of section 84 et seq of the German Commercial Code are only narrowly applicable in such circumstances.

Pursuant to section 92 of the German Commercial Code, different provisions are applicable for a part-time commercial agent, whose business time is not totally occupied by his commercial agency activities. This will not apply to a commercial agent working for several principals at the same time or when working as a commercial agent alongside his full time employment for another company.

The special provisions pursuant to section 92 of the German Commercial Code are only applicable if the commercial agent was explicitly employed part-time when signing the contract.

10.4 DUTIES OF THE COMMERCIAL AGENT

The duties of the commercial agent are only partially regulated by section 86 German Commercial Code; some are regulated by contractual agreement. Principally, the commercial agent must fulfil his duties with the care of a prudent merchant (ss 86 II, 347 I German Commercial Code). The commercial agent is obliged to make efforts towards the solicitation or conclusion of business transactions ('Vermittlungs- und Abschlusspflicht'). Further duties are to be regulated by individual contract; principally, the commercial agent is not obliged to fulfil functions which are not in direct connection to his business, eg collecting sums due or customer services.

In generating business the commercial agent has to be guided by contractual standards or—when in doubt—his duty to solicit business shall pertain to all of the goods of the principal.

Furthermore, the commercial agent has to act in the interests of the principal (ss 86 I, 2 German Commercial Code), and he has to subordinate his own interests to those of his principal, eg his prospect of commission.

As long as it is possible without further costs and difficulties, the commercial agent is obliged to check the credit-status of his clients. Should it become necessary to get further expensive information or should the commercial agent have doubts concerning the credit status, he always has to involve the principal.

Furthermore, the commercial agent has to comply with the obligation not to work for competing principals ('Konkurrenzverbot'), which originates from the obligation to safeguard the principal's interests. In judging competitive activity, court rulings focus on the mere possibility of influencing the interests of the principal. In such circumstances the commercial agent has to inform the principal and has to get his approval. The prohibition not only covers the obligation not to work for competing principals, but also every activity which could influence the interests of any principal, eg activities as shareholders of a competing company. The duties listed in sections 86 I and II of the German Commercial Code are general concepts of law, to be fulfilled by the parties. Section 86, 4 of the German Commercial Code has to be interpreted accordingly. The parties may determine in which way the commercial agent has to safeguard the rights of the principal and therefore may in this context contractually exclude the prohibition on noncompetition. Where the prohibition is infringed, the contractual relationship may be terminated and/or compensatory damage awards may be claimed (s 89 (a) of the German Commercial Code).

Pursuant to the duty to act in the principal's interests, the commercial agent is bound by instructions from the principal. The instructions, however, should not impair the legal self-employment status of the agent and should only focus on the sales policies and the business transactions of the principal.

The commercial agent is obliged pursuant to his fiduciary duties to treat business and trade matters in a confidential manner, especially during but also after the conclusion of the agency agreement pursuant to section 90 of the German Commercial Code.

The commercial agent is obliged to keep and to return all objects given to him for the purpose of representing the principal and may be obliged to insure valuable objects. Pursuant to section 86 II of the German Commercial Code, the commercial agent shall give the principal all necessary information of every solicitation and of every transaction concluded. This duty also includes all detailed information, which the principal needs to know in order to further promote his business, eg the relevant market situation or competitive offers. Again, the frequency of giving all necessary information shall not be detrimental to the legal self-employment status of the commercial agent.

Where the commercial agent guarantees in writing the fulfilment of obligations arising from the transaction towards the principal, he assumes a 'del credere' liability for his transaction (s 86 b I German Commercial Code). This liability has features of a guarantee, so that the commercial agent and the customer are jointly and severally liable. However, the commercial agent formally does not have the defence that the creditor must first unsuccessfully try to execute his claim on the debtor ('Einrede der Vorausklage') according to section 349 of the German Commercial Code. However, the commercial agent will be able to ask that such a provision is included in this contract. The high risk involved with a del credere liability will be compensated with a del credere commission (s 86 II of the German commercial code).

10.5 PRINCIPAL'S DUTIES

Aside from the duties the principal has to the commercial agent, the principal is free to arrange his field of business. However, the Principal may not act arbitrarily or seek to cause damage to the commercial agent.

All obligations under section 86 (a) of the German Commercial Code are mandatory and any agreement therefrom is void. The principal has the duty to support the commercial agent in providing him with necessary materials pursuant to section 86 (a) I of the German Commercial Code. This is a so-called 'Bringschuld', meaning that the material has to be delivered by the principal without further costs of delivery to the place where the commercial agent needs them. The principal holds title to the materials and has to update them regularly.

According to section 86 (a) II, 1 of the German Commercial Code, the principal shall keep the commercial agent generally informed prior to and during the contractual relationship with all information necessary for his business activities. In evaluating necessity in this context, the interests of the commercial agent have to be considered. Pursuant to sections 86 a) II, 2 and 3 of the German Commercial Code, the principal shall inform the commercial agent promptly of any acceptance or rejection of a transaction solicited or concluded by the commercial agent. Further, if the principal wishes to, or is likely to, conclude business on a significantly reduced scale in comparison with what the agent could have expected under normal circumstances, the agent must be informed. The principal is generally obliged to support the commercial agent. The commercial agent must have the opportunity to discharge his duties. In this sense, the principal shall not in any way compete with the commercial agent, either directly or indirectly, eg by way of using another representative.

10.6 COMMISSION OF THE COMMERCIAL AGENT

Section 87 et seq of the German Commercial Code set out the transactions for which commission is due. Commission is to be paid if a transaction is concluded throught the activities of an agent (s 87 1, 1.Alt) or even if the commercial agent is only indirectly involved therewith (s 87, 2).

It is also possible to contractually negotiate a commission which is guaranteed at a certain level. However, that right will not be available if the commercial agent is eligible for a higher amount of commission payment under the German Commercial Code

Section 87 of the German Commercial Code sets out the general rights to commission, whereas section 87 (a) determines specifically when the commission is due and under what conditions the right to commission is enforceable. This division protects the commission claim from contract termination or from changes to the contract conditions, which may occur in the time period after the claim arose but before the claim became due. A valid commercial agency agreement must be in force at the time in which the commercial agent is acting in accordance with the terms of transactions for which commission is due. After the commission is due according to section 87 (a) of the German Commercial Code, the claim for commission is assignable and capable of attachment. A general provision ('Auffangtatbestand') dealing with commission claims is contained in section 345 of the German Commercial Code. According to section 87 of the Code, a transaction having legal effect must be concluded between the principal and the customer for the right to commisson to arise. As to the issue of causation, the commercial agent has to be the contributing factor in promoting the transaction—decisive factors therein are the contractual obligations the commercial agent has to undertake. There are two exceptions:

(i) pursuant to section 87,1 sentence 1, 2nd sub-paragraph, in cases of repeat orders, it is not necessary that the repeat order has to be attributed to the actions of the commercial agent.

(ii) where the commercial agent has been assigned to a specific district or a particular group of customers, he also has a right to commission for transactions whether or not the transactions in question were attributable to the agent. Furthermore the commercial agent has a right to administration commission, eg collection commission, for amounts collected by him pursuant to instructions given by the principal, pursuant to section 87, IV of the German Commercial Code or 'del credere' commission or stockkeeper commission.

10.7 'OVERLAPPING' COMMISSION ('ÜBERHANGPROVISION')

An important provision regarding commission is contained in section 87, III of the German Commercial Code, which deals with two exceptions from the principle that commission is only to be paid if the transaction was concluded during the term of the contractual relationship. These exceptional commissions are called 'overlapping commissions'. According to section 87 III, 1 of the Code, the agent shall have the right to commission for transactions concluded after termination of the contractual agency relationship, if he solicited or was instrumental in obtaining the transactions. The transaction has to be concluded within a reasonable time after termination of the agency agreement. According to the second sentence thereof the agent shall have a right to commission if, prior to the termination of the agency agreement, the offer of a third party has been received by the principal. This shall prevent the principal from holding back contract offers of customers until the agency agreement has been terminated, in order to reduce commission due to the agent.

10.8 CLAIMS FOR COMMISSION ARISING FROM THE GENERAL RIGHT TO COMMISSION

According to section 87 (a) of the German Commercial Code, the commercial agent has a right to commission as soon as and insofar as the principal has completed the transaction. Thus, the right to commission arises immediately and unconditionally, when the customer performs or when it is contractually agreed that the customer will subsequently perform. Even outside of such circumstances, the commercial agent has a right to a reasonable advance according to section 87 (a) I, 2 of the German Commercial Code. 'Reasonable' is what both parties consider to be reasonable pursuant to the circumstances of both parties. The right to this form of commission fails if it is clear that the customer will not pay. Advances which have already been paid have to be returned if the underlying business transaction is cancelled. The right of the principal to repayment is forfeited when advance payments have not been charged against the commissions owed for a period of two years. Furthermore, the commercial agent has a claim to partial commission if the customer only pays in part (s 87 I, 3 of the German Commercial Code) .

If performance of an obligation under the contract is adversely affected, it will have the following influence on the right to commission: Where it has been determined that the customer does not perform because, for example his performance has become impossible, there is no right to commission (s 87 (a) II of the German Commercial Code). Furthermore, the principal has to demand performance of his customer. If the principal does not do so, the commercial agent has the right to commission. A customer's non-performance has to be judged by objective criteria. The right to commission will continue to exist, if substituted performance is made. On the other hand, it is possible that the principal could interfere with the performance—in such situations basically the right to commissions will continue to exist, so that the risk is shifted to the principal after business has been transacted. According to section 87 (a) III 2 of the German Commercial Code no right to commission shall exist in the event of non-performance where that is due to reasons beyond the control of the principal, ie because of force majeure or when the law has been changed. Pursuant to the former situation, one has to judge if it was reasonable for the principal to adhere in good faith to the business transaction with the client, ie where the client's wish to cancel was judged as unreasonable, if in case of non-compliance with that wish the business contact would be lost. According to the latter situation, which only refers to the responsibility of the non-performance of the business transaction, the principal has to carry the risk of all cancellations and the agent will still have the right to commission.

10.9 FORMAL CRITERIA FOR COMMISSION ACCOUNTING

The accounting of the commission due shall be carried out up to the last day of the month following the business transaction in question, if the parties have not agreed upon an extension to a maximum of three months, pursuant to section 87 (c) I of the German Commercial Code. The amount of the commission is most often set out in the contract. Where the amount of commission is not specified, the customary rate is deemed to be agreed upon according to section 87 (b), 1 of the Code. The amount of commission may also be agreed upon impliedly through action, eg payments of a certain amount. The agreed upon amount of commission is valid for all relevant actions of the agent and shall only be changed if the contract provides for such changes or if new contractual terms are agreed upon. The amount of commission shall furthermore not be reduced by way of partial contract termination, which basically is not admissible under the relevant provisions of German law, if not otherwise provided for in the contract. It is, however, possible to terminate a contract with the option to create a new contract under altered conditions ('Änderungskündigung').

When judging the customary rate of commission, the practice in the line of business of each agent's district shall be decisive. When calculating the commission the remuneration which the client or the principal has to pay for the business conducted is decisive. However, the allowance of price reductions for cash-payments or incidental expenses such as freight, package or insurance costs are not taken into account. Contractually-negotiated rebates, however, may be deducted. According to section 87 (b) II, 3 of the German Commercial Code, the commission shall be calculated from the gross amount of the invoice; in practise, however, most often it is agreed upon using the net value of the goods. According to section 12 I of the German Turnover Tax Law, the performance of the agent has to be taxed at the standard tax rate of 16 per cent. In long term contractual relationships, where the remuneration is determined by reference to a certain time period, the commercial agent is entitled either to a one-off commission, calculated for the whole contractual period, or to a sum calculated until the time the client is entitled to terminate the contract. In cases where the commercial agency agreement is terminated during the period of a long term contract, such termination has no effect on the right to commission fixed thereunder.

10.10 CHECKING OF THE COMMISSION PAYMENTS BY THE AGENT

According to section 87 (c) of the German Commercial Code the agent has several ways of checking the commission payments: he may demand a monthly account from the principal (para 1); he may demand an excerpt from the books concerning all transactions in respect of which he has a claim for commission (para 2); he may demand information (para 3) or he may demand the inspection of the business books (para 4).

The principal rights are to demand monthly accounting, and to demand an excerpt from the books. Where reasonable doubts exist as to the accuracy or completeness of the account or the excerpt, the commercial agent may request permission to inspect the business books. The right to an excerpt from the books and the right to inspect the business books may only be pursued consecutively, not concurrently. The final possibility the commercial agent has is to demand an affidavit from the principal. This right is not time-barred parallel to the statute of limitations of the right to commission, but according to section 88 of the German

Commercial Code, where the statute of limitation begins with the coming into existence of each right to check upon the commission. The accounting for the commission has to include the inchoate right to commission, the unconditional right to commission as well as 'del credere' commission or collecting commission. The agent has to declare its intention unequivocally to accept the billing—then the billing is considered as recognising a debt according to section 781 of the German Civil Code.

The agent has a right to claim for an excerpt from the books according to section 87 (c) II of the German Commercial Code until the parties have agreed upon the accounting for the commission. The excerpt has to be provided in written form by the principal and must be precise and complete in order to be understood by the agent.

The right of information according to section 87 III of the German Commercial Code makes it possible for the agent to receive all necessary information which he cannot obtain through books or accounting .

The principal has the option to permit either the agent or an auditor or a certified accountant designated by him to inspect the books according to section 87 (c) IV of the German Commercial Code. The costs shall be borne by the agent, but if it is proved that the accounting of the principal is incorrect to the agent's detriment, the agent then shall have the right to claim against the principal for reimbursement of the costs due to breach of contract.

Furthermore, the agent is able to claim retention of tangible property of the principal that is in his possession (ss 273, 369 of the German Commercial Code). In addition, the merchant's right of retention according to section 369 of the German Commercial Code gives the agent the right to satisfy his claim pursuant to section 371 of the German Commercial Code. However, the right of retention is restricted in 369 III of the German Commercial Code insofar as the retention of the item would conflict with instructions given by the debtor before or upon delivery thereof or would conflict with the creditors duty to deal with the item in a specific way. After termination of the agency agreement, the agent has the right to retain materials placed at his disposal only by reason of unpaid commissions or reimbursement of expenses due to him (s 86 (a) I German Commercial Code). If other claims should exist he may only have the right of retention of other items.

10.11 STATUTE OF LIMITATIONS FOR CLAIMS

Claims for commission and claims arising from the contractual relationship are time barred after four years, beginning with the end of the year in which they became due (s 88 of the German Commercial Code). Excluded are claims for restitution of overpaid commission payments by the principal, which are time barred after 30 years according to section 195 of the German Civil Code.

Although section 88 of the German Commercial Code provides that the statute of limitation begins with the end of the year the claim has become due, section 225 sentence 2 of the German Civil Code allows this period to be shortened if acknowledged interests exist and no interests warranting protection are impaired.

10.12 REIMBURSEMENT OF EXPENSES

The commercial agent may only demand reimbursement of his regular business expenses if this is customary within the trade. The extent of the business shall be in accordance with the agency agreement. His soliciting actions, however, are not included; those costs, such as business entertainment or travel expenses, shall not be reimbursed.

10.13 TERMINATION

Whether the contractual relationship is intended to be of definite or indefinite duration, it may be terminated subject to a certain period of notice. Section 89 of the German Commercial Code, however, excludes the provisions dealing with termination of an employer/employee relationship. Section 89 of the German Commercial Code sets a minimum length of notice period, which will be extended in correspondence to the length of the contractual relationship between the agent and its principal. If a contract of definite duration is changed into a contract of indefinite duration, the total duration of the relationship shall be decisive for calculating the termination notice period. The termination may be done informally but must indicate clearly the intention of the terminating party. During the notice period, the principal shall not release the agent from his duties.

According to section 89 (a) of the German Commercial Code the contractual relationship may be terminated without observing a notice period for an important reason. The important reason—and a high threshold is applied in each case—may arise in relation to either party, for example due to a sudden worsening of the economic situation, which makes a termination of the contract with the agent without notice necessary in order to save the enterprise of the principal. Termination without notice has to be defined as such; the time limit of two weeks according to section 626 II German Civil Code is not applicable; rather, the party terminating the contract has a notice period which is appropriate for each situation. Where termination results from conduct of the other party, that party is obliged to compensate for damages arising from the contract termination (s 89 (a) of the German Commercial Code).

In order to claim damages, the important reason must be given, theoretically—but there is no need to mention it expressly. Hence also a termination with a notice period may establish the claim to compensatory damages, if theoretically there is an important reason. If the party receiving the termination without prior notice could also have terminated the contractual relationship due to an important reason, the claim for compensatory damage will fail.

Furthermore, the contractual relationship between the agent and principal may be terminated through rescission according to section 142 I of the German Civil Code, and the death of the agent, when in doubt, will lead to the extinction of the contract (ss 675, 673 German Civil Code).

10.14 INDEMNITY CLAIM

The commercial agent may, after expiration of the contractual relationship, demand from the principal reasonable indemnity (s 89 (b) of the German Commercial Code). No claim for compensation shall exist, where pursuant to section 89 (b) III,1 of the German Commercial Code, the commercial agent has terminated the contract, unless the actions of the principal constituted sufficient grounds therefor, or when the commercial agent cannot be expected to continue his activities by reason of his age or health.

The sufficient ground need not be assessed in the same way as the important reason for the termination without notice– rather the commercial agent must in good faith get into an unbearable situation, eg an adverse economic development of the enterprise, which cannot further guarantee profitable actions of the commercial agent.

Furthermore, no claim shall exist where according to section 89 (b) III,2 of the German Commercial Code the principal has terminated the contract for an important reason relating to culpable conduct of the commercial agent. Section 89 (b) III, 3 German Commercial Code provides that no claim to compensation shall exist where by reason of an agreement between the principal and the commercial agent a third party assumes the rights and obligations of the commercial agent, because it is assumed that the withdrawing agent will demand a payment from the third party for receiving the rights of the commercial agent.

A precondition for the compensation claim is that the principal retains substantial advantages from business relations with new customers solicited by the commercial agent or from intensified contacts with old customers after termination of the contractual relationship. The business relations with new customers must have a certain intensity, with an expectation of further business transactions. There have to be substantial advantages regarding the theoretical profit expectations resulting from the new clientele. The advantages are substantial if the principal will receive economic usage from the new customer relationships, when transactions in general are in decline. There might also be financial advantages when selling the new established clientele. The commercial agent has the burden of proving the preconditions of a compensation claim. Easing the burden of proof is allowed according to court rulings if—judging by the outward appearance of a long-lasting and successful commercial agent activity—the requirements of section 89 (b) I German Commercial Code are satisfied.

Pursuant to section 89 (b) I of the German Commercial Code, another precondition for a compensation claim is that the commercial agent, by reason of termination of the contractual relationship, loses his right to commission relating to concluded business or business to be concluded in the future with those customers he had solicited. Estimates are required of the quantity and nature of commission from later orders and how many follow-up commissions would have been received if the commercial agent had continued his activities and how long the agent's activities could have been expected to continue—here, court rulings assume a time frame of three to five years. The compensation claim from the agent shall not be reduced if the business turnover is declining due to the principal's fault. Administration commissions are to be excluded therefrom. Unpaid 'overlapping commissions' from business transactions already performed may not be taken into consideration for the debit calculation.

It is assumed that the excess commission shall be paid in accordance with the principles of fairness. In this connection all matters relating to the substantial advantage of the principal and to the losses of the agent, which result from the contractual relationship, must be considered. As an exception the courts have decided that the social situation of the commercial agent and the economic situation of the principal have to be considered if the situation requires it.

Thus, a pension for old age, financed by the principal, will lead to a reduction of compensation. Likewise, other circumstances may be taken into consideration leading either to a reduction or a cancellation of a compensation reduction, owing to the principle of fairness, for example a sudden termination of the principal or a termination with prior notice due to the intention to assign the representation to a person close to the principal.

The actual calculation of the compensatory claim is done in two steps:

First, a rough compensation ('Rohausgleich') is calculated according to the business transaction commission which the agent has made during the last 12 months of his contractual relationship with new clients; the time frame in which he could have terminated from the established clientele; and an allowance for the fluctuation of the clientele. The loss of the commission for the years following the termination of the contractual relationship is based on the calculation of each commission quota per year minus the quota resulting from clientele who leave. All commission losses for all the years together are added up and then added to the total commission loss. From this amount 10 per cent will be discounted, because the amount is paid in full at once and not in installments. The discounted amount then may be adjusted due to reasonableness. Thus the so-called 'Rohausgleich' is established.

In a second step and according to section 89 (b) II of the German Commercial Code, the maximum amount has to be calculated, which only functions as a limit to the rough compensation. The maximum amount is the amount of commission received by the agent in the last five years.

The compensation claim has to be asserted within one year after termination of contractual relationship. After this time limit the claim lapses. The claim may be asserted orally or in writing. To be on the safe side, the agent should be able to show proof that he made the claim within the specified time. In asserting the claim, the agent does not have to specify the amount claimed. The right to claim compensation may not be excluded in advance (section 89 (b) IV of the German Commercial Code). The agent may, however, waive his right to compensation after his claim arose or in connection with a rescission of the contract.

a. Exclusive foreign jurisdiction—avoiding section 89 (b) of the German Commercial Code ?

An interesting issue is whether the explicit negotiation of an exclusive foreign jurisdiction, which does not provide for a compensation claim, will supplant section 89 (b) of the German Commercial Code. Such a situation occurs when the principal resides in a foreign country, but the commercial agent's place of business is in Germany.

According to section 30 of the European Community civil code (EGBGB), one could assume that a stipulation to the exclusive foreign jurisdiction would be invalid due to the mandatory nature of section 89 (b) of the German Commercial Code. However, section 30 of the European Community Civil Code will be strictly interpreted and thus will only apply to safeguard fundamental German legal rules which form the basis of social and public lives. Hence, the German Federal Supreme Court did not assume this for the compensation claim of the commercial agent according to section 89 (b) of the German Commercial Code.

b. Belgian commercial agency law—missing compensation claim?

In Belgian law, only a distributor-contract existed until 1995, and this was applicable to distributors who had received the right from the licensor to sell products on their own account and in their own name. Until then, no legal provision existed for commercial agents and thus no right existed for a compensation claim.

In accordance with the European Community Directive on harmonisation of commercial agency law, the 'Commercial Agency Agreement Act' was passed on 13 April 1995. This new law regulates the relationship between the principal and the self-employed commercial agent. The Belgian word for 'commercial agent' in Article 1 is analogous with the definition of the commercial agent in the German Commercial Code: an agency agreement is an agreement in which one party, the commercial agent, is obliged to solicit or to transact business for the other party, the principal, in the name of and on account of the principal. Furthermore, the commercial agent is not bound by instructions from the principal, but may organise his activities independently.

According to the new Belgian Commercial Agency Law (Art 20) the commercial agent now has a claim for compensation for soliciting new clients or for expanding business transactions with former clients, after his contractual relationship has terminated and if the activity of the commercial agent is of further advantage to the principal. This provision safeguards the agent to a high degree—no distinction is made between a time limited or unlimited agreement, and furthermore the compensation shall be paid even if the commercial agent has to terminate his contract because of his age, incapacity or sickness (Art 20 II no 2, 2). In calculating the compensatory amount the Belgian law refers to the French model that does not cap the compensatory amount and in the alternative refers to the German model which establishes a maximum amount (annual average commission).

According to section 29 of the Belgian Commercial Agency Law, the new right, and thus the mechanisms for the compensation claim, is not applicable to contractual claims which were pending before the commencement of the new act, ie prior to 13 April, 1995.

10.15 AGREEMENT PROHIBITING COMPETITION

Competition between the agent and principal is prohibited during the time of the contractual relationship. After termination, the parties are free to negotiate an agreement prohibiting competition. This agreement must be within the limits set forth in section 90 (a) of the German Commercial Code. According to section 90 (a) I, 2 of the German Commercial Code, the agreement may run for no longer than two years following termination and may only cover the geographical area or group of customers assigned to the agent. The agreement must be in writing and must be signed by the principal. The principal is obliged to pay reasonable compensation to the commercial agent for the duration of the prohibition of competition. In determining the amount of the compensation, the advantages and the disadvantages on both sides have to be considered taking into account the latest received compensations of the agent. The compensation of the agent should not be taken into account (section 89 (b) of the German Commercial Code). Should the parties not agree to the amount, then the court must determine compensation. The compensation may also be paid in material values or other assets which are to the benefit of the commercial agent. The compensation claim arises at the commencement of the prohibition on competition. During the contractual relationship the principal may at any time waive the prohibition on competition (section 90 (a) II, 1 German Commercial Code). However, compensation must be paid to the agent for six months starting with the date of that declaration—even if this time goes beyond the end of the contractual relationship. A waiver of the prohibition on competition by common consent is permissible at all times and does not lead to any compensation payment by the principal. Where the contractual relationship is terminated due to an important reason and without prior notice by either one of the parties, the party terminating the agreement may in writing within one month declare that he is not bound by the terms prohibiting competition. Where the commercial agent offends against the prohibition on competition, the principal is not required to pay any compensation. Furthermore the principal may demand damage compensation, against which the saved compensation payments should be allowed. Where the principal refuses payment of compensation for the agreement prohibiting competition, the commercial agent is liberated from this agreement after setting a time limit with right to rejection according to section 326 of the German civil code ('Fristsetzung mit Ablehnungsandrohung').

11

Commercial Agency Law in France

11.1 INTRODUCTION

IN FRANCE, COMMERCIAL agents have been protected since 1958.[1] The 1958 decree was the first text to recognise commercial agents as independent professionals, acknowledge the specificity of their profession and provide them with compensation on termination. The commercial agency relationship is now regulated by the statute of 1991,[2] which was recently integrated into the new commercial code (Articles L 134–1 to L 134–17). Although the statute implements the Directive of 1986,[3] it nevertheless differs from it since it gives statutory value to certain custom-based rules accepted by French case law for over a century. The peculiarity of the French system compared to the directive can be seen in three main areas; the emphasis on the independence of the commercial agent, the notion of common interest mandate and compensation on termination. These three aspects will be emphasised in this study.

The scope of application of the code

Unlike the Agency Regulations, the code applies to all commercial agents without reference to territory. Although this seems advantageous, the recent case of *SA Allium v Société Alfin Incorporated*,[4] which facts are not dissimilar to those of the case of *Ingmar*,[5] seriously undermines the protection of commercial agents who are established in France but work for a foreign principal within Europe because the decision is in direct contradiction with that of the European Court of Justice (ECJ) in the case of *Ingmar*.[6] The French supreme court, the *Cour de Cassation*, without even referring the matter to the ECJ, upheld the choice of law clause stating that the contract was subject to the law of New York and rejected the claim of

---

[1] Decree 58/1345 of 23 December 1958, D 1959, L 132.

[2] Statute 91/593 of 25 June 1991, OJ 27 June 1991, p 8271. The statute is complemented by the decree 92–506 of 10 June 1992 (D 1992, L 320) and the arrêté of 8 January 1993 (OJ 10 March 1993).

[3] Council Directive on the co-ordination of the laws of the member states relating to self-employed commercial agents, [1986] OJ L382/17–21.

[4] *Cass Com 28 November 2000*, JCP G 2001, II, 10527, p 947. The French commercial agent was in charge of selling perfumes for an American principal in Europe and Israel. The contract stipulated that the law of New York applied. When the contract was terminated, the commercial agent claimed compensation under French law.

[5] Case C–381/98 *Ingmar GB v Eaton Leonard Technologies* [2001] 1 CMLR 9.

[6] *Ibid.*

compensation of the commercial agent under French law. The court held that the 1991 statute, as incorporated in the new commercial code was a public order statute but only domestically and not internationally.

The form of the commercial agency agreement

The code does not require the commercial agency agreement to be entered into in writing and France did not opt for the possibility left by the Directive to require the commercial agency contract to be evidenced in writing.[7] Yet, the parties may request that the agreement and any subsequent covenants be entered into in writing.[8] Such a right is compulsory and cannot be contracted out.[9]

The contract does not have to be formal since an exchange of letters will be sufficient as long as it is accepted by both parties.[10] Although an oral contract will be perfectly valid, it is nevertheless advisable for the parties to enter the contract in writing for evidential purposes. Moreover, two clauses of the commercial agency contract are required to be in writing; the exclusion of the protection of the statute[11] and the post-contractual non-competition clause.[12]

The registration of the commercial agent

France requires commercial agents to be registered in a special registry.[13] Following two recent decisions of the ECJ, it is clear that registration can only be required for administrative purposes and not for questions of validity.[14] Yet, the conditions defined in two statutes are nevertheless heavy.[15] The registration is the responsibility of the commercial agent. Failing to comply with the requirement will lead to various fines. Although it has been remarked that the sanctions are very rarely applied,[16] it is nevertheless advisable to comply with the rules in order to avoid any problems.

Registration must be carried out just after a contract of mandate is entered between a commercial agent and a principal. The commercial agent him/herself,

---

[7] Art 13(2) of the Directive.

[8] Art 2 of the statute as incorporated in Art L 134–2 French commercial code.

[9] Art 16 of the statute as incorporated in Art L 134–16 French commercial code.

[10] *Cass Com 19 January 1993*, JCP G 1993, IV, 688 (this case was decided in relation to the decree of 1958). Position reiterated in relation to the implementing statute in *CA Agen 14 January 1997 SICA Procanar v Sud Ouest Diffusion*, Juriscl Dalloz, fasc 1240, 1.

[11] Art 15(1) of the statute as incorporated in Art L 134–15 al 1 French commercial code.

[12] Art 14 of the statute as incorporated in Art L 134–14 French commercial code. .

[13] The obligation only applies to commercial agents who carry out their activities in France *Cass 9 October 1990*, JCP ed E 1991, II, 211 confirmed by *Cass Com 19 November 1996 Foglino v SA David et Foillard*, JCP G 1997, IV, 68. Both cases relate to the 1958 decree.

[14] Case C–215/97 *Barbara Bellone v Yokohama* and Case C–454/98 *Centrosteel Srl v Adipol GmbH*.

[15] The arête of 1993 deals with the conditions of registration together with decree of 1958 as amended by decree of 1992.

[16] Catoni 'Le registre spécial des agents commerciaux' AC No 63, mai-juin 1985, pp 7–9.

or a representative, must carry out such a duty to the commercial tribunal of his/her place of business.[17] First of all, s/he must sign a declaration that s/he exercises his/her profession in the light of the 1991 statute. Then, s/he must provide a copy of his/her commercial agency contract. The rest of the wide spectrum of documents to provide will vary depending on whether the commercial agent is established as an individual or a legal entity.[18] The registration is valid for a period of five years.[19] Before the expiry of the period, the commercial agent must renew it by providing the same documents provided when registering for the first time.

11.2 DEFINITION OF THE COMMERCIAL AGENT AS AN INDEPENDENT BUSINESSMAN

The commercial agent is defined as

> a self-employed mandated agent who, on a permanent basis, independently and without any subordination link, is in charge of negotiating and possibly concluding agreements for the sale, purchase or hire of goods or the supply of services, in the name and for the account of producers, industrial business men, merchants or other commercial agents. The commercial agent can be a legal or a natural person.[20]

The three characteristics of the commercial agent

The definition is of crucial importance since it defines three characteristics which must be met before an intermediary can be regarded as a commercial agent and be protected by the code. They are as follows: (i) an independent professional who (ii) represents another person (iii) on a permanent basis.

The independence of the commercial agent

The clear emphasis on the independence in the definition (independently and without subordination link) shows its importance. Such an emphasis represents a slight departure from the directive, which remains silent on that aspect. The independence of the commercial agent can be seen in various ways. First of all, the commercial agent is essentially free to conduct the commercial agency as s/he sees fit eg s/he has a place of work independent from that of the principal,[21] s/he can

---

[17] Art 4(2) of the 1958 decree as amended by decree of 1992. Art 4(3) gives details as to precisely where to go when the commercial agent is established in certain departments.

[18] For details, see J M Leloup 'Les agents commerciaux, statuts juridiques, stratégies professionnelles', 5th edn (Delmas, 2001), pp 70–71.

[19] Art 5 of decree of 1958 as amended by decree of 1992.

[20] Art 1(1) of the statute as incorporated in Art L 134–1 al 1 French commercial code.

[21] *CA Angers 7 December 1995 Eclimont v Guibout*, Juriscl Dalloz, fasc 1230, p 1.

structure the activities, determine the hours of work as necessary;[22] use the services of employees or appoint sub-agents and establish the commercial agency as a legal or an individual entity. Secondly, the commercial agent, as an independent businessman, can act for several principals at once. The only restriction is that, should they be in competition with each other, consent of the current principals must be sought.[23] Finally, the commercial agent, as an independent person, can even have another profession alongside the commercial agency. However, the two professions must be compatible and must allow the commercial agent to fully commit him/herself to the commercial agency.[24] The commercial agent can even be linked to the principal with various contracts, such as a distributorship in addition to the commercial agency. In such a case, it will be possible for the parties to stipulate that as soon as the commercial agent spends less time on the commercial agency than on the other profession, the former becomes secondary and the protection of the law can be excluded[25] (see paragraph 11.2.2 for details).

The commercial agent acts for the principal

Although the commercial agent is an independent businessman, s/he does not act for himself but in the name and on behalf of the principal. This fact is of crucial importance since it is one of the elements, which explains why the commercial agent is in need of protection at the stage of termination.[26] If an intermediary, who claims to be a commercial agent, does not act for the principal, the status of commercial agent cannot be granted. In such a case, the courts have the power to regard the supposedly contract of commercial agency as a distributorship, which will prevent the commercial agent from claiming compensation.[27] The emphasis on the fact that the commercial agent represents another person also indicates that the contract is a mandate, which means that the commercial agent is a civil person and not a merchant.[28]

---

[22] In *CA Montpellier 6 May 1988 Fouque v Dutol*, Juriscl Dalloz, fasc 1230, p 1, an intermediary was held not to be a commercial agent because his hours of work were imposed by the manufacturer, he had no freedom to organise the visits to the clients since they were all scheduled by the manufacturer.

[23] Art 3 of the statute as incorporated in Art L 134–3 French commercial code. Such a restriction makes sense in the light of the notion of common interest as detailed later in paragraph 11.3.1.

[24] Failing to do so can be regarded as a breach of good faith and will entitle the principal to terminate the contract without having to pay compensation as in *CA Orléans 9 July 1997 Davault v Sarl Claudine Mary Immobilier*, Juriscl Dalloz, fasc 1250, §48, p 2. In this case, a commercial agent who also held a full time position of negotiator, which required her to be present in an office for 39 hours a week for a period of two months was held in breach of good faith, since her full time position did not allow her to perform the contractual obligations as a good professional towards her principal.

[25] Art 15(1) of the statute as incorporated in Art L 134–15 al 1 French commercial code.

[26] This was very well understood by Reynolds, who stated that because commercial agents do not act for themselves, civil law recognises the risk that once commercial agents have created the customer base for the manufacturers, the latter might terminate the contract, bypass commercial agents and deal directly with the clients which would deny commercial agents their legitimate share of the profits. Reynolds 'Bowstead and Reynolds on Agency' 16th edn (Sweet & Maxwell, 1996), p 688.

[27] *CA Paris 7 March 1996 Malmed v Société Polyphol*, Juriscl Dalloz, fasc 1230, 1.

[28] The civil character of the relationship has several consequences, which cannot all be reviewed. The most pertinent ones are twofold. First, the rules of the civil code on the contract of mandate may apply. Secondly, evidence, for and against the commercial agency can only be done in writing.

The mandate is carried out on a permanent basis

The permanence of the relationship is of crucial importance in the light of the notion of '*common interest mandate*' (see paragraph 11.3.1 for details). Indeed, the permanence of the relationship will allow the commercial agent and the principal to work towards the common goal; the creation/development of the customer base.

Exclusions

The text expressly excludes categories of agents who are already protected by other statutes.[29] They are travel agents, insurance agents, estate agents and '*administrateurs judiciaires*'. Then, France has opted for the possibility to exclude from the protection of the statute commercial agents whose activities are secondary.[30] This rule gives the choice to parties to renounce the protection of the statute. This is therefore different from the agency regulations where secondary activities are automatically excluded. This exclusion must be expressly stipulated in writing in the contract.[31] Moreover, such a renunciation will be invalid, should the activity of commercial agent be primary in reality.[32] This exclusion was introduced in relation to 'car agents' eg garage owners who work under a specific trade mark. As a duty towards the trademark owner, garage owners might be required to sell a few cars of that trademark. It is in this aspect of the relationship that they can be regarded as acting as commercial agents.[33]

Sub-agency

The definition expressly allows commercial agents to use sub-agents. The sub-agent, is a commercial agent in his/her own right and will therefore benefit from the protection of the text (including compensation). The main commercial agent nevertheless remains bound by all the contractual obligations toward the principal. Although the civil code recognises a right of direct action from the principal to the sub-agent (Article 1994 cc), custom shows that the commercial agent remains liable for the acts of the sub-agent to the principal. Similarly, although case law recognises a right of direct action from the sub-agent to the principal,[34] custom shows that sub-agents tend not to use such a right.

---

[29] Art 1(2) of the statute as incorporated in Art L 134–1 al 2 French commercial code.

[30] Art 15(1) of the statute as incorporated in Art L 134–15 al 1 French commercial code.

[31] *Ibid.*

[32] Art 15(2) of the statute as incorporated in Art L134–15 al 2 French commercial code.

[33] There have only been two cases involving such situations. *Cass Com 18 February 2000* and *Cass Com 19 December 2000*. Unreported, mentioned in J M Leloup 'Les agents commerciaux, statuts juridiques, stratégies professionnelles', 5th edn (Delmas, 2001), p 47.

[34] *Cass Com 27 December 1960*, D 1961, 491.

11.3 PERFORMANCE OF THE COMMERCIAL AGENCY CONTRACT: THE OBLIGATIONS OF
THE PARTIES ARE GOVERNED BY THE COMMON INTEREST NOTION

The mandate is entered for the common interest of the parties

Where the directive requires the parties to behave in good faith towards each other, the code stipulates that commercial agency contracts are entered into for the common interest of the parties *'mandat d'intérêt commun'*.[35] The text goes on by explaining what 'common interest' entails for each party. The parties first owe each other a compulsory duty of loyalty and information[36] and secondly, the commercial agent must perform the mandate as a *'bon professionnel'* ie a good professional and the principal must allow the commercial agent to perform the mandate.[37] These duties which are all interlinked cannot be derogated from.[38]

The departure of the implementing text from the directive represents a clear desire to follow a very old legal tradition. Originally, the notion of common interest was introduced by the courts in order to protect the commercial agent on termination.[39] The notion shows that French law regards the commercial agency relationship in quasi-property terms since it describes the economic benefit that each party derives from their collaboration. In a commercial agency relationship, both parties work towards one goal; the creation or the development of a customer base ie the common interest. During the life of the commercial agency contract, both parties benefit from the common interest. At the end though, only the principal can still benefit from it. An imbalance is created, which is why compensation is payable to the commercial agent.

The fact that the notion now governs the relationship as a whole seems to indicate that the common interest is a specific type of good faith,[40] which is associated with the special regime of the commercial agency relationship. Indeed, the common interest is at the very heart of the contract and govern all other duties. Any breach of duty will therefore be assessed in the light of the common interest. A breach of duty, which jeopardises the common interest will be regarded as a serious fault/serious breach and will entitle the other party to terminate the contract immediately. This will have serious consequences at the stage of termination and will therefore be looked at in more detail in paragraph 11.4.

---

[35] Art 4(1) of the statute as incorporated in Art L 134–4 al 1 French commercial code.

[36] Art 4(2) of the statute as incorporated in Art L 134–4 al 2. The obligation of information of the commercial agent remains fairly general since it includes 'any information which is necessary for the performance of the contract' (Art 1 of the decree of 1958 as amended by decree of 1992). The obligation of the principal is more detailed and mirrors the list defined in Arts 4(2) and 4(3) of the directive (Art 2 of the decree of 1958 as amended by decree of 1992).

[37] Art 4(3) of the statute as incorporated in Art L 134–4 al 3 French commercial code.

[38] Art 16 of the statute as incorporated in Art L 134–16 French commercial code.

[39] *Cass Civ 13 May 1885*, DP 1885, 1, 350. For more details, see S. Saintier 'Commercial agency law: a comparative analysis', (Ashgate, forthcoming).

[40] In *Cass Com 16 March 1993*, Bull Civ IV, 109; RTD Com 1994, p 104, the court expressly relied on the notion of good faith to define the common interest.

To pay the agreed commission

In relation to the commission, the rules follow the directive very closely since the previous text was silent. The code follows the definition of the commission adopted in the directive.[41] The parties remain free to decide which method of remuneration to adopt and the rules will apply even when the commercial agent is only partly paid by commission.[42] In the absence of an express agreement on remuneration, the right to be paid will be determined by reference to customs of the area where the commercial agent works. If there is no custom, a fair and reasonable remuneration will apply.[43]

It is important to state that the commission is not only a right of the commercial agent but is also a substantial obligation of the principal in the light of the notion of common interest. Paying the commission forms part of the obligation of the principal, to allow the commercial agent to carry out the mandate '*as a good professional*'. Consequently, failing to pay the commissions due or paying the commission late is regarded as a serious fault by the principal because it jeopardises the economic equilibrium of the relationship. As such, this entitles the commercial agent to repudiate the contract and claim compensation.[44]

The statute remains silent as to which elements will be taken into consideration in order to calculate the commission rate. The main elements are the price of the goods, the volume of sales, the nature of the clients, the number of duties of the commercial agent etc. Once the rate of the commission is agreed upon, in theory, the principal cannot unilaterally modify it.[45]

Entitlement to receive commissions

The commercial agent is entitled to commissions on commercial transactions concluded within the life of the commercial agency contract[46] as well as for transactions concluded after termination of the contract.[47] These articles are not compulsory and the parties may agree on different terms.

With regard to transactions concluded within the life of the contract, the code follows the directive and differentiates between two kinds of transactions, the direct and the indirect transactions. Direct transactions include the transactions concluded through the commercial agent's efforts as well as the repeat orders. The commercial agent will be entitled to commissions on such transactions as long as s/he has been instrumental in getting the transaction concluded.[48] For indirect

---

[41] Art 5(1) of the statute as incorporated in Art L 134–5 al 1 French commercial code.
[42] Art 5(2) of the statute as incorporated in Art L 134–5 al 2 French commercial code.
[43] Art 5(3) of the statute as incorporated in Art L 134–5 al 3 French commercial code.
[44] *Cass Com 9 January 2001 Sarl BGC Vinocor v Merlet*, Journagence, special issue to Les Annonces de la Seine, No 75 of 12 November 2001, p 2.
[45] *Cass Com 14 March 1995 de La Celle v Société Sapaic*, D 1997, SC 52.
[46] Art 6 of the statute as incorporated in Art L 134–6 French commercial code.
[47] Art 7 of the statute as incorporated in Art L 134–7 French commercial code.
[48] Art 6(1) of the statute as incorporated in Art L 134–6 al 1 French commercial code.

transactions, the text stipulates that commercial agents who are in charge of a geographical area or a group of customers, will be entitled to a commission on all transactions entered into by these customers in the given area.[49]

In relation to transactions concluded after the contract has ended, the same pattern applies. The commission will arise when the transaction is concluded through the commercial agent's efforts during the life of the contract and if the transaction is sent within a reasonable time after termination.[50] In the case of a repeat order, commission will arise when the order has reached the principal or the commercial agent before the end of the commercial agency. However, the commercial agent will not be entitled to a commission, if, following the previous article, the commission belongs to a predecessor unless it is equitable because of the circumstances that the commission be shared between the commercial agents.[51]

When commission is acquired and must be paid

Commission is acquired when the principal has performed the transaction or should have done so according to the agreement with the third party or when the third party has performed the transaction.[52] The commission shall become due at the latest when the third party has performed his part of the transaction or should have done so if the principal had performed his part.[53] Finally, commission must be paid, no later than the last day of the month following the quarter in which it became due.[54] This article can only be derogated from to the advantage of the commercial agent.[55] The parties are therefore free to define more frequent payment times.

Information on the commission due

The principal must supply the commercial agent with a statement of the commission due, no later than on the last day of the month following the quarter in which the commission has become due. This statement must set out the main components used in calculating the commission.[56] This new obligation is compulsory and cannot be derogated from to the detriment of the commercial agent.[57] Should the principal fail to comply with such a requirement, the commercial agent can demand to be provided with all the information and in particular an extract of the books, which is available to the principal, in order to check the amount of commission due to him.[58]

---

[49] Art 6(2) of the statute as incorporated in Art L 134–6 al 2 French commercial code.
[50] Art 7 of the statute as incorporated in Art L 134–7 French commercial code.
[51] Art 8 of the statute as incorporated in Art L 134–8 French commercial code.
[52] Art 9(1) of the statute as incorporated in Art L 134–9 al 1 French commercial code.
[53] Art 9(2) of the statute as incorporated in Art L 134–9 al 2 French commercial code.
[54] *Ibid.*
[55] Art 16 of the statute as incorporated in Art L 134–16 French commercial code.
[56] Art 3 of 1958 decree as amended by decree 1992.
[57] Art 3–1 of 1958 decree as amended by decree 1992.
[58] Art 3 of 1958 decree as amended by decree 1992.

Such a possibility is in direct application of the obligation of information and loyalty that the principal owes to the commercial agent. Should the principal refuse to grant access to the books to the commercial agent, the latter can require the courts to force the principal.[59]

When commission is lost

The entitlement to a commission is only lost when a transaction between the principal and the customer has not been performed through no fault of the principal.[60] In such a case, the commercial agent must refund any undue commissions.[61] This article is mandatory, and therefore cannot be derogated from.

11.4 TERMINATION OF THE COMMERCIAL AGENCY CONTRACT AND THE RIGHT OF THE COMMERCIAL AGENT TO CLAIM COMPENSATION

How to terminate the commercial agency contract and the notice due

Following the directive, the text differentiates between fixed-term and indeterminate contracts; a notice being required only for the latter. The notice, which varies according to the length of the contract, is of one month for the first year, two months for the second year and three months afterwards.[62] Unless otherwise agreed, the end of the notice will coincide with the end of the calendar month. A recent case shows that the notice starts from the day that the letter is received by the commercial agent rather than the day it is sent by the principal.[63] The notices are the minimum required and cannot be derogated from, but the parties may choose to opt for longer periods on the condition that they are the same for both parties.[64] The statute remains silent on the manner by which the notice must be communicated, it seems that a letter, sent by registered post, is an acceptable way of doing it.

Because notices are compulsory, when a party fails to comply with them, s/he will be liable for damages for breach of contract. For the commercial agent, this

---

[59] *CA Orléans 19 November 1996 SA Draoger Industries v T'Kindt*, Journagence, special issue of Les Annonces de la Seine, No 37 of 26 May 1997, p 8.

[60] Art 10(1) of the statute as incorporated by Art L 134–10 al 1 French commercial code.

[61] Art 10(2) of the statute as incorporated by Art L 134–10 al 2 French commercial code An example of undue commission is for instance when the principal grants advance commission to the commercial agent. If the commercial agent does not pass any orders on to the principal, s/he must give back the commissions given in advance of orders as in *CA Paris 5 July 1996 Ets Bernard Heuchet v Société Cifat*, Juriscl Dalloz, fasc 1240, p 3.

[62] Art 11(4) of the statute as incorporated in Art L 134–11 al 4 French commercial code.

[63] *CA Reims 22 June 1996 Lagneau v Colot*, Juriscl Dalloz, fasc 1250, § 62, p 2 where a letter of termination including a notice was sent on the first day of the month but was only received on 5th of the month. The court held that the one month notice, which should have stopped on 5th of the following month was prolonged until the first day of the following month.

[64] Art 11(5) of the statute as incorporated in Art L 134–11 al 5 French commercial code.

means that s/he will have to pay contractual damages to the principal when termination is regarded as abusive and has caused a damage.[65] For the principal, this means that s/he will have to pay the commissions that the commercial agent should have been entitled to receive during the notice period. It is up to the commercial agent to prove how much commission s/he should be entitled to. Should s/he fail to do so, the courts will look at the past commissions and award damages on such a basis.

It must be noted that such a reparation is different from the compensation due to the commercial agent when termination by the principal is not justified. As a consequence, they are cumulative.[66]

No notice is required when the commercial agency contract is entered for a fixed period since termination will merely occur on expiry of the term of the agreement. Yet, when both parties continue to perform a fixed-duration contract beyond the expiry date, the contract is presumed to be transformed into an indefinite duration contract.[67] In which case, the duration of the fixed-term contract will be taken into consideration in order to calculate the notice.[68]

No notice is required either when termination is triggered by a case of force majeure or by a serious fault / serious breach of one party.[69] Whoever wants to rely on this article must prove the seriousness of the fault. As already mentioned, a serious fault is proven when either party has acted in breach of the common interest. Yet, in this matter, specific rules of the civil code apply. The code stipulates that unless the breach committed was of a duty expressly stipulated to be a repudiatory breach, the victim cannot automatically treat the contract as repudiated but must ask a judge to do so.[70]

The right of the commercial agent to receive compensation for the damage suffered

Following the choice left by the directive, France has kept its own system of compensation. Yet, the French rules depart from the directive in order to follow the French legal tradition. In fact, where the directive gives specific examples of situations when a damage is supposed to have occurred (see Article 17(3)), the code remains silent and merely stipulates that on termination, the commercial agent has a right to receive compensation for the damage suffered.[71] This article cannot

---

[65] *CA Versailles 26 June 1997 Sarl Liota v Lecoq*, Juriscl Dalloz, fasc 1250, p 2.

[66] This point was made clear in two instances: *Cass Com 14 June 1994, France Alfa v Marchal* (unreported) and *Cass Com 30 November 1993 Décathlon v Hannant* (unreported). Both cases listed J M Leloup 'Les agents commerciaux, statuts juridiques, stratégies professionnelles', 5th edn (Delmas, 2001).

[67] Art 11(1) of the statute as incorporated in Art L 134–11 al 1 French commercial code. This presumption can be rebutted. The parties can therefore do so, in writing.

[68] Art 11(3) of the statute as incorporated in Art L 134–11 al 3 French commercial code.

[69] Art 11(6) of the statute as incorporated in Art L 134–11 al 6 French commercial code.

[70] The commercial agency contract is a bilateral contract and as such the parties are bound by *Art 1184–3 French civil code.*

[71] Art 12(1) of the statute as incorporated in Art L 134–12 al 1 French commercial code.

be derogated from to the detriment of the commercial agent.[72] Another slight difference with the directive is the fact that the text stipulates that compensation is due '*à la cessation du contract*' eg when the contract ceases to be and not 'termination' as in the directive. Non-renewal of a fixed-term duration contract can therefore give rise to compensation when the conditions are met.[73]

What damage is compensated?

As seen earlier, France looks at the commercial agency in quasi property terms and compensation represents the part of the market lost by the commercial agent which was part of the common interest. On termination of the commercial agency, the commercial agent is regarded as having suffered a damage because of the loss of his/her ability to generate an income via the commissions[74] or the ability to assign the agency to another commercial agent.[75] Compensation is therefore due as of right.

Scope of application of the compensatory award

The rule is straightforward: termination of the commercial agency contract by the principal, unless justified, entitles the commercial agent to receive compensation. Only a serious fault of the commercial agent will be a justified cause for the principal to terminate the contract and avoid paying compensation. Any other reason will be regarded as unjustified and abusive. In order to protect the commercial agent, the courts have interpreted the notion of 'unjustified termination' reasonably widely. When the principal terminates the contract for economic reasons, such as the reorganisation of the business,[76] or even because s/he wants to stop the production of the goods that the commercial agent was in charge of selling,[77] compensation will be due. However, if the reorganisation of the business or the stopping of the production is motivated by a case of *force majeure*, compensation will not be due. *Force majeure* is however very rarely accepted by the courts.

Is also regarded as an abusive termination when the commercial agent has to terminate the contract because of '*circumstances attributable to the principal*'.[78]

---

[72] Art 16 of the statute as incorporated in Art L 134–16 French commercial code.

[73] In *CA Paris, 15 December 1995 Société Harco v SA Moulinex*, Juriscl Dalloz, fasc 1250, p1, the principal did not renew a contract of fixed duration after the commercial agent had provided him with lucrative orders, this was regarded as an abuse of the right not to renew the contract and the commercial agent successfully claimed compensation.

[74] *Cass Com 9 January 2001 Sarl BGC Vinocor France v Merlet*, Journagence, special issue to Les Annonces de la Seine No 75, 12 November 2001, pp 2–3.

[75] *CA Amiens 19 December 2000 Scwartz v Société Max Perles & Cie*, Journagence, special issue to Les Annonces de la Seine of 30 July 2001.

[76] *CA Angers 18 October 1999*, Journagence, special issue to Les Annonces de la Seine, No 32 of 26 April 2001.

[77] *CA Rennes 19 June 1985 Treficable-Pirelli v SA Burgeot*, unreported.

[78] Art 13(2) of the statute as incorporated in Art L 134–13 al 2 French commercial code.

This is effectively the case when an act of the principal forces the commercial agent to terminate the relationship. Only an act of the principal which is regarded as a serious fault/breach and which negates the common interest will entitle the commercial agent to terminate and still claim compensation. The onus is on the commercial agent to prove the seriousness of the fault in order to be able to claim compensation.[79] Only a fault, which is in breach of the common interest will be regarded as serious. The main example of a serious fault is when the principal fails to comply with the obligation to 'allow the commercial agent to perform the contract' as imposed by Article L 134–4 al 3 new commercial code[80] by failing to pass some information, by failing to pay the commission[81] etc.

Is also regarded as a serious fault when the principal acts in a disloyal manner. Such will be the case when s/he acts in breach of an exclusivity clause by selling directly to customers or even by appointing a new commercial agent to cover the same territory as the existing one, without informing him/her of such an appointment or without any good reason to do so.[82] A final example of a serious breach would be if the principal refused to allow the commercial agent his/her right to assign the agency for no valid reason.[83]

Other examples of a serious fault of the principal are related to general rules of contract law. The commercial agency contract is a bilateral contract and therefore cannot be modified without the consent of both parties (Article 1134–1 cc). If the principal wishes to change a substantial element of the contract, s/he can only do so with the consent of the commercial agent, otherwise it affects the equilibrium of the relationship. Substantial elements of the commercial agency contract are the commission, the territory of the commercial agent[84] and the goods that the commercial agent is in charge of selling.[85] A unilateral modification of such areas by the principal, without the consent of the commercial agent and with no valid economic reason to do so would be regarded as a serious fault and would entitle the commercial agent to terminate and claim compensation.[86]

---

[79] *Cass Com 17 January 1995.* Failing to prove the seriousness of the fault, the commercial agent cannot claim compensation.

[80] In *Cass Com 24 November 1998, Chevassus-Marche v Danone*, RTDCiv 1999, p 646, the principal was held in breach of his duty imposed by Art 4 of the implementing statute by not allowing the commercial agent to impose lower prices in line with its competitors. The commercial agent, whose prices were too high was unable to sell any of the products of the principal.

[81] *Cass Com 9 January 2001 Sarl BGC Vinocor France v Merlet*, Journagence, special issue to Les Annonces de la Seine No 75, 12 November 2001, pp 2–3.

[82] *CA Lyon 4 February 1994*, Juriscl Dalloz, fasc 1250, §29, p 1.

[83] *CA Orléans 18 February 1999 Brcc v Guibert Express*, Journagence, special issue to Les Annonces de la Seine, No 32, 26 April 2001.

[84] *CA Poitiers 30 April 1980.*

[85] *T Com Annonay 27 February 1970*, unreported, mentioned in J M Leloup 'Agents commerciaux, statuts juridiques, stratégies professionnelles', 5th edn (Delmas, 2001), p 194.

[86] *Cass Com 14 March 1995 de La Celle v Société Sapaic*, JCP G 1995, IV, 1156 where decrease of the commission rate by the principal was held to be valid since it was motivated by economic factors.

How to calculate the compensatory award

A long established custom considers that compensation should be two years worth of commission. Two years is regarded as the time that it will take the commercial agent to build a commercial agency of similar value to the one s/he has just lost. Yet the rule will only apply if such an amount is regarded as a true assessment of the damage suffered by the commercial agent. In fact, French courts regularly insist that such a custom cannot be seen as a 'tariff compensation'.[87] The courts will therefore award more if the commercial agent proves that two years does not represent the reality of the damage suffered.[88] In such cases, the courts will take into consideration the age of the commercial agent, the length of the commercial agency and the speciality of the goods. Vice versa, on proof by the principal that two years is too generous, the courts will award less. Usually, the courts will award less than the custom when the relationship has lasted less than two years.

Compensation is calculated on all remunerations, not just commissions.[89] Therefore, any additional duties performed by the commercial agent such as delivery of the goods, storage of the goods, del credere obligations etc will be taken into consideration. Yet, the most reliable element on which to base compensation is the commission due, which includes outstanding commissions.[90] Calculation is carried out on gross figures and there is no practice to reduce for professional costs. More importantly, the courts make no distinction between old and new customers.[91] It is therefore of no importance that the commercial agent did not bring new customers to the principal.[92] This is the essential difference between France and Germany. Whilst the former looks at the damage suffered at the time of termination, the latter concentrates on the goodwill brought by the commercial agent to the principal.

Because the award aims at compensating the commercial agent of the part of the market lost, the loss is fixed at the moment of termination. As a consequence, future events will have no impact on the evaluation of the damage suffered. The fact that the principal ceases to trade or that the commercial agent can work with the same clients cannot be a valid argument by the principal as a way to reduce the value of the compensatory award. Finally, the commercial agent has no obligation to mitigate the loss.

---

[87] Such a principle is regularly reiterated by the courts as seen in *Cass Com 3 October 2000 Société SineuGraff v M Card*, Journagence, special issue to Les Annonces de la Seine, No 75 of 12 November 01, pp 4–5.

[88] There are only a few decisions where the court awarded 3 years of commission for compensation. *CA Paris, 5 July 1975 Bongrain v Richot*, les Petites Affiches 24 December 1975, 3; *T Com Nanterre 8 November 1991*, Les Annonces de la Seine 9 December 1991, p 2.

[89] *Cass Com 22 December 1969.*

[90] *CA Aix 9 October 1996* Journagence, special issue to Les Annonces de la Seine, No 57 of 26 May 1997.

[91] Principle adopted in *Cass Com 14 October 1974*, RTDCom 1975, 590. Principle consistently reiterated ever since. For instance, see *Cass Com 9 January 2001 Sarl BGC Vinocor v Merlet*, Journagence, special issue to Les Annonces de la Seine, No 75 of 12 November 2001, p 2.

[92] *Cass Com 14 October 1997 Société Vogelsang France v M Lacauste*, Journagence, special issue to Les Annonces de la Seine, No 75 of 12 November 2001.

Loss of the right to claim compensation

Only three situations will deny the commercial agent the right to claim compensation on termination.[93] Firstly, when the principal terminates the contract with a just cause to do so, eg a serious fault of the commercial agent. Secondly, when the commercial agent terminates the contract with no justified cause to do so. Thirdly, when the commercial agent, with the principal's consent, assigns the agency to a third party. Such an article can only be derogated from to the benefit of the commercial agent.[94] In addition, compensation will be lost if commercial agent fails to claim his/her right within one year after termination.[95] The statute remains silent on the manner by which the claim must be made. It seems that a letter sent by the counsel of the commercial agent is acceptable.[96] It must be pointed out that such a restriction only applies for the claim of compensation. It does not affect the claim for contractual damages for breach of notice or claim of arrears in the payment of commission.

Serious fault of the commercial agent

A serious fault is the only type of fault that will cause the commercial agent to lose his/her right to compensation.[97] In addition, the commercial agent will also have to pay contractual damages for loss to the principal, if the need occurs.[98] The principal must prove the seriousness of the fault. Failing to do so, compensation will be due.[99] The courts have been very strict in their appreciation of what a serious fault is. Yet, they have been consistent with their appreciation of the seriousness of the fault of the principal since only a fault of the commercial agent, which jeopardises the common interest, goes at the heart of the contract and hence renders the continuation of the relationship impossible will be regarded as serious.

When looking at case law, there are several recurring themes used by principals in order to try to avoid paying compensation. They are that the commercial agent has failed to reach a particular target or quota or that the commercial agent has been disloyal. In relation to the failure to reach the target, the strictness of the courts in appreciating the seriousness of the fault is particularly clear. It is not enough for the principal to prove that the commercial agency has not been as

---

[93] Art 13 of the statute as incorporated in Art L 134–13 French commercial code.

[94] Art 16 of the statute as incorporated in Art L 134–16 French commercial code. The principal cannot impose a probation period and use it as a way of terminating the contract, without any notice and without having to pay compensation. *CA Paris 11 March 1993, Dalmasso v Mécanoto*, unreported, mentioned in J M Leloup 'Les agents commerciaux, statuts juridiques, stratégies professionnelles', 5th edn, Delmas, 2001).

[95] Art 12(2) of the statute as incorporated in Art L 134–12 al 2 French commercial code.

[96] *CA Nancy, 22 September 1999*, D 2000, J 62.

[97] Art 13(1) of the statute as incorporated in Art L 134–13 al 1 French commercial code.

[98] *Cass Com 7 March 1995*, RTDCom 1995, 836.

[99] *Cass Com 17 October 2000 Allanic Immobilier v Ubertini*, Journagence, special issue to Les Annonces de la Seine No 55, 30 July 2001.

profitable as had been envisaged.[100] Likewise, the decrease in the volume of sales[101] or the fact that the activity of the commercial agent does not give rise to new contracts[102] are not in themselves sufficient reasons to terminate and refuse to pay compensation. The reason for such an attitude by the courts is that the absence of results or the decrease in business could be explained by a multitude of reasons other than the commercial agent's actions. For instance, an economic slowdown, the bad quality of the products, failure by the principal to deliver the goods on time, failure to provide information on the goods or even failure to produce enough goods to satisfy the customers.[103] The principal must therefore establish very precise facts that show that the commercial agent has acted in breach of his/her duties, and that such a breach has caused the lack of profits.[104] In other words, the principal must prove that the commercial agent failed to perform his/her obligations as a good professional as required under Article L 134–4 al 3 new commercial code. The courts considered that the commercial agent was guilty of a serious fault when he failed to prospect any of the clients of the principal.[105] It is also considered to be a serious fault if the commercial agent continuously refuses to follow the methods of sales advocated by the principal,[106] or if the commercial agent assigns the commercial agency without the consent of the principal.[107]

In relation to an act of disloyalty as serious fault, such an act exists when the commercial agent acts for a competing principal without the consent of the principal.[108] A breach of good faith by the commercial agent such as claiming commissions, which in fact do not exist or are not due[109] is also regarded as disloyal.

Unjustified termination by the commercial agent

If the commercial agent terminates the contract with no justified cause such as age, death, incapacity or illness, or circumstances attributable to the principal, no compensation is due.[110] The latter has already been considered (see paragraph 11.4.2). Death automatically terminates the contract and entitles the heirs of the

---

[100] *CA Agen 14 January 1997*, Les Annonces de la Seine 1997, 13.

[101] *TGI Blois 12 January 2001 Sarl Pouplet Représentation v Sarl Vernantes*, Journagence, suppl to Les Annonces de la Seine No 75, 12 November 2001, p 9.

[102] *Cass Com 14 October 1997 Société Vogelsang France v M Lacauste*, Journagence, special issue to Les Annonces de la Seine No 75, 12 November 2001, pp 7–8.

[103] *Cass Com 13 October 1998 Cadiou v Société Annunziata France*, Juriscl Dalloz, fasc 1250, p 3.

[104] *CA Amiens 19 December 2000*, Journagence, special issue to Les Annonces de la Seine No 55, 30 July 2001.

[105] *Cass Com 28 November 2001.*

[106] *Cass Com 20 February 2001.*

[107] *Cass Com 14 January 1997 Société d'exploitation des établissements Hubert v Sarl Borie-Manoux*, Juriscl Dalloz, fasc 1250, p 3.

[108] *Cass Com 14 March 1995 Malka v Société Kempel et Liebfried GmbH*, Juriscl Dalloz, fasc 1250, 1.

[109] *Cass Com 17 October 2000 Allanic Immobilier v Ubertini*, Journagence, special issue to Les Annonces de la Seine No 55, 30 July 2001.

[110] Art 13(2) of the statute as incorporated in Art L 134–13 al 2 French commercial code.

commercial agent to claim compensation.[111] With age, incapacity and illness however, the rules are different. The commercial agent will only be entitled to terminate the commercial agency and claim compensation by proving that in these three circumstances, the principal cannot reasonably require him/her to pursue the commercial agency. The best way to do so is to obtain a medical certificate.

Assignment of the commercial agency

Assigning the commercial agency, with the consent of the principal, is the third exception to the right of the commercial agent to claim compensation.[112] If the commercial agent fails to obtain the consent of the principal, this is regarded as a serious breach and will entitle the principal to terminate the contract immediately and not to pay compensation.[113] The principal however can only refuse to consent to the assignment with valid reasons. If the principal refuses with no such reasons, the commercial agent will be entitled to terminate the contract and claim compensation.

Post contractual clauses

It is possible for the parties to enter into a post contractual non-competition clause.[114] Such a clause is already valid during the notice period.[115] However, following the directive closely, the rules are strict. The clause must be entered in writing and it must be reasonably precise since it must refer to the geographical area[116] or the group that the commercial agent is in charge of as well as to the type of goods and/or services.[117] Finally, the clause cannot exceed two years after termination.[118]

---

[111] Art 12 (3) of the statute as incorporated in Art L 134–12 al 3 French commercial code.
[112] Art 13(3) of the statute as incorporated in Art L 134–13 al 3 French commercial code.
[113] *Cass Com 14 January 1997*, D 1997, IR 33.
[114] Art 14(1) of the statute as incorporated in Art L 134–14 al 1 French commercial code.
[115] *CA Paris, 13 January 1994*, jurisdata 020592.
[116] If the clause applies to the French territory as a whole, this will be regarded as invalid: *CA Paris, 3 July 1998 Rimbault v Sarl Société nationale d'incendie*, Juriscl Dalloz, fasc 1240, §45, p 2.
[117] Art 14(2) of the statute as incorporated in Art L 134–14 al 2 French commercial code.
[118] Art 14(3) of the statute as incorporated in Art L 134–14 al 3 French commercial code.

12

Conclusion

T HE PREVIOUS CHAPTERS have traced the thinking behind the appointment of
agents, the process leading up to the adoption of the Directive, the development of the Regulations and comment on their detailed terms. The following
points are clear:

—The Regulations marked a major change in English law relating to agents.
—Principals and their advisers, in particular, will need to continue to exercise care
in every case—even where careful consideration was given to this issue before
1 January 1994 the case law has thrown up surprises and will continue to do so.
—The Regulations largely mirror the wording of the Directive but for this reason
they import into English law concepts which, while known in continental countries, were not formerly a part of English law—eight years on from implementation uncertainty continues.
—The confused and ambiguous drafting, the failure to clarify novel concepts and
the existence of large numbers of important unanswered questions, are likely to
lead to continued uncertainty, and to even more expensive litigation.

The authors' view, and that of most if not all of the others who have written on
this subject since the Regulations came into force, is that this confusion and uncertainty has been and is likely to continue to be extremely damaging. It has led to the
dismissal of agents, to the adoption by businesses of strategies which are less effi-
cient than agency might have been, to higher bills for legal advice on the drafting
of agency contracts and to large quantities of litigation before the domestic courts
and before the European Court of Justice.

The government's approach to the Directive appears to have been characterised
by a mixture of antipathy and apathy and the government may only have agreed
to the adoption of the Directive because, in the run-up to the execution of the
Single European Act, it was faced with a limited window of opportunity in which
it could vary the terms of the Directive before qualified majority voting enabled
other member states to adopt the Directive against the UK Government's wishes.

Naturally, following the adoption of the Directive, the UK Government had no
option but to implement it into English law. The DTI often expresses its intention
to keep the legislative burden on business to a minimum and to assist business
generally, and this comment is repeated throughout the documentation relating to
the Regulations. The authors' view, however, is that the DTI has failed in its duty
to business in taking few steps to clarify the meaning of the Regulations, and in
dropping the few clarificatory additions which it had adopted in the drafts in

favour of merely mirroring the wording of the Directive in what seems to have been an unsuccessful attempt to reduce the possibility of actions on the *Francovich* principle. Outwardly at least the DTI seems to have made little attempt to draft so as to take into account the serious objections raised in the consultation process, or to consult the Commission as regards the terms of the Directive with a view to clarifying the terms of the Directive whilst implementing it properly. The objections noted by the House of Lords Select Committee and by the Law Commission 25 years ago can still legitimately be levelled at the Regulations.

Another failure was the slow pace of drafting and consultation and the seeming reluctance to implement the Directive early with a view to giving business an opportunity to consider the terms of the Regulations and to take action in advance of the implementation date: much of the uncertainty and litigation which has resulted and will continue to result from the hurried implementation of the Regulations could have been avoided had this simple step been taken. Instead, the final form of the Regulations was not readily available before mid-December 1993 despite the fact that that version (contrary to the DTI's earlier statements) involved several major changes of direction, such as the introduction of the indemnity model as an alternative, the altering of position as regards territorial scope of application and so forth.

Six years after the first edition of this work, we find ourselves reiterating that the English courts have yet to become fully acquainted with the Regulations, although the position is improving.

Finally, it is vitally important to remember that the present Regulations are based on an EC Directive and that as such, they must be interpreted in a purposive manner. Therefore, regard must be given to the fact that the Directive itself was heavily based on existing continental law, in particular French and German law. There are many instances, hopefully highlighted in this work, where the Regulations are less than clear or are plainly confusing. In such circumstances research as to how the Directive has been implemented in other member states of the European Union and how national courts in those jurisdictions have tackled specific issues may be of value.

Appendix 1—The Commercial Agents (Council Directive) Regulations 1993

(SI 1993/3053)

Made on 7 December 1993 by the Secretary of State in exercise of the powers conferred on him by s 2(2) of the European Communities Act 1972, operative from 1 January 1994.

ARRANGEMENT OF REGULATIONS

PART I—GENERAL

Regulation

PART II—RIGHTS AND OBLIGATIONS

PART III—REMUNERATION

PART IV—CONCLUSION AND TERMINATION OF THE AGENCY CONTRACT

13 Right to signed written statement of terms of agency contract
14 Conversion of agency contract after expiry of fixed period
15 Minimum periods of notice for termination of agency contract
16 Savings with regard to immediate termination
17 Entitlement of commercial agent to indemnity or compensation on termination of agency contract
18 Grounds for excluding payment of indemnity or compensation under regulation 17
19 Prohibition on derogation from regulations 17 and 18
20 Restraint of trade clauses

PART V—MISCELLANEOUS AND SUPPLEMENTAL

21 Disclosure of information
22 Service of notice etc.
23 Transitional provisions

SCHEDULE

PART I—GENERAL

Citation, Commencement and Applicable Law

1(1)   These Regulations may be cited as the Commercial Agents (Council Directive) Regulations 1993 and shall come into force on 1st January 1994.
1(2)   These Regulations govern the relations between commercial agents and their principals and, subject to paragraph (3), apply in relation to the activities of commercial agents in Great Britain.
1(3)   [A Court or tribunal shall:
   (a) apply the law of the other member State concerned in place of regulations 3 to 22 where the parties have agreed that the agency contract is to be governed by the law of that member State;
   (b) (whether or not it would otherwise be required to do so) apply these regulations where the law of another member State corresponding to these regulations enables the parties to agree that the agency contract is to be governed by the law of a different member State and the parties have agreed that it is to be governed by the law of England and Wales or Scotland.

interpretation, application and extent

2(1) In these regulations:

'**commercial agent**' means a self-employed intermediary who has continuing authority to negotiate the sale or purchase of goods on behalf of another person (the 'principal'), or to negotiate and conclude the sale or purchase of goods on behalf of and in the name of that principal; but shall be understood as not including in particular:

(i) a person who, in his capacity as an officer of a company or association, is empowered to enter into commitments binding on that company or association;

(ii) a partner who is lawfully authorised to enter into commitments binding on his partners;

(iii) a person who acts as an insolvency practitioner (as that expression is defined in section 388 of the Insolvency Act 1986, or the equivalent in any other jurisdiction;

'**commission**' means any part of the remuneration of a commercial agent which varies with the number or value of business transactions;

'**EEA Agreement**' means the Agreement on the European Economic Area signed at Oporto on 2 May 1992 as adjusted by the Protocol signed at Brussels on 17 March 1993;

'**Member State**' includes a State which is a contracting party to the EEA Agreement;

'**restraint of trade clause**' means an agreement restricting the business activities of a commercial agent following termination of the agency contract.

2(2) These regulations do not apply to:

(a) commercial agents whose activities are unpaid;

(b) commercial agents when they operate on commodity exchanges or in the commodity market;

(c) the Crown Agents for Overseas Governments and Administrations as set up under the Crown Agents Act 1979, or its subsidiaries.

2(3) The provisions of the Schedule to these Regulations have effect for the purpose of determining the persons whose activities as commercial agents are to be considered secondary.

2(4) These regulations shall not apply to the persons referred to in paragraph (3) above.

2(5) These regulations do not extend to Northern Ireland.

PART II—RIGHTS AND OBLIGATIONS

Duties of a commercial agent to his principal

3(1) In performing his activities a commercial agent must look after the interests of his principal and act dutifully and in good faith.

---

[1] The words in brackets were substituted by the Commercial Agents (Council Directive) (Amendment) Regulations 1998 (SI 1998/2868).

3(2)   In particular, a commercial agent must:
    (a) make proper efforts to negotiate and, where appropriate, conclude the trans-
        actions he is instructed to take care of;
    (b) communicate to his principal all the necessary information available to him;
    (c) comply with reasonable instructions given by his principal.

Duties of a principal to his commercial agent

4(1)   In his relations with his commercial agent a principal must act dutifully and in good
faith.

4(2)   In particular, a principal must:
    (a) provide his commercial agent with the necessary documentation relating to the
        goods concerned;
    (b) obtain for his commercial agent the information necessary for the performance
        of his agency contract, and in particular notify his commercial agent within a
        reasonable period once he anticipates that the volume of commercial trans-
        actions will be significantly lower than that which the commercial agent could
        normally have expected.

4(3)   A principal shall, in addition, inform his commercial agent within a reasonable
period of his acceptance or refusal of, and of any non-execution by him of, a commercial transaction which the commercial agent has procured for him.

Prohibition on derogation from regulations 3 and 4 and consequence of breach

5(1)   The parties may not derogate from regulations 3 and 4 above.

5(2)   The law applicable to the contract shall govern the consequence of breach of the
rights and obligations under regulations 3 and 4 above.

PART III—REMUNERATION

Form and amount of remuneration in absence of agreement

6(1)   In the absence of any agreement as to remuneration between the parties, a commercial agent shall be entitled to the remuneration that commercial agents appointed for
the goods forming the subject of his agency contract are customarily allowed in the
place where he carries on his activities and, if there is no such customary practice, a
commercial agent shall be entitled to reasonable remuneration taking into account
all aspects of the transaction.

6(2)   This regulation is without prejudice to the application of any enactment or rule of
law concerning the level of remuneration.

6(3)   Where a commercial agent is not remunerated (wholly or in part) by commission,
regulations 7 to 12 below shall not apply.

Entitlement to commission on transactions concluded during agency contract

7(1) A commercial agent shall be entitled to commission on commercial transactions concluded during the period covered by the agency contract:

    (a) where the transaction has been concluded as a result of his action; or

    (b) where the transaction is concluded with a third party whom he has previously acquired as a customer for transactions of the same kind.

7(2) A commercial agent shall also be entitled to commission on transactions concluded during the period covered by the agency contract where he has an exclusive right to a specific geographical area or to a specific group of customers and where the transaction has been entered into with a customer belonging to that area or group.

Entitlement to commission on transactions concluded after agency contract has terminated

8 Subject to regulation 9 below, a commercial agent shall be entitled to commission on commercial transactions concluded after the agency contract has terminated if:

    (a) the transaction is mainly attributable to his efforts during the period covered by the agency contract and if the transaction was entered into within a reasonable period after that contract terminated; or

    (b) in accordance with the conditions mentioned in regulation 7 above, the order of the third party reached the principal or the commercial agent before the agency contract terminated.

Apportionment of commission between new and previous commercial agents

9(1) A commercial agent shall not be entitled to the commission referred to in regulation 7 above if that commission is payable, by virtue of regulation 8 above, to the previous commercial agent, unless it is equitable because of the circumstances for the commission to be shared between the commercial agents.

9(2) The principal shall be liable for any sum due under paragraph (1) above to the person entitled to it in accordance with that paragraph, and any sum which the other commercial agent receives to which he is not entitled shall be refunded to the principal.

When commission due and date for payment

10(1) Commission shall become due as soon as, and to the extent that, one of the following circumstances occurs:

    (a) the principal has executed the transaction; or

    (b) the principal should, according to his agreement with the third party, have executed the transaction; or

    (c) the third party has executed the transaction.

10(2) Commission shall become due at the latest when the third party has executed his part of the transaction or should have done so if the principal had executed his part of the transaction, as he should have.

10(3) The commission shall be paid not later than on the last day of the month following the quarter in which it became due, and, for the purposes of these regulations, unless otherwise agreed between the parties, the first quarter period shall run from the date the agency contract takes effect and subsequent periods shall run from that date in the third month thereafter or the beginning of the fourth month, whichever is the sooner.

10(4) Any agreement to derogate from paragraphs (2) and (3) above to the detriment of the commercial agent shall be void.

Extinction of right to commission

11(1) The right to commission can be extinguished only if and to the extent that:
  (a) it is established that the contract between the third party and the principal will not be executed; and
  (b) that fact is due to a reason for which the principal is not to blame.

11(2) Any commission which the commercial agent has already received shall be refunded if the right to it is extinguished.

11(3) Any agreement to derogate from paragraph (1) above to the detriment of the commercial agent shall be void.

Periodic supply of information as to commission due and right of inspection of principal's books

12(1) The principal shall supply his commercial agent with a statement of the commission due, not later than the last day of the month following the quarter in which the commission has become due, and such statement shall set out the main components used in calculating the amount of the commission.

12(2) A commercial agent shall be entitled to demand that he be provided with all the information (and in particular an extract from the books) which is available to his principal and which he needs in order to check the amount of the commission due to him.

12(3) Any agreement to derogate from paragraphs (1) and (2) above shall be void.

12(4) Nothing in this regulation shall remove or restrict the effect of, or prevent reliance upon, any enactment or rule of law which recognises the right of an agent to inspect the books of a principal.

PART IV—CONCLUSION AND TERMINATION OF THE AGENCY CONTRACT

Right to signed written statement of terms of agency contract

13(1) The commercial agent and principal shall each be entitled to receive from the other, on request, a signed written document setting out the terms of the agency contract including any terms subsequently agreed.

13(2) Any purported waiver of the right referred to in paragraph (1) above shall be void.

Conversion of agency contract after expiry of fixed period

14   An agency contract for a fixed period which continues to be performed by both parties after that period has expired shall be deemed to be converted into an agency contract for an indefinite period.

Minimum periods of notice for termination of agency contract

15(1) Where an agency contract is concluded for an indefinite period either party may terminate it by notice.

15(2) The period of notice shall be—
   (a) 1 month for the first year of the contract;
   (b) 2 months for the second year commenced;
   (c) 3 months for the third year commenced and for the subsequent years;
   and the parties may not agree on any shorter periods of notice.

15(3) If the parties agree on longer periods than those laid down in paragraph (2) above, the period of notice to be observed by the principal must not be shorter than that to be observed by the commercial agent.

15(4) Unless otherwise agreed by the parties, the end of the period of notice must coincide with the end of a calendar month.

15(5) The provisions of this regulation shall also apply to an agency contract for a fixed period where it is converted under regulation 14 above into an agency contract for an indefinite period subject to the proviso that the earlier fixed period must be taken into account in the calculation of the period of notice.

Savings with regard to immediate termination

16   These Regulations shall not affect the application of any enactment or rule of law which provides for the immediate termination of the agency contract—
   (a) because of the failure of one party to carry out all or part of his obligations under that contract; or
   (b) where exceptional circumstances arise.

Entitlement of commercial agent to indemnity or compensation on termination of agency contract

17(1) This regulation has effect for the purpose of ensuring that the commercial agent is, after termination of the agency contract, indemnified in accordance with paragraphs (3) to (5) below or compensated for damage in accordance with paragraphs (6) and (7) below.

17(2) Except where the agency contract otherwise provides, the commercial agent shall be entitled to be compensated rather than indemnified.

17(3) Subject to paragraph (9) and to regulation 18 below, the commercial agent shall be entitled to an indemnify if and to the extent that—

    (a) he has brought the principal new customers or has significantly increased the volume of business with existing customers and the principal continues to derive substantial benefits from the business with such customers; and

    (b) the payment of this indemnity is equitable having regard to all the circumstances and, in particular, the commission lost by the commercial agent on the business transacted with such customers.

17(4) The amount of the indemnity shall not exceed a figure equivalent to an indemnity for one year calculated from the commercial agent's average annual remuneration over the preceding five years and if the contract goes back less than five years the indemnity shall be calculated on the average for the period in question.

17(5) The grant of an indemnity as mentioned above shall not prevent the commercial agent from seeking damages.

17(6) Subject to paragraph (9) and to regulation 18 below, the commercial agent shall be entitled to compensation for the damage he suffers as a result of the termination of his relations with his principal.

17(7) For the purpose of these regulations such damage shall be deemed to occur particularly when the termination takes place in either or both of the following circumstances, namely circumstances which—

    (a) deprive the commercial agent of the commission which proper performance of the agency contract would have procured for him whilst providing his principal with substantial benefits linked to the activities of the commercial agent; or

    (b) have not enabled the commercial agent to amortize the costs and expenses that he had incurred in the performance of the agency contract on the advice of his principal.

17(8) Entitlement to the indemnity or compensation for damage as provided for under paragraphs (2) to (7) above shall also arise where the agency contract is terminated as a result of the death of the commercial agent.

17(9) The commercial agent shall lose his entitlement to the indemnity or compensation for damage in the instances provided for in paragraphs (2) to (8) above if within one year following termination of his agency contract he has not notified his principal that he intends pursuing his entitlement

Grounds for excluding payment of indemnity or compensation under regulation 17

18   The [indemnity or]² compensation referred to in regulation 17 above shall not be payable to the commercial agent where—

    (a) the principal has terminated the agency contract because of default attributable to the commercial agent which would justify immediate termination of the agency contract pursuant to regulation 16 above; or

    (b) the commercial agent has himself terminated the agency contract, unless such termination is justified—

---

² The words in square brackets were added by the Commercial Agents (Council Directive) (Amendment) Regulations 1993 (SI 1993/3173).

(i) by circumstances attributable to the principal, or

(ii) on grounds of the age, infirmity or illness of the commercial agent in consequence of which he cannot reasonably be required to continue his activities; or

(c) the commercial agent, with the agreement of his principal, assigns his rights and duties under the agency contract to another person.

Prohibition on derogation under regulations 17 and 18

19   The parties may not derogate from regulations 17 and 18 to the detriment of the commercial agent before the agency contract expires.

Restraint of trade clauses

20(1) A restraint of trade clause shall be valid only if and to the extent that—

(a) it is concluded in writing; and

(b) it relates to the geographical area or the group of customers and the geographical area entrusted to the commercial agent and to the kind of goods covered by his agency under the contract.

20(2) A restraint of trade clause shall be valid for not more than two years after termination of the agency contract.

20(3) Nothing in this regulation shall affect any enactment of rule or law which imposes other restrictions on the validity or enforceability of restraint of trade clauses or which enables a court to reduce the obligations on the parties resulting from such clauses.

PART V——MISCELLANEOUS AND SUPPLEMENTAL

Disclosure of information

21   Nothing in these Regulations shall require information to be given where such disclosure would be contrary to public policy.

Service of notice etc.

22(1) Any notice, statement or other document to be given or supplied to a commercial agent or to be given or supplied to the principal under these regulations may be so given or supplied:

(a) by delivering it to him;

(b) by leaving it at his proper address addressed to him by name;

(c) by sending it by post to him addressed either to his registered address or to the address of his registered or principal office;

or by any other means provided for in the agency contract.

22(2) Any such notice, statement or document may—
- (a) in the case of a body corporate, be given or served on the secretary or clerk of that body;
- (b) in the case of a partnership, be given to or served on any partner or on any person having the control or management of the partnership business.

Transitional provisions

23(1) Notwithstanding any provision in an agency contract made before 1 January 1994, these Regulations shall apply to that contract after that date and, accordingly any provision which is inconsistent with these regulations shall have effect subject to them.

23(2) Nothing in these regulations shall affect the rights and liabilities of a commercial agent or a principal which have accrued before 1 January 1994.

THE SCHEDULE

Regulation 2(3)

1   The activities of a person as a commercial agent are to be considered secondary where it may reasonably be taken that the primary purpose of the arrangement with his principal is other than as set out in paragraph 2 below.

2   An arrangement falls within this paragraph if—
- (a) the business of the principal is the sale, or as the case may be purchase, of goods of a particular kind; and
- (b) the goods concerned are such that—
  - (i) transactions are normally individually negotiated and concluded on a commercial basis, and
  - (ii) procuring a transaction on one occasion is likely to lead to further transactions in those goods with that customer on future occasions, or to transactions in those goods with other customers in the same geographical area or among the same group of customers, and

that accordingly it is in the commercial interests of the principal in developing the market in those goods to appoint a representative to such customers with a view to the representative devoting effort, skill and expenditure from his own resources to that end.

3   The following are indications that an arrangement falls within paragraph 2 above, and the absence of any of them is an indication to the contrary—
- (a) the principal is the manufacturer, importer or distributor of the goods;
- (b) the goods are specifically identified with the principal in the market in question rather than, or to a greater extent than, with any other person;
- (c) the agent devotes substantially the whole of his time to representative activities (whether for one principal or for a number of principals whose interests are not conflicting);
- (d) the goods are not normally available in the market in question other than by means of the agent;

(e) the arrangement is described as one of commercial agency.

4   The following are indications that an arrangement does not fall within para 2 above—

(a) promotional material is supplied direct to potential customers;

(b) persons are granted agencies without reference to existing agents in a particular area or in relation to a particular group;

(c) customers normally select the goods for themselves and merely place their orders through the agent.

5   The activities of the following categories of persons are presumed, unless the contrary is established, not to fall within paragraph 2 above—

Mail order catalogue agents for consumer goods.

Consumer credit agents.

Appendix 2—Council Directive 86/653

On the coordination of the laws of the member states relating to self-employed commercial agents
(18 December 1986, OJ 1990 L382/17)

The Council of the European Communities

Having regard to the Treaty establishing the EEC, and in particular Articles 57(2) and 100 thereof,

Having regard to the proposal from the Commission,

Having regard to the opinion of the European Parliament,

Having regard to the opinion of the Economic and Social Committee,

Whereas the restrictions on the freedom of establishment and the freedom to provide services in respect of activities of intermediaries in commerce, industry and small craft industries were abolished by Directive 64/224/EEC;

Whereas the differences in national laws concerning commercial representation substantially affect the conditions of competition and the carrying-on of that activity within the Community and are detrimental both to the protection available to commercial agents vis-à-vis their principals and to the security of commercial transactions; whereas moreover those differences are such as to inhibit substantially the conclusion and operation of commercial representation contracts where principal and commercial agent are established in different member states;

Whereas trade in goods between Member States should be carried on under conditions which are similar to those of a single market, and this necessitates approximation of the legal systems of the Member States to the extent required for the proper functioning of the common market; whereas in this regard the rules concerning conflict of laws do not, in the material of commercial representation, remove the inconsistencies referred to above, nor would they even if they were made uniform, and accordingly the proposed harmonisation is necessary notwithstanding the existence of those rules;

Whereas in this regard the legal relationship between commercial agent and principal must be given priority;

Whereas it is appropriate to be guided by the principles of Article 117 of the Treaty and to maintain improvements already made, when harmonising the laws of the Member states relating to commercial agents;

Whereas additional transitional periods should be allowed for certain Member States which have to make a particular effort to adapt their regulations, especially those concerning indemnity for termination of contract between the principal and the commercial agent, to the requirements of this Directive,

has adopted this Directive:

CHAPTER I—SCOPE

Article 1

1(1)   The harmonisation measures prescribed by this Directive shall apply to the laws, regulations and administrative provisions of the Member States governing the relations between commercial agents and their principals.

1(2)   For the purposes of this Directive, '**commercial agent**' shall mean a self-employed intermediary who has continuing authority to negotiate the sale or the purchase of goods on behalf of another person, hereinafter called the 'principal', or to negotiate and conclude such transactions on behalf of and in the name of that principal.

1(3)   A commercial agent shall be understood within the meaning of this Directive as not including in particular:
  —a person who, in his capacity as an officer, is empowered to enter into commitments binding on a company or association,
  —a partner who is lawfully authorised to enter into commitments binding on his partners,
  —a receiver, a receiver and manager, a liquidator or a trustee in bankruptcy.

Article 2

2(1)   This Directive shall not apply to:
  —commercial agents whose activities are unpaid,
  —commercial agents when they operate on commodity exchanges or in the commodity market, or
  —the body known as the Crown Agents for Overseas Governments and Administrations, as set up under the Crown Agents Act 1979 in the United Kingdom, or its subsidiaries.

2(2)   Each of the Member States shall have the right to provide that the Directive shall not apply to those persons whose activities as commercial agents are considered secondary by the law of that member state.

CHAPTER II—RIGHTS AND OBLIGATIONS

Article 3

3(1)   In performing his activities a commercial agent must look after his principal's interests and act dutifully and in good faith.

3(2)   In particular, a commercial agent must:
  (a) make proper efforts to negotiate and, where appropriate, conclude the transactions he is instructed to take care of:
  (b) communicate to his principal all the necessary information available to him;
  (c) comply with reasonable instructions given by his principal.

Article 4

4(1)   In his relations with his commercial agent a principal must act dutifully and in good faith.

4(2)   A principal must in particular:

(a)   provide his commercial agent with the necessary documentation relating to the goods concerned;

(b)   obtain for his commercial agent the information necessary for the performance of the agency contract, and in particular notify the commercial agent within a reasonable period once he anticipates that the volume of commercial transactions will be significantly lower than that which the commercial agent could normally have expected.

4(3)   A principal must, in addition, inform the commercial agent within a reasonable period of his acceptance, refusal, and of any non-execution of a commercial transaction which the commercial agent has procured for the principal.

Article 5

5   The parties may not derogate from the provisions of Articles 3 and 4.

CHAPTER III—REMUNERATION

Article 6

6(1)   In the absence of any agreement on this matter between the parties, and without prejudice to the application of the compulsory provisions of the Member States concerning the level of remuneration, a commercial agent shall be entitled to the remuneration that commercial agents appointed for the goods forming the subject of his agency contract are customarily allowed in the place where he carries on his activities. If there is no such customary practice a commercial agent shall be entitled to reasonable remuneration taking into account all the aspects of the transaction.

6(2)   Any part of the remuneration which varies with the number or values of business transactions shall be deemed to be commission within the meaning of this Directive.

6(3)   Articles 7 to 12 shall not apply if the commercial agent is not remunerated wholly or in part by commission.

Article 7

7(1)   A commercial agent shall be entitled to commission on commercial transactions concluded during the period covered by the agency contract:

(a)   where the transaction has been concluded as a result of his action; or

(b)   where the transaction is concluded with a third party whom he has previously acquired as a customer for transactions of the same kind.

7(2)   A commercial agent shall also be entitled to commission on transactions concluded during the period covered by the agency contract:
—either where he is entrusted with a specific geographical area or group of customers,
—or where he has an exclusive right to a specific geographical area or group of customers, and where the transaction has been entered into with a customer belonging to that area or group.
member states shall include in their legislation one of the possibilities referred to in the above two indents.

Article 8

8   A commercial agent shall be entitled to commission on commercial transactions concluded after the agency contract has terminated:
(a) if the transaction is mainly attributable to the commercial agent's efforts during the period covered by the agency contract and if the transaction was entered into within a reasonable period after that contract terminated; or
(b) if, in accordance with the conditions mentioned in Article 7, the order of the third party reached the principal or the commercial agent before the agency contract terminated.

Article 9

9   A commercial agent shall not be entitled to the commission referred to in Article 7, if that commission is payable, pursuant to Article 8, to the previous commercial agent, unless it is equitable because of the circumstances for the commission to be shared between the commercial agents.

Article 10

10(1) The commission shall become due as soon as and to the extent that one of the following circumstances obtains:
(a) the principal has executed the transaction; or
(b) the principal should, according to this agreement with the third party, have executed the transaction, or
(c) the third party has executed the transaction.
10(2) The commission shall become due at the latest when the third party has executed his part of the transaction or should have done so if the principal had executed his part of the transaction, as he should have.
10(3) The commission shall be paid not later than on the last day of the month following the quarter in which it became due.
10(4) Agreements to derogate from paragraphs 2 and 3 to the detriment of the commercial agent shall not be permitted.

Article 11

11(1) The right to commission can extinguished only if and to the extent that:
—it is established that the contract between the third party and the principal will not be executed, and
—that fact is due to a reason for which the principal is not to blame.

11(2) Any commission which the commercial agent has already received shall be refunded if the right to it is extinguished.

11(3) Agreements to derogate from paragraph 1 to the detriment of the commercial agent shall not be permitted.

Article 12

12(1) The principal shall supply his commercial agent with a statement of the commission due, not later than the last day of the month following the quarter in which the commission has become due. This statement shall set out the main components used in calculating the amount of commission.

12(2) A commercial agent shall be entitled to demand that he be provided with all the information, and in particular an extract from the books, which is available to his principal and which he needs in order to check the amount of the commission due to him.

12(3) Agreements to derogate from paragraphs 1 and 2 to the detriment of the commercial agent shall not be permitted.

12(4) This Directive shall not conflict with the internal provisions of member states which recognise the right of a commercial agent to inspect a principal's books.

CHAPTER IV—CONCLUSION AND TERMINATION OF THE AGENCY CONTRACT

Article 13

13(1) Each party shall be entitled to receive from the other on request a signed written document setting out the terms of the agency contract including any terms subsequently agreed. Waiver of this right shall not be permitted.

13(2) Notwithstanding paragraph 1 a member state may provide that an agency contract shall not be valid unless evidenced in writing.

Article 14

14 An agency contract for a fixed period which continues to be performed by both parties after that period has expired shall be deemed to be converted into an agency contract for an indefinite period.

Article 15

15(1) Where an agency contract is concluded for an indefinite period either party may terminate it by notice.

15(2) The period of notice shall be one month for the first year of the contract, two months for the second year commenced, and three months for the third year commenced and subsequent years. The parties may not agree on shorter periods of notice.

15(3) Member States may fix the period of notice at four months for the fourth year of the contract, five months for the fifth year and six months for the sixth and subsequent years. They may decide that the parties may not agree to shorter periods.

15(4) If the parties agree on longer periods than those laid down in paragraphs 2 and 3, the period of notice to be observed by the principal must not be shorter than that to be observed by the commercial agent.

15(5) Unless otherwise agreed by the parties, the end of the period of notice must coincide with the end of a calendar month.

15(6) The provisions of this Article shall apply to an agency contract for a fixed period where it is converted under Article14 into an agency contract for an indefinite period, subject to the proviso that the earlier fixed period must be taken into account in the calculation of the period of notice.

Article 16

16   Nothing in this Directive shall affect the application of the law of the Member States where the later provides for the immediate termination of the agency contract:

(a) because of the failure of one party to carry out all or part of his obligations;

(b) where exceptional circumstances arise.

Article 17

17(1) Member States shall take the measures necessary to ensure that the commercial agent is, after termination of the agency contract, indemnified in accordance with paragraph 2 or compensated for damage in accordance with paragraph 3.

17(2) (a) The commercial agent shall be entitled to an indemnity if and to the extent that:

—he has brought the principal new customers or has significantly increased the volume of business with existing customers and the principal continues to derive substantial benefits from the business with such customers, and

—the payment of this indemnity is equitable having regard to all the circumstances, and, in particular, the commission lost by the commercial agent on the business transacted with such customers. member states may provide for such circumstances also to include the application or otherwise of a restraint of trade clause, within the meaning of Article 20;

(b) The amount of the indemnity may not exceed a figure equivalent to an indemnity for one year calculated from the commercial agent's average annual remuneration over the preceding five years and if the contract goes back less than five years the indemnity shall be calculated on the average for the period in question;

(c) The grant of such an indemnity shall not prevent the commercial agent from seeking damages.

17(3)   The commercial agent shall be entitled to compensation for the damage he suffers as a result of the termination of his relations with the principal.

Such damage shall be deemed to occur particularly when the termination takes place in circumstances:

—depriving the commercial agent of the commission which proper performance of the agency contract would have procured him whilst providing the principal with substantial benefits linked to the commercial agent's activities,

—and/or which have not enabled the commercial agent to amortise the costs and expenses that he had incurred for the performance of the agency contract on the principal's advice.

17(4)   Entitlement to the indemnity as provided for in paragraph 2 or to compensation for damage as provided for under paragraph 3, shall also arise where the agency contract is terminated as a result of the commercial agent's death.

17(5)   The commercial agent shall lose his entitlement to the indemnity in the instances provided for in paragraph 2 or to compensation for damage in the instances provided for in paragraph 3, if within one year following termination of the contract he has not notified the principal that he intends pursuing his entitlement.

17(6)   The Commission shall submit to the Council, within eight years following the date of notification of this Directive, a report on the implementation of this Article, and shall if necessary submit to it proposals for amendments.

Article 18

18   The indemnity or compensation referred to in Article 17 shall not be payable:

(a) where the principal has terminated the agency contract because of default attributable to the commercial agent which would justify immediate termination of the agency contract under national law;

(b) where the commercial agent has terminated the agency contract, unless such termination is justified by circumstances attributable to the principal or on grounds of age, infirmity or illness of the commercial agent in consequence of which he cannot reasonably be required to continue his activities;

(c) where, with the agreement of the principal, the commercial agent assigns his rights and duties under the agency contract to another person.

Article 19

19   The parties may not derogate from Articles 17 and 18 to the detriment of the commercial agent before the agency contract expires.

Article 20

20(1)   For the purposes of this Directive, an agreement restricting the business activities of a commercial agent following termination of the agency contract is hereinafter referred to as a restraint of trade clause.

20(2) A restraint of trade clause shall be valid only if and to the extent that:
   (a) it is concluded in writing; and
   (b) it relates to the geographical area or the group of customers and the geographical area entrusted to the commercial agent and to the kind of goods covered by his agency under the contract.
20(3) A restraint of trade clause shall be valid for not more than two years after termination of the agency contract.
20(4) This Article shall not affect provisions of national law which impose other restrictions on the validity or enforceability of restraint of trade clauses or which enable the courts to reduce the obligations on the parties resulting from such an agreement.

CHAPTER V—GENERAL AND FINAL PROVISIONS

Article 21

21   Nothing in this Directive shall require a Member State to provide for the disclosure of information where such disclosure would be contrary to public policy.

Article 22

22(1) Member States shall bring into force the provisions necessary to comply with this Directive before 1 January 1990. They shall forthwith inform the Commission thereof. Such provisions shall apply at least to contracts concluded after their entry into force. They shall apply to contracts in operation by 1 January 1994 at the latest.
22(2) As from the notification of this Directive, Member States shall communicate to the Commission the main laws, regulations and administrative provisions which they adopt in the field governed by this Directive.
22(3) However, with regard to Ireland and the United Kingdom, 1 January 1990 referred to in paragraph 1 shall be replaced by 1 January 1994.
   With regard to Italy, 1 January 1990 shall be replaced by 1 January 1993 in the case of the obligations deriving from Article 17.

Article 23

23   This Directive is addressed to the Member States.

Appendix 3—The Law Commission

(LAW COM. No. 84)
Law of Contract
Report on the Proposed E.E.C. Directive on The Law Relating to Commercial Agents
Advice to the Lord Chancellor Under Section 3(1)(e) of the Law Commissions Act
(1965) (Footnotes omitted)

The proposed EEC directive on the law relating to commercial agents

CONTENTS

THE PROPOSED EEC DIRECTIVE ON
THE LAW RELATING TO COMMERCIAL AGENTS

Advice to the Lord Chancellor under section 3(1)(e) of the
Law Commissions Act 1965

To the Right Honourable the Lord Elwyn-Jones, C.H.,
  Lord High Chancellor of Great Britain

PART I—INTRODUCTION

1. In April 1973 the Directorate for Social Affairs and the Directorate for the Internal market of the EEC prepared a document for consultation with Denmark, Ireland and the United Kingdom. This document consisted merely of a draft directive together with an explanatory memorandum. The Commission of the European Communities proposed that the draft directive be discussed by representatives of the Commission and representatives of Denmark, Ireland and the United Kingdom at a Conference on 21 and 22 June 1973 and that after this Conference a proposed directive taking into account the views of the new members would be sent by the Commission to the Council of Ministers. The draft directive had been prepared by the Commission after detailed discussions with the Six over a period of some years. The Commission considered it to be in virtually final form, so that the proposed directive could be sent to the Council of Ministers shortly after the Conference.

2. The Solicitor of the Department of Trade and Industry asked the Law Commission whether they could assist the Department in handling the draft directive. The legal staff of the Law Commission gave the Department assistance between May 1973 and May 1975. A member of the legal staff of the Law Commission was made available for the meeting on 21 and 22 June 1973 (where the draft directive was discussed by representatives of the Commission of the European Communities and representatives of Denmark, Ireland and the United Kingdom) and further assistance was given to the Department at meetings with members of the staff of the EEC and in discussion of the detailed provisions of the directive. The Department was also assisted in dealing with the consultation which they conducted on the draft directive and at meetings with representatives of the Manufacturers' Agents' Association, the Confederation of British Industry, the Bar Council, the Law Society and other bodies.

3. At that stage the Law Commission's function was confined to assisting and advising the Department on the first draft of the directive, and between May 1975 and the end of 1976 no further assistance was requested of them. On 14 December 1976, the Commission of the European Communities sent to the Council of Ministers a proposed directive which differs in some respects from the previous draft. A copy of the directive and the explanatory memorandum under cover of a letter from the Commission of the European Communities to the Council of Ministers dated 5 January 1977 is attached as Annex A. The Law Commission had played no part in the new draft. By letter dated 1 March 1977 we were asked to tender you our advice in accordance with section 3(1)(e) of the Law Commissions Act 1965 on the attitude which we would recommend the United Kingdom to adopt towards the proposed

directive. You will appreciate that our advice was asked for as a matter of some urgency and we have not therefore been able to follow our usual practice of extensive consultation through the publication of a working paper.

PART II—OUR GENERAL APPROACH

4. Before we consider the content of the directive as such, we should say something about its vires in terms of the Treaty of Rome and its status as an instrument of community law. The Commission of the European Communities have indicated that the directive is based on Articles 57 and 100 of that Treaty. Article 57 imposes on the Council of Ministers a duty to issue directives for the co-ordination of laws in Member States concerning the taking up and pursuit of activities as self-employed persons. Since Article 2 of the directive declares a defining characteristic of a commercial agent to be that he must be self-employed, it seems that the directive is intra vires Article 57 of the Treaty. Article 100 of the Treaty lays upon the Council of Ministers the duty to issue directives for the approximation of such laws in Member States as "directly affect the establishment or functioning of the Common Market". It is, we think, possible to contend with some justification that the differences in the laws of Member States relating to commercial agents do affect the functioning of the Common Market in that they inhibit the commercial agent's freedom of establishment in the EEC and may interfere with the freedom of movement of goods and services between Member States. Our conclusion is that the directive as a whole is almost certainly intra vires the Treaty of Rome.

5. A directive is, by Article 189(3) of the Treaty of Rome, "binding as to the result to be achieved, upon each Member State to which it is addressed, but shall leave to the national authorities the choice of form and method". Our view is that the directive, as presently drafted, contains provisions of such a detailed and complex nature as would in effect deprive the national authorities of the choice as to the method by which they should be implemented. We think that the contents of the directive are thus to some extent inconsistent with the status of a directive as an instrument of community law, and that the directive is an inappropriate vehicle for the creation of this kind of detailed set of rules of private law.

6. The proposed directive contains detailed rules regulating the legal relationship between "commercial agents", as defined by Article 2, and their principals. These rules relate to the rights and duties of the parties, remuneration and reimbursement of expenses, *del credere* commercial agents, bankruptcy of the principal and the making and cessation of the contract. It constitutes a fairly comprehensive codification of the law relating to the legal relationship between the commercial agent and his principal. Some of the rules are declaratory of terms of a general character that are implicit in the relationship of principal and agent, for example, the mutual obligations of good faith; others deal in detail with matters, such as the entitlement to remuneration, which one would expect to find provided for expressly in the agency contract, probably after negotiation. Many of the rules are made mandatory by Article 35; this article provides that any stipulation whereby the parties derogate, to the detriment of the agent, from a provision incorporating a mandatory rule is rendered void.

7. The proposed directive thus has three main features:—

(a) it contains provisions, out of which the parties cannot contract, for the protection of the commercial agent;

(b) it contains provisions which, in the absence of contrary agreement, will form the basis of the legal relationship between the principal and the commercial agent: it thus provides what might be described as a "model contract" for commercial agents;

(c) it provides a codification of that part of the law of agency which deals with the relationship between the commercial agent and the principal.

8. Before we discuss any of these three features of the directive it is obviously necessary to determine precisely the category of persons who are called "commercial agents" and who thus fall within the scope of the directive.

The scope of the directive and its rationale

9. "The word 'agency', to a common lawyer, refers in general to a branch of the law under which one person, the agent, may affect the legal relations of another person, the principal, as regards other persons, called third parties, by acts which the agent is said to have the principal's authority to perform, and which are often regarded as the principal's acts and not as those of the agent". "The mature law recognises that a person need not always do things that change his legal relations in person: he may utilise the services of another to change them, or to do something during the course of which they may be changed".

10. Under the directive a commercial agent is an intermediary who has authority to negotiate and/or to conclude commercial transactions in the name or for the account of his principal. Under Article 9(1) he only has authority to conclude agreements when the principal empowers him to do so. To the extent that the power to affect the legal relations of the principal appears to be the exceptional situation rather than the normal one, the typical commercial agent differs from the typical agent of the English common law.

11. It is also necessary to comment on the categories of the business intermediaries who are *not* within the definition in Article 2. Under the article the intermediary must be self-employed and this serves to exclude a large number of representatives and commercial travellers who are employees and who are paid partly by wage or salary and partly by commission. Under the article the intermediary must negotiate or transact in the name of and for the account of another person. This will exclude distributors who carry out sales and services in their own name.

12. The term "commercial agent" has no precise connotation in English law. It does not represent a category of persons who have a common identifiable legal characteristic. Indeed, we are not convinced that the term has any precise connotation. Article 2 refers to the commercial agent's authority to negotiate or conclude "commercial transactions". Again, the English lawyer can attach no precise meaning to the term "commercial transaction".

The directive and the German law

13. The "commercial agent" of the directive is clearly based on the German *Handelsvertreter* and the provisions of the directive are based on sections 84–92c of the German Commercial Code, which were introduced in 1953. "The concept of '*Handelsvertreter*' or '*Handelsvertreter*' is of an entirely different nature from either that of *Vertretung* or that of agency (in the English sense). A *Vertreter* or an agent (in the

English sense) is a person who performs a certain function, no matter for whom and no matter whether he does so permanently or temporarily and in commerce or privately. A *Handelsagent*, too, is one who performs certain functions, but he must do so permanently in commerce and for a principal who must be his standing client. The law on *Handelsagenten* is thus a specialised branch of commercial law dealing with the affairs of a certain type of businessman, not one dealing with a technical legal function. It is the law of a social group, framed with due regard to the special social and economic needs and requirements of this group and of those who come into contact with it. The closeness of the definition (on which more will have to be said soon) has enabled the legislature to be definite in regard to the provisions which it could enact".

14. It is important to recognise that in German law the commercial agent is identifiable as a member of a particular social group with special social and economic needs. He appears to be a sort of quasi-employee, who, although he nevertheless retains some independence, is substantially dependent on his principal and so needs to be protected. "Commercial agents in the view of most contemporary continental laws, including German and Swiss law, are a group of men who deserve and require the special protection of the law in regard to their contractual relations. They are, or tend to be, it is thought, an exploited class so that the law must step in, in order to prevent or at least restrict their exploitation. The provisions intended to afford this protection are rules of strict law and in consequence incapable of being derogated from by these parties". The directive contains provisions similar to the mandatory provisions of sections 84–92c of the German Commercial Code and in addition contains further far-reaching mandatory provisions for the protection of the commercial agent.

15. All the rules in sections 84–92c of the German Commercial Code, the mandatory provisions and the other provisions, are, of course, understood by german lawyers and applied by the German courts in the context of the remainder of the German Commercial Code and the general provisions of German civil law. german lawyers and German courts will have this context to assist them in applying these sections, and in particular, they will be able to draw upon rules of German law in regard to interpretation of the rules, the ambit of the rules and the remedies available for the enforcement of the rules. However, an English lawyer in applying the directive will have no such body of law upon which to draw. The equivalent rules of English law will be inappropriate and may indeed be distorted by being so used.

16. There are two particularly striking mandatory provisions in the German law which we will mention at this stage:—

   (i) Section 89b of the German Commercial Code entitles the commercial agent to a special adjustment claim on termination, a type of redundancy or severance payment. A similar, although more elaborate and less flexible, provision appears in the directive (Articles 30 and 31). This payment is called by the directive "a goodwill indemnity".

   (ii) Section 90a of the German Commercial Code provides that the principal must pay reasonable compensation, not provided for by his contract, to the agent, during the currency of a restraint clause by which he is bound after the termination of his contract. Again, a similar, although more elaborate and less flexible, provision appears in the directive (Article 32). This payment we will call an "Article 32 payment".

17. Professor Cohn points out that the agent's entitlement to the goodwill indemnity under section 89 of the German Commercial Code is "intended to compensate him for the fact that as a rule the agent's work increases the goodwill of the principal and

not that of the agent and that on termination of the agency the principal thus derives a benefit from this accrued goodwill, while the agent suffers a corresponding loss". Presumably the rationale of section 90a of the German Commercial Code is the assumed inferior bargaining position of the agent.

18. Section 84(1) of the German Commercial Code defines a commercial agent in much the same way as Article 2 of the directive. It seems that commercial agents comprise a social group, with particular social and economic needs, that can be identified in Germany.

The directive and English law

19. We are unable to identify such a social group in England. We are aware that there exists a class of persons who may be described as manufacturers' selling agents. We are also aware that the Manufacturers' Agents' Association is a body in this country which represents the interests of a number of such agents. We are also aware that this Association has been making representations to the relevant Department for many years for legislation to be enacted to protect its members' interests and that it has been making strenuous representations to the relevant Department in support of the proposed directive. We assume that the majority of its members fall within the scope of Article 2, although we do not know whether it is exceptional for such agents to be authorised to conclude transactions on behalf of their principals.

20. We do not know whether the present law sufficiently protects the social and economic needs of manufacturers' agents. It may be that they often have unequal bargaining power as compared with their principals, although it must be remembered that in English commerce and industry not all manufacturers are large corporations of great bargaining power and not all manufacturers' agents are one-man businesses of poor financial standing. It may of course be that there is a mischief and that manufacturers' agents do, as they contend, require special protection from English law. Such limited consultation as we have been able to engage in leaves us in doubt as to whether this is so. But manufacturers' agents do not comprise the whole, nor even a great proportion, of the persons who appear to be covered by Article 2. In the next paragraph we point out that wide categories of other intermediaries appear to be caught within the definition in Article 2. It is by no means clear that their social and economic needs are the same as those of manufacturers' agents and it seems highly improbable that they are in need of the extensive protection provided by the mandatory provisions of the directive.

21. It seems to us that, as drafted, Article 2 may very well catch persons such as travel agents, literary and theatrical agents, advertising agents, stockbrokers, loading brokers and forwarding agents to the extent that they act for particular principals over a period of time. Of course, to fall within Article 2 they must be self-employed and they must act in the name of and for the account of their principal, but it is suggested that this would not be an unusual relationship for many members of these classes of person. Indeed, solicitors, accountants and patent agents instructed on a retainer basis may also fall within Article 2. These examples are given by way of illustration only: in Germany it has even been held that a man employed to win customers for a dancing master fell within section 84 of the German Commercial Code, upon which Article 2 of the directive is based.

22. It is clear therefore that Article 2 extends to cover a large and amorphous body of very different persons. It is our view that although such persons have a continuing relationship with their principals, it would be wrong to assume that they have similar economic and social needs. [. . .] With regard to many of them it would be misleading

to assume a mischief arising from an interior bargaining position It is inconceivable to us that all the detailed mandatory provisions of the directive would be appropriate to all, or even to many, of them. It is also inconceivable to us that the provisions of the directive would constitute a desirable or an appropriate model contract for all, or perhaps for any, of them. Our reading of the decided cases on the present rules of the English law of agency has not suggested to us that these rules need amending to do justice to all, many, or indeed any, of these persons.

23. Before turning to the detailed provisions of the directive it will be convenient to make some general remarks about the mandatory provisions. We start with the two provisions which we have mentioned above, because they are the most important and will lead to most practical difficulties, and we then turn to a few of the difficulties to which the mandatory nature of some of the other provisions of the directive may give rise.

Goodwill indemnity

24. It is stated in the explanatory memorandum that "The indemnity is, of course, payable inter alia to the agent because on his side he provides a consideration which is not fully paid for by the normal remuneration". The equivalent claim granted to the agent by section 89b of the German Commercial Code is intended to compensate him for the fact that his work increased the goodwill of his principal. Articles 30 and 31 of the directive "zig-zag" between the two bases of entitlement; between remunerating the agent for his work and the principal paying for benefits which he has received. Thus Article 30(1) indicates that the entitlement is based on the benefit accruing to the principal as a result of the commercial agent's activities, while Articles 30(2) and (3) indicate that the computation of the amount of the indemnity is based on the effort expended by the commercial agent measured by the time over which this effort was expended.

25. When a principal and an agent enter into an agency contract in England the terms of the contract reflect the principal's assessment of the benefits accruing to him as a result of the agent's activities and the agent's assessment of the value of the efforts to be expended by him. It is difficult to see why in general the agent should receive a payment, for which he has not bargained, when the contract terminates. This is particularly so where the agency contract is for a fixed period and makes no provision for such a payment. Surely in such a case the commercial agent takes the risk that the particular source of income will dry up at the end of the period, and this risk will no doubt be reflected in his rate of commission. The argument is even stronger when the agency contract is for a relatively short period (and no qualifying period is included in Article 30(1)). It seems even more difficult to justify such a payment where the agent terminates the contract of his own free will, perhaps to retire or to take up more remunerative work. On what commercial or moral grounds is the right to such a payment based? The general position in England is that self-employed persons themselves have to make provision for their own retirement. No convincing case has been made for any special favourable treatment for commercial agents.

26. In some ways the directive treats the agent's connection with his principal as his property. Thus it provides that if the agent dies during the period of the contract, his "heirs" are entitled to the goodwill indemnity. The explanatory memorandum, commenting on Article 31(b) explains that "there is the situation where the principal continues to contract with the agent's successor by agreement either of the agent or of his heirs, the new agent succeeding to all the rights and duties of the old. One would, no doubt, be

justified in supposing that in these circumstances the old agent will receive a lump sum payment from his successor which will include the goodwill indemnity". Accordingly, Article 31(b) provides that there shall be no claim where the principal maintains the contract on foot with the agent's successor who was introduced by the agent or by his "heirs". Another surprising feature of the claim is that there is no entitlement where the principal closes down his business, even though substantial benefits would have continued to accrue to him had he remained in business.

27.   It is interesting to compare the commercial agent's entitlement to his goodwill indemnity with the employee's entitlement to redundancy pay under English law. For the commercial agent there is no qualifying period; the commercial agent gets his goodwill indemnity if he dies or retires; the commercial agent is not entitled to his goodwill indemnity if the principal closes his business down. In the first and second respects the commercial agent is better off than the employee and in the third respect he is worse off.

28.   Section 89b of the German Commercial Code is simpler and more flexible than Articles 30 and 31. The German Commercial Code provides for payment which is "fair and reasonable in all the circumstances". As will appear from our detailed discussion of Articles 30 and 31 below, the rules relating to entitlement under the directive are complex and give rise to much difficulty. We believe that it would be quite inappropriate to incorporate the provisions of Articles 30 and 31 into English law, and that no case has been made out for granting such compensation to *all* the persons who fall within the scope of Article 2, although it might be argued that some or all manufacturers' agents should be entitled to some compensation in certain circumstances on the termination of their contract. It is suggested, however, that the normal and acceptable way to provide for such compensation would be to ascertain the extent of the mischief; that is to say, to ascertain the class of persons who suffer hardship in this country, the precise circumstances in which this hardship arises and the type of compensation to which they should be entitled to alleviate this hardship. Apart from the detailed criticisms of Articles 30 and 31 which we make in the next Part of this paper, we consider these provisions to be wholly unacceptable

"Article 32 payment"

29.   The explanatory memorandum to the directive refers to this payment in the following manner: "After termination of the contract the principal must pay to the agent a suitable indemnity throughout the whole period of currency of the agreement restricting competition". It is difficult to see the need for this type of payment. When the commercial agent and the principal are negotiating the terms of their contract, the restraint clause will be bargained for in the normal way and its inclusion will thus be reflected in the other provisions of the contract and in particular in the agreed rate of commission. Why should the commercial agent get an extra payment for observing it? Article 32 extends to restraint clauses entered into as part of an agreement made on the termination of the agency contract, and in these circumstances it seems particularly objectionable for the agent to receive such a payment. It also seems inappropriate for the agent to receive payment if he voluntarily terminates the contract in order, for example, to retire altogether or to take up more remunerative work in another area, or by selling other goods.

30.   Section 90a of the German Commercial Code merely provides for the payment of "reasonable compensation in respect of the period of the restriction on competition".

Cohn comments: "Perhaps the best advice that a draftsman can give to his clients in view of the existing provisions may well be not to provide for a non-competition clause in respect of the period following upon the termination of the agreement, though this is in some cases not a very fortunate solution from the point of view of the principal".

31. Article 32 of the directive is more complicated than section 90a and gives rise to many difficulties, as appears from our detailed discussion of Article 32 below.

32. Article 32 would put the commercial agent in a better position than the employee who is, of course, entitled to no such payment during the currency of a period of a valid restraint clause. As a matter of policy we see no basis for such a payment and, in any event, Article 32 as drafted would be quite unjustified, even if there were a basis for some such payment to some agents in some circumstances.

Mandatory nature of the provisions

33. Although the rules regarding the goodwill indemnity and the Article 32 payment are the most striking of the mandatory provisions there are many others. Most of the others concern topics (such as the circumstances in which commission is payable) which would in the ordinary way be dealt with in the contract by express provision. Such express terms would be overridden by the directive with the result that the parties would find themselves bound by terms quite different from those that they had agreed. The directive thus represents a substantial, and, we believe, unwarranted interference with freedom of contract. This general point is most easily illustrated by supposing the following set of facts:—

> A UK company wishes to promote the sale of certain drinks on the Italian Riviera. An Italian company, with a paid up capital of 1 000 000 EUA or less, is engaged to canvass for orders, over a 12-month period, from customers on the Italian Riviera and, in particular, from hoteliers and bar proprietors. An agreement is negotiated and reduced into writing which requires the Italian company to organise and pay for a poster campaign (promoting the drinks in question) and to collect, and guarantee, payment in respect of orders placed during the 12-month period by customers introduced by them. The UK company agrees to pay a substantial monthly retainer together with 25% of the value of the first order (only) placed and paid for by each customer introduced by the Italian company during the 12-month period. The agreement provides that no commission will be payable in any other circumstances and that there will be no reimbursement for expenses. The agreement provides that the Italian company may deduct the agreed commission from monies collected and remit the balance at the end of each month, and that they are not entitled to a lien over goods or samples entrusted to them by the UK company. Finally the agreement provides that there is a possibility of "passing off" proceedings in Italy in respect of a new vermouth that the UK company is marketing; the canvassing of orders for this product is to be at the Italian company's own risk; there is to be no right of indemnity by the UK company if the promotion of this product by the Italian company results in proceedings.

34. An agreement along the lines indicated above would fall foul of the directive in a number of respects:

   (a) The Italian company would be entitled to *extra* payments (notwithstanding the terms expressly agreed):—

    (i) for the cost of the poster campaign (Article 20(2));

   (ii) for collecting money (Article 14);

  (iii) for guaranteeing payment (Article 21(3));

  (iv) for repeat orders from customers introduced by the Italian company (Article 12(1)(*b*));

   (v) for orders from customers in the area introduced by persons other than the Italian company (Article 12(1)(*c*))'

  (vi) for repeat orders from old customers (Article 12(1)(*c*));

 (vii) for orders executed but not paid for (Article 15(2)(*a*)).

(b) On the other hand the Italian company would be in breach of Article 5(2)(*b*) in deducting commission from money received and in not paying over the balance until the end of the month.

(c) The guarantee would be invalidated by Articles 21(2)(*a*) *and* 21(2)(*b*) and 21(2)(*c*).

(d) The Italian company *would* be entitled to a lien (Article 29(2)).

(e) If the Italian company were involved in court proceedings over the new vermouth there *would* be a right of indemnity (Article 8(1)).

There are thus many respects in which the directive prevents the principal and the commercial agent from making a binding agreement which is acceptable to them both. However sensible, reasonable and fair it may be in its effect, it is liable to be converted by the directive into something which is intrinsically unfair and which makes a nonsense of the bargain that was made.

Uncertainty created by the directive

35. The explanatory memorandum states that the directive is intended to remove the uncertainties that may at present exist as to what the rights of commercial agents are. So far from removing uncertainties the mandatory provisions, just considered, are likely to create them wherever there is a conflict between what the directive provides and what the parties have in fact agreed. This might be acceptable if the mandatory provisions were themselves simple and clear, but they are intricate, confusing and inconsistent one with another. Our detailed analysis of the provisions in the directive follows, in Part III; a recurring theme is that even if the policy behind the directive is sound, which we doubt, its provisions are likely to produce great uncertainty across a very wide area.

PART III—THE DETAILED PROVISIONS OF THE DIRECTIVE

36. In this Part we consider the detailed provisions of the directive article by article. We draw attention, in particular, to—

(a) the policy considerations on which the mandatory provisions appear to be based and the relevance of these policy considerations to the various different groups of people who come within the Article 2 description of "commercial agents";

(b) the policy considerations on which the non-mandatory provisions appear to be based and the extent to which the model contract thus produced is appropriate to the needs of the various different kinds of "commercial agent" (see (È), above);

    (c) the consequences of superimposing the provisions of the directive upon the English law of contract;

    (d) the obscure, complex and unsatisfactory nature of the directive's provisions.

37. There are, however, some general observations to be made about the preparation and drafting of the directive and about the legal concepts incorporated into it which it is convenient to deal with first.

General points on the drafting of the directive

38. We realise that directives are not prepared by utilising the same drafting techniques which are used by Parliamentary Counsel when drafting English statutes. We also realise that the style of drafting is that of states whose legal system is based on civil law rather than on common law. We think, however, that the points we are going to make are nevertheless valid and that their validity can be appreciated when a detailed comparison is made between the articles of the directive and the corresponding provisions of the German Commercial Code (sections 84–92c). Many of the criticisms which we make below cannot, or cannot to any great extent, we levelled at the German text. There are many faults in the directive which may merely be faults of translation or be minor drafting errors, but only part of our criticism is directed to these faults. The German provisions have been extensively adapted, changed and elaborated and many of our comments relate to these alterations. This does not mean that as a matter of content we would welcome any or all of the German rules, but at least we understand, or think we do, the meaning and ambit of most of the German rules, whereas we have found the directive much harder to follow and in places completely incomprehensible.

39. There are three major drafting defects which run through the directive:—

    (a) it lays down rules without specifying what consequences flow from their breach (see, for example, Articles 21(1), 23, 24, 26(1) and 27(2));

    (b) it uses a number of different words to express the same idea (a list of examples is included in an Annex, identified as Annex C);

    (c) it uses the same word to express a number of different ideas (a list of examples is included in the Annex referred to above).

40. There are other points to be made about the draftsmanship which merit general comment not just because they make this particular directive hard to construe but because unless exception is taken to them they are likely to occur in other instruments within the Commission of the European Communities:—

    (a) there is a tendency to make the same point twice, once positively and once negatively (compare, for example, Article 3 (first 7 lines) with Article 2; also Article 7(1) and Article 7(2));

    (b) statements of general principle are followed by non-exhaustive, ill-chosen and misleading lists of illustrations (Articles 5 and 10);

    (c) particular instances are given of a general principle which is nowhere stated (Article 8);

    (d) a technique of descriptive drafting is used which does not exhaust all the possibilities (see, for example, articles 9(2) and 11(1)).

41. We draw attention, in our article by article analysis, to provisions in the directive which we consider are badly drafted, unclear, ambiguous, internally inconsistent or which contain lacunae or are otherwise objectionable. We recognise that some of these points, taken in isolation, are of minor importance. But we suggest that the cumulative effect

is that, irrespective of the objections that there are to the policies in the directive and the content of its rules, the directive in its present form is quite unworkable.

Problems for the common law

42. There are a number of legal concepts and techniques which underlie or are found in the provisions of the directive which have no counterpart in English law. This does not, of course, in itself render them objectionable. Indeed, they should be considered as possible reforms of the law and evaluated as such. They do need to be examined, however, in the light of the wide scope of the directive which would make major changes in a broad, but quite ill-defined, area of the law of agency. Any uncertainty so engendered has to be balanced against the advantages, if any, that these new concepts might bring to English law. Three examples may be given:—
    (a) extraordinary termination;
    (b) secondary activities; and
    (c) the effect of failure to comply with the requirement of writing in the formation of the contract.

(a) Extraordinary termination

43. Article 27(1)(b) provides that either party may terminate a contract at any time—
    "where some circumstance arises which makes it impossible to perform the contract, or which seriously prejudices its performance, or which substantially undermines the commercial basis of the contract, so that the party who terminates cannot be required to keep it in being until the end of the period of notice or until the end of its agreed period of duration."
    This provision is mandatory. Section 89a of the German Commercial Code provides that
    "(i) the contractual relationship may be put to an end by either party without notice for important reasons. This provision may not be excluded or limited."
    Professor Cohn comments thus: "No doubt this rule introduces some measure of uncertainty into the relationship between principal and agent. German lawyers do not mind this so very much; they are accustomed to the principle embodied in section 89a from numerous other instances in which it applies. The rule that a contract may be terminated for 'important reasons' is, in fact, a fundamental principle of German law applicable to all contracts concluded for a period of any length. It finds its explanation in part in the desire not to tie parties for too long to obligations undertaken at a time when the future turn of events could not well be appreciated. No doubt, the turbulent history of the country during its last fifty years has contributed to rendering such a rule commendable". Perhaps English lawyers would be surprised at this measure of uncertainty. The concept of "extraordinary termination" is very much wider than the English doctrine of frustration, and "the colourful variety of grounds of termination" to be found in German decisions and in German legal writings would be new to the common law. In addition, whereas in English law the frustrating event brings the contract to an end without more, Article 27(2) requires that there should be an act of termination as such. These differences are likely to cause problems if Article 27 is superimposed upon the English law of contract. We are not convinced that the innovation is necessary or desirable.

(b) Secondary activities

44. An important distinction is drawn in the directive between the main category of commercial agents and those who act as commercial agents by way of "secondary activity" only (Article 4(1)).

45. Unfortunately, the directive does not way what is to constitute a "secondary activity". Apparently, (from what is said in the explanatory memorandum) a person may be an agent as a secondary activity although he has no other form of commercial activity that may be described as "primary". He may, it seems, carry on secondary activities with more than one principal. The explanatory memorandum fairly concedes that it is impossible to lay down suitable criteria which apply in every case, and yet the directive provides, in Article 4, that the question whether the activity is carried on by way of secondary activity is to be determined "in accordance with commercial usage in the State whose law governs the relations between principal and agent". Since there is, so far as we know, no established commercial usage in England regarding persons who act as commercial agents by way of secondary activity, any legislation introducing such a classification would, in order to comply with the directive, have to be cast in very general terms. This might well give rise to considerable litigation in a wide variety of agency relationships.

(c) The function of writing in the formation of the contract

46. Article 23 of the directive provides that either party shall be entitled to receive from the other a signed written document setting out the terms of the contract and any terms subsequently agreed, and that any purported waiver of this right shall be invalid. Section 85 of the German Commercial Code provides:

> "Either party is entitled to demand that the terms of the contract together with any subsequent additional agreements thereto shall be set out in writing and signed by the other party thereto. This provision may not be excluded by agreement."

As Professor Cohn points out, "the German legislator's desire to protect the agent begins literally with the moment of the conclusion of the agency agreement". He continues: "the right to demand written fixation is not merely academic: it can be enforced by proceedings in court which will lead to a judgment in which the court will lay down authoritatively the terms which the parties have been found to have agreed. Although little use has been made of these sweeping and beneficent powers of the court, the rule may well serve to illustrate the wide powers entrusted by the legislature to the judiciary. That the court will not make the contract for the parties is not a proposition with which a modern civilian will be able to find himself in agreement".Whilst a procedure could no doubt be devised in this country for compelling the principal to deliver a written agency agreement to the agent and for the agent to deliver one to the principal, we doubt whether such a procedure would be appropriate in the present broad but uncertain context.

Article by article analysis

47. In the rest of this Part we analyse the directive article by article.

Article 1

We make no comment on this article at this stage although its terms are relevant to what we say about the directive's provisions in relation to third party rights (Articles 5(1) and 9) and rights on bankruptcy (Article 22).

Article 2

(a) The main thrust of the directive seems to be to provide protection for commercial agents who are engaged to canvass orders for their principals' goods. Although the directive does not distinguish between buying agents and selling agents it seems that selling agents are the ones that the directive aims to protect: Article 17 (which provides that the commission should be geared to the gross amount of the invoice) and Article 30(1)(a) (which mentions "new customers") would produce some strange results if applied to buying agents. Similarly, although the directive covers the supply of services as well as goods it is clear from Articles 10(2)(a) and (b) that goods are the directive's prime concern.

(b) Article 2 is far too wide to be acceptable to English law and wider, it seems, than is necessary to serve the policies on which the directive is based. There is, we believe, no ground for extending its scope beyond selling agents dealing in goods. In particular no case is made out for the inclusion of buying agents and agents for services and we think they should be omitted.

(c) The policy of protection may be justified in regard to those individuals who rely for their livelihood on the sale of their principals' products (quasi-employees) but we can see no justification for extending the protection to
   (i) legal persons other than private individuals (for example, limited companies) or to
   (ii) intermediaries such as travel agents, advertising agents, literary and theatrical agents, stockbrokers, loading brokers, forwarding agents, solicitors, accountants, patent agents, etc.

(d) The policy of providing protection may be appropriate where the agent's income is derived wholly or partly from commission, but it is clearly inappropriate where his services are paid for by a fixed retainer. We think that Article 2 ought to limit the directive to commercial agents who are remunerated either wholly or in part by commission.

(e) The requirement that the agent should have a "continuing authority for a fixed or indeterminate period" would seem to be satisfied in the case of an agent appointed for the duration of a motor show; we would have expected the definition to include a requirement of "permanence" as a characteristic of the agent's appointment.

(f) The requirement that the agent's authority must extend to "an unlimited number of commercial transactions" is likely to lead to confusion. Presumably a manufacturer who limited his agent's sales by a quota system of so many sales a year would be outside the scope of Article 2.

Article 3

(a) The first and third exclusions seem to be otiose as they add nothing to what is already excluded by Article 2 itself.

(b) The second exclusion causes difficulties where the agent has authority to act in his own name but doesn't use it and also where the agent has no such authority but acts as if he had.

(c) The exclusion of "those who carry on their activities in the insurance or credit fields" seems to be wider than the exclusion of those who act for insurance or financial institutions. The looser terminology of the directive is likely to lead to uncertainty.

(d) We should, perhaps, add that the very wide definition of commercial agents given by Article 2 would not be made acceptable by adding further specific exclusions, such as travel agents, stockbrokers etc. This would not be a satisfactory way of identifying the social group to whom the directive's provisions should apply.

Article 4

(a) The term "by way of secondary activity" corresponds with the term "*Nebenberuf*" in section 92b of the German Commercial Code. The Code does not contain a definition of "*Nebenberuf*". In German law the test seems to be whether there is another, not necessarily commercial, activity which may be treated as primary. For these purposes students, pensioners and housewives who do agency work in their spare time are doing it by way of secondary activity. Presumably the full-time employee who does agency work on the side (whether during or out of his ordinary hours of employment) is acting "by way of secondary activity" whatever relation his income from one activity bears to his income from the other. Plainly there will be much uncertainty as to what constitutes a secondary activity; the entitlement to a goodwill indemnity may depend on which side of the line the particular agency falls.

(b) Assuming that those who act as commercial agents by way of secondary activity can be identified as a group (the housewife with a mail-order agency seems to be regarded as typical) the group should be excluded altogether from the scope of the directive, on the ground that its members are not quasi-employees and do not need special protection.

Article 5

(a) This article purports to set out the subsidiary duties of the agent (to keep proper accounts, etc.) and to say how he should conduct himself (fairly and carefully) without saying what his main duty is. What seems to be missing is a general duty that the agent should obtain business for his principal.

(b) Article 5(1) requires the agent to act fairly vis-à-vis third parties. The rights of third parties vis-à-vis agents are a matter for national law and there is no justification for legislating for third parties in this directive.

(c) The references to the standard of care exercised by a sound businessman (Articles 5(1) and 5(2)(d)) derive from section 86(3) of the German Commercial Code. We are not altogether clear how English courts would fit this novel duty into the English law of agency.

(d) Articles 5(2)(a) to (e) pose various difficulties of construction, for example:—

    (i) under (a) is it sufficient for the principal to supply such information as he has?

    (ii) under (b) does "without delay" mean "the same day" "at the end of each month" or what?

    (iii) under (e) what kind of instructions "basically affect the agent's independence"? What if the principal were to require the agent to visit certain named principals at certain stated intervals?

Article 6

(a) "The principles of a sound businessman" is a novelty for English lawyers and it is doubtful whether it is apt here; a standard of "fair dealing" rather than "sound business" might be more appropriate.

(b) The directive precludes the agent from making disclosures to third parties even where this is justified by the public interest, or so it seems. How are the English courts to apply this article to facts such as occurred in *Initial Services Ltd. v Putterill*?

Article 7

(a) The drafting of Articles 7(1) and 7(2) is cumbersome and apparently self-contradictory whereas, presumably, all the directive means to say is that the agent may not compete with the principal in relation to the goods (or services) in question without the principal's consent.

(b) We doubt whether this article is appropriate for inclusion in a model contract. It runs contrary to the English law approach which is, broadly, that if the principal wants to restrict the agent from working for other principals at the same time he must say so. Why should not a housewife who runs an agency for one mail order firm be allowed to run one for another firm as well, unless of course the contract expressly provides that she should not?

(c) There is a more general objection to Article 7 and, more particularly Article 7(3), that it would appear to make covenants in restraint of trade binding which would otherwise be invalid in English law. The conflict between this article and the existing state of English law is likely to lead to much confusion and uncertainty.

[Analysis of Articles 8–12 omitted]

Article 13

(a) No doubt difficulties arise when one agent takes over from another. However, instead of allowing the principal and his agents to work out transitional provisions by agreement Article 13 lays down a set of circumstances in which the predecessor is to have the commission and his successor accordingly gets none. There seems no good reason why this crude all-or-nothing solution should be made mandatory.

(b) The rules that entitle the predecessor to his commission depend on fine distinctions (for example between "negotiation" and "preparatory work") and difficult questions of fact (like who is "mainly" responsible and what period after the change-over would be "reasonable" having regard to the type and volume of the transaction in question). The rules are singularly inappropriate for a model agency contract and would cause problems if superimposed on English law.

Article 14

(a) The requirement that a commercial agent must be paid a special commission for collecting payment has no justification that we can see and is likely to lead to great difficulty in cases where the parties treat the remuneration from collecting payment as a factor in calculating the overall rate of commission or retainer.

(b) The "special commission" is not defined. No guidance is given as to when it becomes payable or on what basis or at what rate the commission is to be calculated.

(c) It is not clear whether the *del credere* agent is entitled to Article 14 commission when he makes the payment out of his own pocket.

Article 15

(a) The provision that the right to commission should arise at the moment when the principal and third party enter into a commercial transaction is presumably intended to link up with the bankruptcy provision in Article 22, which provides that natural persons whose income is mainly derived from a commercial agency shall, as regards sums owing to them for remuneration and reimbursement of expenses, be treated as employees on the principal's bankruptcy. The policy, according to a somewhat bland statement in the explanatory memorandum, is to allow the commercial agent to prove in the bankruptcy for commission that has not yet become available, as if it were already due. We believe that this is inconsistent with the principles of bankruptcy law and with honest dealing, and as such should find no place in a directive on agency.

(b) There appears to be a conflict both in the explanatory memorandum and in Article 15 of the directive as to the policy on which the entitlement to receive the commission is based. The explanatory memorandum asserts that payment of the commission is generally dependent on payment by the third party and states that "The general rule is that the principal is not bound to pay commission unless the third party performs his part of the transaction". This seems inconsistent with a later statement that "The agent knows that where the third party has not performed his part of the contract, and however long that state of affairs continues, commission will be paid *as a general rule* at the end of the third month following that in which the principal performs his part. The exceptions to this are set out in Article 16". Article 15(2)(a), however, starts with a proposition that conflicts with the "general rules" in the explanatory memorandum, namely, that the commission is to be payable as soon as and to the extent that the principal has performed his part of the transaction, even if he fails to carry out his obligations fully in the manner agreed or satisfies some of them only partially. This provision is mandatory and yet Article 15(4) (which is also mandatory in some cases) allows the parties to agree that commission shall be payable at a later time so long as the third party has not performed his obligations! Article 15(4) provides a back stop of three months from performance by the principal as the date beyond which payment of the commission may not be postponed by agreement, but this depends on complete performance by the principal whereas Article 15(2) does not. The principal might postpone the payment of commission beyond three months by holding back say the last 5 of 100 articles that were due for delivery. This article is riddled with gaps and inconsistencies.

(c) It seems that although the agent has a "right to commission" when the principal and the third party first enter into the commercial transaction, no commission is ever payable if neither party performs the contract at all or if the contract is cancelled by mutual agreement. It is all very puzzling.

(d) Article 15(3) is badly drafted, complex in its structure and would be very difficult to apply in practice. Likewise with Article 15(5) it seems ridiculous, having regard to the wide variety of persons to whom Article 2 is likely to apply, to restrict them to monthly or quarterly accounting periods.

Article 16

(a) Article 16(1)(a) extinguishes the agent's right to commission for breach of his duty under Article 5(2)(a). However Article 5(2)(a) describes a general duty to supply the principal with information that he needs and also a special duty as regards information on the solvency of third parties. Is the right to commission extinguished for breach of the general duty (which seems too wide) or only for breach of the special duty to keep the principal informed about the solvency of customers? The explanatory memorandum suggests the latter which is obviously too narrow.

(b) Article 16(1)(c) envisages that the principal has reasonable grounds for supposing that the third party will not perform but that the contract has not been frustrated and the third party is not actually in breach and has not repudiated. In English law this gives the principal no legal excuse for not performing the contract with the third party. There is thus likely to be a difficulty if Article 16 (which is mandatory) is superimposed on English law. Moreover, under Article 16(1)(c) the principal is absolved from having to pay commission as soon as "serious grounds for non-performance" exist even though the third party later defies expectations and performs after all. The explanatory memorandum points out that it is impossible to spell out in the directive the precise meaning of "serious grounds", the scope and significance of which has been "settled by the law or by the case law or in the juristic writings in the Member States". However, this is a novel concept in English law where its introduction is likely to cause considerable confusion and uncertainty.

Article 17

(a) It is doubtful whether this provision (that commission should as a general rule be calculated on the gross amount of the invoice) is appropriate for a model contract. Sometimes the cost of transit may represent a large part of the amount of the invoice.

(b) The reference to "invoiced separately" is confusing. It is not clear whether it means "stated as separate items on the same invoice" or "stated in a separate invoice".

Article 18

(a) Article 18 is mandatory and gives the commercial agent a right to see copies of extracts from the principal's books and, in certain circumstances, access to the books themselves. It is not clear whether this is necessary (having regard to the principal's duties under Article 10(1)) or desirable.

(b) If the requirement in Article 18(1) is necessary and desirable (which we doubt) surely the procedure for its enforcement should be left to the laws of Member States. Article 18(2) is an absurdly over-elaborate rule. Its implementation (and it is of course mandatory) would entail the creation of a new category of auditors, "auditors-on-oath" and the making of special rules of procedure.

(c) The option allowed by Article 18(2) enables the principal to compel the agent *not* to employ a professional adviser. We find this objectionable.

Article 19

(a) The policy underlying this article is unclear. It seems to go beyond the requirement that the principal should act in good faith (Article 10). Why should the agent be entitled to "fall-back" pay when he has merely "taken steps" towards performing his obligations or has fulfilled them by doing nothing more strenuous than caring for the samples? It will be remembered that he has no general obligation under Article 5 to promote his principal's business.

(b) The circumstances in which the principal is *not* required to make payments under Article 19 are likely to cause confusion in English law since they depend on a concept of "circumstances beyond his control" and this is not the same as the legal doctrine of frustration.

(c) Assuming that money is payable under Article 19 it is by no means clear when the right to payment arises. As for the basis of the computation, Article 19(2), which is geared to the loss of expected earnings, seems to be in conflict with Article 19(3) which is geared to the amount of money expended by the agent in setting up the agency.

Article 20

(a) We can see no justification for including Article 20(2) in the directive. Why should the parties not be allowed to agree that "special activities" should be at the agent's expense or that they should be taken into account in fixing the level of commission or retainer?

(b) Article 20(2) is extremely loosely drafted. How is the court to decide what are "*special activities?*"

Article 21

(a) The entitlement to a "separate commission" in respect of certain *del credere* transactions is in some circumstances mandatory. It is likely to cause confusion when it runs contrary to what the parties have expressly agreed.

(b) Nowhere in the article is it provided when the agent becomes entitled to be paid his separate commission. Payment cannot be governed by Article 15 as that article depends on performance by (principal or third party) and a *del credere* agent is paid his commission for his promise.

(c) Article 21(1) requires that *del credere* agreements be evidenced in writing. Such agreements are not within the provisions of our Statute of Frauds and accordingly are not required by English law to be evidenced by writing. Confusion is likely to arise where some of the activities of an English *del credere* agent are affected by the directive and some are not.

(d) The effect of non-compliance with the requirement of written evidence (Article 21(1)) is not clear. Presumably the agent is not liable to the principal if the third party does not pay, but suppose the third party does pay. Can the agent get his *del credere* commission under Article 21(3) or is he barred by want of written evidence?

(e) Article 21(4) allows the parties to derogate from the earlier provisions as regards transactions "which the agent has been given full power to agree and to carry out". It is hard to see what situations are described by this provision; it seems to allow "contracting out" in every case.

(f) There are various obscurities in the text that are likely to cause difficulty:—,

    (i) Who are "particular parties . . . specified" (Article 21(b))? Do they have to be named or will a class description suffice? If the latter, can the class be "any customer introduced by the commercial agent"?

    (ii) Does "unlimited" (Article 21(2)(c)) mean "without financial limit"? If so, the provision is useless unless a financial limit is specified. Will 99% pass muster?

    (iii) What is "the place of business" (Article 21(4)(a)) where the principal (or the third party) has several?

Article 22

(a) This article goes beyond the relations between self-employed commercial agents and their principals (Article 1). It seeks to change the laws on insolvency so as to give commercial agents preferential rights against the general body of creditors. We can see no justification for such provisions in this directive and doubt whether they have a sound jurisdictional basis.

(b) Remarkably this article is not mandatory. This is particularly odd because Article 15(1), which *is* mandatory, provides that a right to commission arises at the moment when the principal and the third party enter into the commercial transaction and so gives the agent improved rights on bankruptcy.

(c) It is by no means clear how Articles 15(1) and 22 are meant to work when the principal becomes insolvent. Article 15(1) is intended to allow the agent to prove for commission although neither the principal nor the third party have performed at all; but for what sum does he, in fact, prove?

(d) The broad aim of Article 22 is to make the agent a preferred creditor in respect of his commission as if he were an employee claiming for wages. However the agent may only so prove where his income is "mainly derived from a commercial agency" (Article 22(1)). The relevance of the agent's other income (for example from investments) is not clear. Moreover, the line may often be hard to draw in practice and is not effective to exclude stockbrokers, forwarding agents and so on, nor even to exclude those who act as agents as a secondary activity. It is unsatisfactory in every possible way.

(e) Employees are preferred creditors in English law for some of the wages that are payable but unpaid at the date of bankruptcy. Articles 15(1) and 22 do not merely put self-employed commercial agents on a par with wage-earners—although this would be hard enough to justify—but they purport to give the agent a preferential right to prove for commission that is not even payable at the date of the bankruptcy.

Article 23

The explanatory memorandum makes it clear that the entitlement by the principal and the agent to receive a signed written document from each other arises on the request of the other party. What is the effect of failure to comply with the request? Under Article 23 no consequences appear to flow. It would be absurd if the result was that the contract was void. Does it impose a duty, the breach of which might justify termination and could give rise to damages, if it should lead to loss? Is it mere exhortation?

Article 24

(a) Presumably failure to comply with Article 24 has no more effect than failure to comply with Article 23. This being so it is hard to see why the parties should bother to comply with Article 24.

(b) It is odd that the provision in Article 24 is not mandatory whereas Article 23 is. Presumably the invalidation of any waiver of rights given by the article is imported from Article 23, so that the parties, in order to release each other from the right to receive a written document upon request setting out the terms of the mutual termination, would have expressly to provide in their contract that Article 24 was not to apply. This is a good example of a wholly inappropriate provision for insertion into a model contract.

Article 25

No comment.

Article 26

(a) Article 26(1) is mandatory and provides, amongst other things, that the period of notice must be the same for both sides. This is not always appropriate and confusion will arise where the parties make more sensible arrangements in breach of the article.

(b) No sanction is specified where the notice of termination is not given in writing. The contract presumably continues (?)

(c) It is not clear what happens when the proper period of notice is not observed. One would have expected the notice to be ineffective but Article 28(1) seems to contemplate that an agreement may be "terminated" by a defective notice.

Article 27

(a) This article provides that the agreement may be terminated on grounds that are not recognised in the English law of contract. Difficulties are likely to follow from the superimposition of this article upon English law. One of the novel grounds of termination is the other party's "fault"; an idea that may be well-established in civilian systems but is not part of the English law of contract.

(b) Another novel ground is the happening of "events which justify termination". It is clear that this goes beyond the English doctrine of frustration since the example given in the explanatory memorandum is of an agent who finds it impossible to continue in business for reasons of health, old age or serious and unforeseeable family circumstances. We can only guess at the other kinds of "events" that might justify termination. What about Japanese competition which undermines the financial prospects of the agency after it has run for two years? What is the principal (as opposed to the agent) becomes old or ill or has family problems? Or where it has become unprofitable for him to sell a particular line of goods? The inter-relation between the grounds for termination under this article and the grounds for non-payment of commission under Article 16(1)(c) remains unclear.

(c) Article 27(1)(b) differs from frustration in another respect which is likely to cause difficulties in English law, namely that the events justifying termination do not by themselves end the agreement: one party or the other has to "terminate" as well.

(d) The relation between this article and Article 13 should be noted. It seems that the agent may still be entitled to commission on a transaction negotiated by him, even though "at fault" in relation to the very transaction justifying his dismissal. Is this a desirable rule?

(e) Article 27(1)(a) uses the phrase "cannot be required", whereas in Article 16(1)(c) the phrase is "cannot reasonably be required". A similar point occurs in Article 27(1)(b). Is the difference intended to have a significance or is it just sloppy drafting?

(f) Article 27(2) refers to "termination vis-à-vis the other party". Presumably the communication would have to be in writing; otherwise the provision that the reasons for termination have to be given in writing is anomalous. But the point is not dealt with expressly.

Article 28

(a) Article 28(1) seems to draw a distinction between "termination" and "declaring the contract to be at an end" although it is not clear what it is; it is unknown to English law. It is likely to cause uncertainty.

(b) Article 28 tells us nothing about the effects of failure to give *written* notice under Article 26(1) or to give *written* reasons under Article 27(2). In other words, it does not tell us what happens where the notice is good in substance but bad in form. Does the notice terminate the contract or does the contract nevertheless continue?

(c) Article 28(2) introduces the concept of the "lump sum indemnity" which is a novelty in our law of agency. It seems that the agent gets his average monthly earnings for the unexpired contract period, subject to the two year limit. Why should he get the whole "average remuneration" without allowing for the fact that he does not have to incur the expense of earning it? Why are the factors, relevant under Article 19(3)(b), not also relevant here? The English law requires that employees who have been wrongfully dismissed should only recover their real loss, after taking into account the extent to which the loss was or should have been mitigated. The directive aims to put the commercial agent in a better position, in this regard, than the ordinary employee.

Article 29

There seems no reason why the agent's right of lien should be mandatory and in full force in all cases. There may be circumstances in which it would be fair and reasonable for the agent to contract for a qualified right of lien, or, perhaps, no such right at all. Furthermore Article 29(2) seems to allow a general lien covering, for example, goods entrusted to the agent for use only; this is in conflict with the existing English law and must result in uncertainty.

Articles 30 and 31

Policy considerations relevant to whether there should be any payment at all

(a) We have already pointed out that we are not satisfied that any case has been made out that a goodwill indemnity should ever be payable unless the principal and the agent, in their contract, have bargained for such a payment.

(b) However, even if a case were made out for such a mandatory entitlement it should only be payable where the agency is for an indeterminate period and it certainly could never be justified where the agency is for a fixed term.

(c) Whatever justification there might be for giving the "quasi-employee" a goodwill indemnity there certainly can be none for giving it to:—

　　(i) persons such as advertising agents, theatrical agents, stockbrokers, etc., who are caught by Article 2;

　　(ii) persons acting as commercial agents as a secondary activity;

　　(iii) companies or corporations; although Article 33(1) permits large companies to contract out of Article 30 we are of the view that not only is the mandatory rule inappropriate for small companies, but the entitlement is also inappropriate as a term of a model contract for large companies.

(d) We can see no justification for allowing the agent to claim the indemnity when he retires and terminates the contract by notice under Article 30(4). The agency is treated by the directive as alienable. If it is worth something then presumably the agent should be able to recover its value by selling it; if it is not worth anything then presumably he should not be entitled to anything. Furthermore, a principal may be prejudiced by having to pay out a lump sum at a time not of his own choosing. The right of indemnity on resignation could be abused by the agent if, after an interval (so that 30(1)(b) is satisfied) he begins to negotiate transactions between the customers he introduced to his former principal and a new principal with whom he subsequently has taken up work.

(e) Even if the goodwill indemnity ought sometimes to be payable to the agent whose services are dispensed with—so as to provide him with something comparable to redundancy money—it does not follow that the right to the indemnity should automatically pass to his estate if he dies while the contract is still on foot (as Article 30(1) appears to contemplate).

(f) On the other hand if the policy behind the goodwill indemnity provisions is that the agent should get a reward for effort it is hard to see why he should be deprived of it just because he receives something by virtue of Article 13. If under Article 13 the commercial agent receives commission on one or two transactions entered into after the contract has come to an end with two customers introduced by him, it seems that his right to goodwill indemnity is excluded. Can this be right? The position seems to be different if he gets Article 13 commission in respect of one customer and not in respect of the other: that is, he is then entitled to the *full* goodwill indemnity. Is this distinction defensible? The general policy of Article 30(1)(c) seems to be that the commercial agent is not to get goodwill indemnity in respect of a source of income that is in fact continuing. But the attempt to express this policy has been unsuccessful.

(g) Assuming, as in (f), that the basis of the goodwill indemnity is to provide a reward for effort it is remarkable that the agent who puts in many years of work gets no recompense if the principal does not as a result receive "substantial benefits [that] will continue to accrue", for example, where the principal decides to close down his business because it is no longer profitable.

Policy considerations relevant to the calculation of the amount payable

(h) Articles 30 and 31 "zig-zag" between two different principles for calculating the remuneration, one that it should be a reward to the agent for the work he has done, the other that the principal should account for the benefit that he is left with when the agent has left. The result is confusing and must create difficulties for the courts.

(i) There is no direct relationship between the conditions in which the right arises (Article 30(1)) and the amount to which the agent is entitled (Article 30(2)). Suppose the principal gets a slight benefit by introducing two new customers while also negotiating transactions with 98 old customers (with whom the volume of business is not "appreciably increased"). The minimum amount of the goodwill indemnity under Article 30(2) is based on the *whole* of his average annual remuneration—not on the *extra* amount attributable to the new customers. This might be adjusted under Article 30(3). But this confused position shows that sensible rules for computation have not been formulated: and, because of the conflicting bases of the entitlement (benefit/efforts), certainly cannot be formulated.

(j) The first sentence of Article 30(4) envisages payment to the agent who terminates by notice without justification of an indemnity not exceeding the amount payable under Article 30(2), whereas the second sentence of Article 30(4) provides that the agent who terminates without justification might be entitled to the maximum indemnity in Article 30(3). It is quite possible, if the agent has worked for 20 years, for his minimum entitlement under Article 30(2) to be equal to his maximum entitlement under Article 30(3): the effect or providing a different way of calculating the indemnity is not clear. In any event, where the agent's termination was justified by the principal's conduct, the agent would presumably have his remedy in damages for breach.

(k) Article 30(4) provides for a very unsatisfactory mixture of goodwill indemnity and some form of punitive damages. The principal becomes liable to the maximum amount (whether it is otherwise available or not) simply because he is in breach, even though the loss to the agent is much less.

Points which are likely to give rise to difficulties in practice

(l) The question whether a right to goodwill indemnity exists may be very hard to answer in view of the words "appreciably" in Article 30(1)(a) and "substantial" in Article 30(1)(b). The latter provision also prompts the question for how long must the benefit continue to accrue? Is one month long enough after ten years of agency?

(m) In Article 30(2) it is not clear what "the preceding five years" precedes. If it is intended to denote the five years preceding the cessation of the contract, then it appears to be inconsistent with the provision that the basis for the calculation for the indemnity should include Article 13 commission in respect of transactions concluded *after* the cessation of the contract. If the words are not intended to mean that period, it is hard to see what they do mean.

(n) Article 30(4), second sentence, seems to create some anomalies. It only applies (so as to give the commercial agent the right to the "maximum amount"—that is, two years' average pay) if the commercial agent gives due notice *and* the termination is justified; at least this seems to follow from the phrase "*such* termination". Why, if termination is "justified" must the notice periods be observed for this purpose? What, moreover, is meant by "justified"? Is the reference to "the principal's conduct" one to "fault" within Article 27(1)(a)? If so, why is this not stated? If not, what *does* "the principal's conduct" mean? Is the reference to a kind of constructive dismissal but without breach by the principal? What are "reasons which are particular to the agent"? Is the reference to circumstances listed in Article 27(1)(b) or is it to something wider? Do the words cover the case where the commercial agent is simply too old to carry on and wants to retire? What, finally, is supposed to be the effect of the last four words? Do they once again leave the assessment completely at large? Although Article 30(4) is concerned with quantification rather than entitlement, it contains many obscurities and badly needs clarification.

(o) Article 31(c) provides that the commercial agent loses his right to goodwill indemnity if he miscalculates the period of notice by so much as one day. Should not the test rather be whether his failure to give proper notice causes serious prejudice to the principal? A somewhat similar point can be made about a commercial agent who terminates (or purports to do so) believing in good faith, and reasonably, that he has grounds under Article 27(1), but who then finds that he cannot substantiate those grounds. In view of the obscurity of Article 27(1)(b), this is no improbable contingency.

(p) Article 31(b) exempt the principal from having to pay the goodwill indemnity where one agent is replaced by another whom he has introduced. In English law there would, in such circumstances, either be an assignment of the agency by one agent to the other or (more likely) a new contract with the new agent. The directive contemplates that the old contract may be "maintained on foot" with the new agent being "substituted entirely". It is not clear whether this would apply to an assignment and very doubtful whether it would apply where there was a new contract. The article is likely to cause confusion and uncertainty in this country.

Article 32

(a) It is extraordinary that this is not one of the articles which, under Article 4(1), Member States need not apply to persons who act as commercial agents by way of secondary activity.

(b) The weakness of Article 32(2) is that it will often be impossible to tell, when the agreement restricting competition is drafted, whether it is going to be valid. The agency agreement may last for many years; but in the last few months the agent may cease to be "entrusted" with a small part of his original territory. The result is that the restrictive agreement no longer satisfies the test of Article 32(2), though when made it did satisfy the test. What is the effect? Is the agreement wholly void? Can it be severed? Article 32(1) says nothing about failure to comply with substantive requirements,

(c) It should be noted that the restraint clause may be void by English law even if it is for a period of less than two years and this possibility does not seem to have been envisaged in Article 32.

(d) The meaning of Article 32(3) is unclear. Does it mean that only restrictive covenants of two years' duration are valid? If a restrictive covenant is for more than two years, would it be void *in toto*, or could the court sever the covenant, holding the first two years to be valid and the rest to be void?

(e) Is the payment provided for in Article 32(4) only available if the restrictive covenant is valid, or also, if it is invalid, but nevertheless observed?

(f) It is not clear what happens if the contract of agency is terminated by principal and agent, by mutual consent. Does the restriction run on under Article 32(3)? Can it not be ended by agreement of the parties? Presumably not since Article 32(3) is mandatory.There is a related problem under Article 32(5)(b). What happens if the agent terminates the contract under Article 32(5) but does not terminate the restriction in writing? Apparently it continues in force.

(g) In Article 32(6), line 1, why only "before the contract has come to an end" and not after?

(h) What, for instance, if after giving notice, the principal goes out of business? Why must he pay the indemnity for six months even though during those six months the agent is free to compete, does so, and suffers no loss of earnings at all?

(i) Article 32(6) provides that if the agent gives notice of termination in accordance with Article 26, then the principal during the currency of the notice can terminate the restrictive covenant, but only to release himself of the obligation to pay indemnity after a period of six months has elapsed. There seems no good reason why the principal should still have to pay the indemnity to the agent during the part of this period falling after the termination of the contract.

(j) Why should the agent who voluntarily resigns to work for another principal either in another area or selling other goods, be paid goodwill indemnity under Article 30, plus (possible) Article 13 commission, plus an Article 32 payment equivalent to a maximum two years' remuneration.

Article 33

Article 33 attempts to distinguish between small companies which require protection granted by all the mandatory provisions of the directive and large companies which, presumably because of their financial standing, only require the protection of some of the mandatory provisions. The distinction is turned on the paid-up capital of the company. In our view, the paid-up capital of the company is not a reliable index of its financial strength and to turn the distinction on it is totally unrealistic.

Article 34

No comment.

Article 35

Article 35(2) permits the parties to derogate from the mandatory provisions in the directive in relation to activities which the agent carries on outside the EEC. If would obviously be cumbersome to have an agreement which was partly valid and partly invalid.

PART IV—OUR CONCLUSIONS

48. As we have seen, the directive attempts:—
    (a) to isolate a social group, "commercial agents", with special economic and social needs;
    (b) to lay down mandatory rules to give these agents protection commensurate with these needs;
    (c) to provide a model contract incorporating terms that ought to be implied between these agents and their principals unless the contract provides to the contrary;
    (d) to produce a clear and rational statement in the form of a code covering the relationship between these agents and their principals, in particular the rules governing the formation, performance and termination of their contracts.
49. With regard to (a) we are satisfied that the social group has not been identified and no case seems to have been made out for the alleged social and economic needs of all the persons falling within the ambit of the directive.

50. With regard to (b) we consider the directive to be one-sided and the mandatory rules to consist of an elaborate advancement of a sectional interest for which no case has been made out. The rules, as drafted, appear to us to be cumbersome and unworkable. Moreover, parties who devise clearer or more sensible rules to suit themselves do so at their peril.

51. With regard to (c) we do not consider that the provisions of the directive would constitute in English law appropriate terms to be incorporated in a model contract between any agent and any principal. With regard to many of them it seems inconceivable that the parties to such a contract would wish them to govern their mutual relationship. Yet this is what they will do, unless the parties expressly provide that they should not.

52. With regard to (d) we do not consider that the attempted codification has done anything to clarify the existing law. On the contrary, the rules which the directive purports to declare are full of uncertainties, gaps and inconsistencies and, in many respects, offend against basic principles of the English law of agency. Furthermore, they depend for their operation upon a corpus of law which is not stated in the directive. Their introduction would necessitate the distortion of the common law of agency and of other areas of commercial law. In our opinion, no justification, social or legal, has been made out for such a step.

53. Our conclusion is, therefore, that the directive's defects of substance, presentation and drafting are such that it fails even to provide a basis for negotiation.

Appendix 4—House of Lords Select Committee Fifty-First Report

WEDNESDAY 27 JULY 1977

By the Select Committee appointed to consider Community proposals whether at draft or otherwise, to obtain all necessary information about them, and to make reports on those which, in the opinion of the Committee, raise important questions of policy or principle, and on other questions to which the Committee consider that the special attention of the House should be drawn.

ORDERED TO REPORT:—

1. R/3/77: DRAFT COUNCIL DIRECTIVE TO CO-ORDINATE THE LAWS OF THE MEMBER STATES RELATING TO (SELF-EMPLOYED) COMMERCIAL AGENTS

1. The proposed Directive deals with the legal relationship between "commercial agents" and their principals. For the purposes of the Directive a "commercial agent" is, broadly speaking, an independent person acting on a continuing basis in the name of a manufacturer or trader and negotiating or concluding contracts on his behalf for the supply of goods or services. The Directive if adopted would require standardised rules to be implied into the agency contract under which the commercial agent acts for the manufacturer or trader; in many instances departure from these standardised rules to the detriment of the commercial agent would not be permitted; the rules concern the rights and duties of the agent and of his principal, the remuneration of the agent, the agent's rights in the insolvency of the principal, and the making and cessation of the agency contract. Some of the Member States already have statutory codes, the content of which varies, concerning the legal relationship between these parties; the other Member States, including the United Kingdom, have no such code. One of the main purposes of the Directive is to introduce harmonised rules in the Member States about this kind of agency, since it is considered by the Commission that the existing differences are detrimental to the functioning of the Common Market; the other main purpose is to strengthen the position of the commercial agent vis-à-vis his principal by requiring the existence in all Member States of rules which favour the agents.

2. At the outset, those concerned in drafting the Directive seem to have encountered difficulty in defining the expression "commercial agent". Article 2 of the draft defines the expression to mean "a self-employed intermediary who has continuing authority for a fixed or indeterminate period to negotiate and/or to conclude an unlimited number of commercial transactions in the name and on account of another person (who is hereinafter called 'the principal')." This is a wide definition, and the draftsmen seem to have

been so much impressed by its width that in Article 3 they proceed to exclude from the definition two classes of persons who in any case would not have been within it. The exact area that could be covered by the definition is very indeterminate; it has been suggested that it could include such persons as travel agents, advertising agents, stockbrokers, loading brokers, and forwarding agents to the extent that they act for particular principals over a period of time. It could cover buying agents, though later articles suggest that this is not intended. Agents in the insurance and credit fields are expressly excluded. It becomes clear, at a late stage in the draft, that it is intended to cover companies acting as agents as well as individuals so acting. Generally speaking, the Committee found the drafting of the Directive loose and uncertain.

3. The Committee take the true intended effect of the Directive to be to protect independent commercial agents who are engaged to canvass for orders for the principal's goods or services as distinct from "commercial travellers" who are employees of the persons whom they serve. The draft Directive contains rules concerning commission which considerably favour the commercial agent. Of the other detailed rules which compliance with the Directive would cause to be implicit in the agency contract, the most important would be those which would confer on the agent (a) the right on cessation of the contract to be paid a "goodwill indemnity" where he has brought new customers to the principal or appreciably increased the volume of business with existing customers, and as a result substantial benefits will continue to accrue to the principal (Article 30); (b) the right, where the commercial agent is for a period after cessation of the contract bound by an agreement restricting his business activities, to be paid remuneration during that period (Article 32); and (c) a right to preferential treatment in the insolvency of the principal. The inclusion in the agency contract of rights of the kind mentioned under (a) or (b) above, though required by the laws of some of the Member States, is not compulsory according to the law of the United Kingdom; in that country they are a matter for negotiation between the parties, and the inclusion of (b) would, it is thought, be very unusual. If the Directive were adopted in its present form these rights would, under the law in each of the Member States, have to be conferred on the agent, save that the right to the goodwill indemnity would be excluded if the agent were a company with a paid-up capital exceeding 100,000 European Units of Account ("EUA") (about £67,000). It would not, however, be difficult to avoid being excluded on this ground; the company could operate on loan capital, or several companies each having a capital less than 100,000 EUA could be formed.

4. While therefore the law of the United Kingdom includes, at present, no special rules governing the relationship between commercial agents and their principals, the laws of the continental Member States do include rules for the protection of these agents, but these it appears vary very considerably from country to country. Thus the Sub-Committees (B and E) which have considered the Directive were informed in evidence that the degree of protection for agents in France goes much further than that provided for in the Directive, and had been raised so high that "principals were not interested in entering into contracts with French agents." The rules in Germany are evidently less favourable to the agents, and it is said that even after the protective law was introduced "the commercial agency was still the cheapest means of marketing goods in Germany."

5. The purpose of the present report is not to review the Directive in detail and to criticize its drafting, but to consider whether there is any justification in principle for introducing a Directive on this subject at all. The justification put up by the Commission is summarised as follows in the Commission's Explanatory Memorandum at page 2.

"Basically, the proposal has two objectives. The first is to remove the differences in law which are detrimental to the proper functions of the common market. They affect the conditions of competition and create considerable legal uncertainty. This applies, for example, in relation to the goodwill indemnity, which is known in some Member States but not in others. It is more expensive for the principal to have an agent in those countries in which the goodwill indemnity is already compulsory by law, and this operates very much to the economic advantage of principals who are not under an obligation to pay any indemnity after the contract has terminated. The second objective is to safeguard or improve the protection that already exists for commercial agents. Although they are self-employed, most commercial agents are economically in a weak position vis-à-vis their principals. In so far as the proposal envisages minimum rules it does not affect those provisions of national law which are more favourable to the commercial agent and does not stand in the way of progress. From a more general point of view the proposal is aligned on the principles set out in Article 117 of the EEC Treaty, and, in harmonising the law, endeavours to achieve a levelling-up."

6. This statement on the part of the Commission is notable for the boldness of its asser-tions. It is, for example, insupportable to lay down as a general proposition that "it is more expensive for the principal to have an agent in those countries in which the good-will indemnity is already compulsory by law, and this operates very much to the eco-nomic advantage of principals who are not under (such) an obligation . . .". Obviously, the question whether the one principal has a competitive advantage over another depends as much, if not more, on the rates of remuneration which they each pay dur-ing the period of the contract, to say nothing of the other terms of the contract. It may suit both principal and agent to dispense with a provision for goodwill indemnity in favour of a higher rate of commission during the currency of the contract. There would seem no justification for prohibiting them from making what bargain they please about this. The statement that "most commercial agents are economically in a weak position vis-à-vis their principals" appears to be simply a matter of assertion. The preamble to the Directive is couched in more cautious terms and states that "in many cases com-mercial agents are as a rule, though in differing degrees, economically in a weak posi-tion vis-à-vis their principals." The evidence given on the part of the Manufacturers' Agents' Association of the United Kingdom was that there are twenty thousand agents in this country. It is difficult to believe that the Commission knows the conditions under which "most" of these persons work, and their economic strength. The evidence of the Association was that "the agent used to have to get the best terms he could from his principal, today we have a form of agreement which is ever increasingly being accepted by British principals". The evidence further was that the standard form of contract "goes rather further than the directive which you are now considering, partic-ularly in respect of the goodwill compensation clause"; and that "there is no question . . . whatever that there is now a greater demand, especially in the economic situation in which we live today, for manufacturers' agents than ever before." The Association stated in its written submission that "it is generally conceded that the commercial agent is invariably the weaker party as between himself and his principal." Dr R A Haumann, a German lawyer who gave helpful evidence about the law of that country, stated that "in general, the manufacturer's agent is in a weaker position and this weaker position is a bad thing for him. It leads to insecurity." But he went on to say that "we are not in favour of compulsory provision overall in Germany . . . there must be some

compulsory provisions in agency law, but in my opinion there is a little too much in this respect in the EEC draft Directive." On the other hand, the Confederation of British Industry stated that "the realities of commercial and industrial life being what they are, it is probable that proper investigation would show that principals are very often at the mercy of commercial agents and in at least equal general need of 'protection', and that the relative economic positions (which in effect means sizes and physical or financial resources) are very frequently irrelevant in determining which party is the dominant one in practice." The Association of British Chambers of Commerce, in their submission, said:

"The guiding principle behind the Commission's proposals is that commercial agents are believed to be in a weaker negotiating position than their principals, and thus need protected and inalienable rights. The ABCC does not believe this premise is correct. The Commission claims that in countries where a preferential regime has been introduced for commercial agents (for example Belgium) there has been a resulting increase in their numbers. This is evidence of nothing more than the fact that the people take advantage of a preferential status if it is offered to them. It does not mean that in the absence of this preferential status those who might otherwise act as commercial agents would be severely disadvantaged. On the contrary, the ABCC considers that an agent is frequently in a reasonably strong position and is not therefore always in need of the extended protection proposed.

The Commission is particularly keen to impose protection where a principal in one country appoints a selling agent in another country. The ABCC believes that this relationship will most frequently occur when a comparatively small manufacturer wishes to break into an export market and, having neither the resources nor the immediate sales potential for setting up a full time distributor or his own office in the country, hires an agent with specialised and local knowledge to do the job on his behalf. In this type of situation, there is very little likelihood of the principal being in such a strong negotiating position that the agent is in need of special protection.

In the UK, at least, there exist various established trade associations, most notably the Manufacturers' Agents' Association, who protect the interests of members, and presumably provide their membership with clear advice and guidelines as to acceptable conditions of agency contracts."

7. In the result therefore, the facts, so far as they are ascertainable at all, seem to emerge very much as might be expected. At one end of the scale it seems that there are agents who are at the mercy of their principals; at the other end, principals at the mercy of their agents; in the middle, there appears to be a substantial body of agents whose services, according to the evidence of their Association, are much in demand and who are steadily improving their position. To impose, on this variegated pattern of agents, one body of inflexible legal rules seems to the Committee to be incapable of justification. What is needed is a flexibility which enables the parties to the agency contract to arrange terms which suit their respective needs.

8. In general, the Committee question the desirability of imposing strict standards in these commercial matters. If terms which favour the commercial agents are imposed, then the principals will find other means of selling their goods, by employing their own travellers, by employing commission agents who act in their own names, or by forming subsidiary companies. Distortions of business are a common result of imposing inflexible rules.

9. The Commission's other justification for the Directive is that it would remove "a continuing and quite definite inequality of the conditions of competition." Here, again, the Committee feel the lack of any supporting evidence. In so far as a manufacturer wishes to sell his goods in a particular country there seems to be no room for distortion of competition. Each manufacturer will be in the same position, according to whether or not the country in question has adopted rules resembling those in the Directive. The notion that a manufacturer will be positively debarred from selling in a country where agencies are so favoured seems to the Select Committee to be fanciful.

10. It should be observed that the Directive is not intended only to govern international transactions in which the manufacturer is in one Member State and the agent in another. The Directive would apply to trade which is being carried on entirely in one Member State, so that an English manufacturer dealing through English commercial agents entirely with English customers in the domestic market would have to accord to his agents the terms laid down in the Directive. For this, the Commission relies on the proposition that "trade in goods and the provision of services should always be effected under conditions which are similar to those of a single market." The Committee do not entirely accept this far-reaching proposition; but if there is to be a single market of the size of the Community, the need for flexibility in the ways in which commercial transactions can be carried out seems to be all the greater.

11. The Committee have recently noted with concern a tendency on the part of the Commission to interfere, in ways which are not altogether judicious, with particular segments of the national legal systems. They instance, in particular, the draft Directive on liability for Defective Products on which they reported in their 63rd Report of last Session, and the draft Directive on Contracts negotiated away from Business Premises ("Doorstep Selling") on which they are about to report. No doubt the operation of the Community requires the steady, though not hasty, development of some uniformity of general law in the commercial field throughout the Community. But caution is needed. The present Directive, for example, would, if adopted, apply to a particular and relatively small section of the field of agency, some hard and fast rules quite unknown to the general agency law of the United Kingdom. As to product liability, paragraph 8 of the Committee's 63rd Report points out that "the two legal systems of the United Kingdom, like those of the majority of the other Member States, accept as a general rule the principle that non-contractual liability for loss or damage caused to others should be based on fault—in the case of product liability the tort or delict of negligence. To incorporate into such a legal system a special rule whereby liability for loss or damage of a particular kind from a particular cause is made independent of all fault raises legal and practical problems of great complexity . . .". The draft Directive on Doorstep Selling might jeopardise many sales activities in the United Kingdom which are open to abuse only to a very limited extent, and which can provide a valuable service to the consumer. The Committee are unconvinced that these interferences are, as the Commission contends, called for so as to prevent competition from being distorted. The general law of a nation is not something which has come into existence by accident; it arises from the local circumstances, habits, and sentiments of the people' changes in it must be effected only with care and where real need can be demonstrated.

Recommendation

12. The Committee are of the opinion that this draft Directive raises important questions of policy and principle. They recommend that this Report should be debated by the House.

Appendix 5—Department of Trade and Industry Guidance Notes on the Commercial Agents (Council Directive) Regulations 1993

CONTENTS

PART I

(a) *Historical background to the Directive*

The main purposes of the Directive were to harmonise the laws of member states, which the Council of Ministers considered detrimental to the functioning of the Single Market, and to strengthen the position of the commercial agent in relation to his principal.

Independent commercial agents can be in a weak position when dealing with their principals, although it is acknowledged that this is not always the case. Agents have found difficulty obtaining written contracts and access to all the information they need to verify that they were being paid the correct amount of commission, and some have suffered financially because their commission has not been paid promptly and because their contracts were terminated with little or no notice.

(b) *Preamble to the Directive*

The preamble to the Directive includes the following recitals which are at the heart of the thinking behind the need for the Directive:

> 'Whereas the differences in national laws concerning commercial representation substantially affect the conditions of competition and the carrying-on of that activity within the Community and are detrimental both to the protection available to commercial agents vis-a-vis their principals and to the security of commercial transactions; whereas moreover those differences are such as to inhibit substantially the conclusion and operation of commercial representation contracts where principal and commercial agent are established in different member states.
>
> Whereas trade in goods between member states should be carried on under conditions which are similar to those of a single market, and this necessitates approximation of the legal systems of the member states to the extent required for the proper functioning of the common market; whereas in this regard the rules concerning conflict of laws do not, in the matter of commercial representation, remove the inconsistencies referred to above, nor would they even if they were made uniform, and accordingly the proposed harmonisation is necessary notwithstanding the existence of those rules.'

(c) *Implementation of the Directive*

The Directive has been implemented as regards the law of England and Wales, and Scotland by Statutory Instrument No. 1993/3053 as amended by Statutory Instrument No. 1993/3173. Separate implementing provision is made in relation to Northern Ireland by the Commercial Agents (Council Directive) Regulations (Northern Ireland) 1993 (Statutory Rules for Northern Ireland No. 1993/483).

(d) *Purpose of the guidance notes*

The purpose of these notes is to assist commercial agents, principals, and their legal advisers to understand the effect of the Commercial Agents (Council Directive) Regulations 1993 by explaining why particular options for implementing the Directive were chosen and by setting out the Department's view on a number of points of difficulty. It must be emphasised that the Department's view is no more than that. As with other Community legislation, the Directive has to be interpreted uniformly throughout the Community and ultimately only the European Court can do that.

The guidance notes are in two parts. Part I continues by setting out, by regulation, the Department's general interpretation of the intention behind the Directive and hence the Regulations. Part II deals with other more specific and general points which arose during the consultation.

The notes deal only with those provisions which are novel or about which, during consultation, specific queries were raised. IN THAT CONNECTION IT SHOULD BE NOTED THAT THE TEXT OF REGULATIONS 5, 13, 14, 15, 18, 19, 21, 22 AND 23 IS NOT PRINTED, NOR DO THESE NOTES CONTAIN ANY SPECIFIC COMMENT ON THEM. Further issues on particular provisions may arise in the future, and the contact point is:

Christopher Farthing
Consumer Affairs Division 2a
Room 325
10–18 Victoria Street
London SW1H 0NN
Tel: 071 215 3302
Fax: 071 215 3396

The Department has taken the view that, for the most part, the substantive provisions of the Directive leave the member states with little or no discretion as to implementation of the Directive in national law and therefore, the wording of the Regulations follows that of the Directive very closely.

(e) Details of the Regulations and the Department's Interpretation

REGULATION 1

1(1) These Regulations may be cited as the Commercial Agents (Council Directive) Regulations 1993 and shall come into force on 1 January 1994.

1(2) These Regulations govern the relations between commercial agents and their principals and, subject to paragraph (3), apply in relation to the activities of commercial agents in Great Britain.

1(3) Regulations 3–22 do not apply where the parties have agreed that the agency contract is to be governed by the law of another member state.

INTERPRETATION

This Regulation sets out the circumstances in which the Regulations will apply to an agency contract. If the agent carries out his activities as a commercial agent in Great Britain, then the Regulations will apply *unless* the parties expressly choose the law of another member state as the law which is to apply to the agency contract. If the law of a non-EU country is chosen then the provisions of the Regulations are intended to override that choice of law in so far as any of the activities of the commercial agent are carried out in Great Britain.

Regulation 1(2) provides that the Regulations govern relations between commercial agents and their principals and apply in relation to the activities of commercial agents in *Great Britain* (whether or not the agent is physically based in Great Britain).

The provisions of the Regulations, where the agent carries on his activities outside Great Britain, do not, however, prevent the parties from choosing the law of a part of Great Britain (for example the law of England and Wales) and incorporating in the agency agreement some or all of the provisions of the Regulations which the parties might wish to agree should apply as though the agents' activities were, in fact, to be carried on in Great Britain. However, in such a case, if litigation arises, the court hearing the action may or may not:

  (i) uphold the choice of law, and

  (ii) accept the validity of such incorporation.

The state of the law of the other member states relating to commercial agents will depend, in part, on the manner in which the Directive has been implemented in those States, and advice as to the relevant foreign law (both within the EU and outside) should be sought in appropriate cases.

Some examples appear in the Annex to these notes which are intended to show the application (or otherwise) of the Regulations where the principal is based in one country and his agent performs his activities in another.

The Regulations apply to *Great Britain* (Regulation 2(5)). The Directive has been implemented separately in relation to Northern Ireland by the Commercial Agents (Council Directive) Regulations (Northern Ireland) 1993 (Statutory Rules for Northern Ireland No. 1993/483).

REGULATION 2

(*Articles 1 & 2 of the Directive*)

2(1) In these Regulations—

    'commercial agent' means a self-employed intermediary who has continuing authority to negotiate the sale or purchase of goods on behalf of another person (the 'principal'), or to negotiate and conclude the sale or purchase of goods on behalf of and in the name of that principal; but shall be understood as not including in particular:

(i) a person who, in his capacity as an officer of a company or association, is empowered to enter into commitments binding on that company or association;

(ii) a partner who is lawfully authorised to enter into commitments binding on his partners;

(iii) a person who acts as an insolvency practitioner (as that expression is defined in section 388 of the *Insolvency Act* 1986) or the equivalent in any other jurisdiction;

'commission' means any part of the remuneration of a commercial agent which varies with the number or value of business transactions;

'restraint of trade clause' means an agreement restricting the business activities of a commercial agent following termination of the agency contract.

2(2) These Regulations do not apply to—

(a) commercial agents whose activities are unpaid;

(b) commercial agents when they operate on commodity exchanges or in the commodity market;

(c) the Crown Agents for Overseas Governments and Administrations, as set up under the *Crown Agents Act* 1979, or its subsidiaries.

2(3) The provisions of the Schedule to these Regulations have effect for the purposes of determining the persons whose activities as commercial agents are to be considered secondary.

2(4) These Regulations shall not apply to the persons referred to in paragraph (3) above.

2(5) These Regulations do not extend to Northern Ireland.

INTERPRETATION

The Regulation sets out the definitions of the terms used within the Regulations and also excludes those agents where the activities are considered secondary.

The expression 'self-employed' is derived from Articles 52 and 57 of the Treaty of Rome (which deal with freedom of establishment and freedom to provide services) and is consistent with Community law, to be understood as including, for example, companies as well as self-employed individuals.

If an agent is appointed for a specified number of transactions, then he would be excluded from the scope of the Regulations, owing to his lack of continuing authority.

'Goods' clearly has to be interpreted in accordance with the EC Treaty and, for that reason, the Regulations do not define the word. However, it is considered that the definition of 'goods' in section 61(1) of the *Sale of Goods Act* 1979 as including, inter alia, all personal chattels other than things in action (eg shares) and money, may offer a reasonable guide, without necessarily being absolutely co-extensive with the Directive meaning.

Interpretation of the term 'secondary activities' and the provisions of the Schedule to the Regulations are dealt with later in these notes.

Some agents only effect introductions between their principals and third parties. The question arises as to whether such agents are commercial agents for the purposes of the Regulations. Such agents are sometimes known as 'canvassing' or 'introducing' agents. As such, they generally lack the power to bind their principals and are not really agents in the true sense of the word. However, to the extent that such an agent 'has continuing authority to negotiate the sale or purchase of goods' on behalf of his principal, even though, as a matter of fact, he merely effects introductions, it seems that he would fall within the definition of 'commercial agent' in Regulation 2(1). It is clear that an 'introducing' agent who lacks such authority falls outside the scope of the definition of 'commercial agent'. It may be that the courts would give a wide interpretation to the word 'negotiate' and that, as a result, 'introducing' agents will, in general have the benefit of the Regulations.

It is thought that the Regulations do apply to *del credere* agents who exhibit the characteristics set out in the definition of 'commercial agent'. The Department does not consider that the additional features of a del credere agency cause the agent to fall outside the definition. Questions can, however, arise as to whether a person is an agent at all who, in consideration of extra remuneration, guarantees to his principal that third parties with whom he enters into contracts on behalf of the principal will duly pay any sums becoming due under those contracts (and thus appears to be a del credere agent), or, whether that person is really acting on his own account.

Regulation 2(2)(b) provides that the Regulations do not apply to commercial agents when they operate on commodity exchanges or in the commodity market. A 'commodity' is any tangible good. So called 'commodity exchanges' deal in such goods and, to a large extent, in commodity 'futures' ie the right to buy or sell a particular commodity at a particular price at a particular time in the future, hence eg 'coffee futures'.

REGULATION 3
(*Article 3 of the Directive*)

3(1) In performing his activities a commercial agent must look after the interests of his principal and act dutifully and in good faith.

3(2) In particular, a commercial agent must—

(a) make proper efforts to negotiate and, where appropriate, conclude the transactions he is instructed to take care of;

(b) communicate to his principal all the necessary information available to him;

(c) comply with reasonable instructions given by his principal.

INTERPRETATION
This Regulation sets out the duties which the agent owes to the principal and, in effect, restates the duties owed at common law by an agent to his principal.

It is not certain how an agent's duty to 'communicate to his principal all the necessary information available to him' is to be fulfilled where an agent is acting for several principals. However, parties to contracts of commercial agency will doubtless wish to explore the possibility of agreeing on express terms to cover that situation.

REGULATION 4
(*Article 4 of the Directive*)

4(1) In his relations with his commercial agent a principal must act dutifully and in good faith.

4(2) In particular, a principal must—

(a) provide his commercial agent with the necessary documentation relating to the goods concerned;

(b) obtain for his commercial agent the information necessary for the performance of the agency contract, and in particular notify his commercial agent within a reasonable period once he anticipates that the volume of commercial transactions will be significantly lower than that which the commercial agent could normally have expected.

4(3) A principal shall, in addition, inform his commercial agent within a reasonable period of his acceptance or refusal of, and of any non-execution by him of, a commercial transaction which the commercial agent has procured for him.

INTERPRETATION

This Regulation deals with the principal's duties to the commercial agent. It is thought that these duties merely amplify the position at common law.

A principal is required to inform his commercial agent accordingly once the principal knows that business will decrease significantly or where an order will not be concluded.

REGULATION 6
(*Article 6 of the Directive*)

6(1) In the absence of any agreement as to remuneration between the parties, a commercial agent shall be entitled to the remuneration that commercial agents appointed for the goods forming the subject of his agency contract are customarily allowed in the place where he carries on his activities and, if there is no such customary practice, a commercial agent shall be entitled to reasonable remuneration taking into account all the aspects of the transaction.

6(2) This Regulation is without prejudice to the application of any enactment or rule of law concerning the level of remuneration.

6(3) Where a commercial agent is not remunerated (wholly or in part) by commission, Regulations 7–12 shall not apply.

INTERPRETATION

This Regulation is applicable only where the parties have not agreed on the remuneration payable by the principal to the agent. In the event of a dispute as to the remuneration payable, the court would be likely to have regard to custom in the commercial area concerned.

Should there be no identifiable custom in the area concerned, then it is considered that the agent would be entitled to a reasonable amount of remuneration. The position under the Regulations is thought to be similar to the position at common law.

It should be noted that where the commercial agent is not remunerated (wholly or in part) by commission, Regulations 7–12 do not apply.

REGULATION 7
(*Article 7 of the Directive*)

7(1) A commercial agent shall be entitled to commission on transactions concluded during the period covered by the agency contract—

(a) where the transaction has been concluded as a result of his action; or

(b) where the transaction is concluded with a third party whom he has previously acquired as a customer for transactions of the same kind.

7(2) A commercial agent shall also be entitled to commission on transactions concluded during the period covered by the agency contract where he has an exclusive right to a specific geographical area or to a specific group of customers and where the transaction has been entered into with a customer belonging to that area or group.

INTERPRETATION

This Regulation sets out the circumstances in which the agent may be considered to have earned his commission, and in that connection the view is taken that a transaction is 'concluded' when the principal and the third party have entered into a contract. The provisions of (2) include so called 'House Accounts' held by the principal ie where the principal deals directly with the third party although the agent has the rights to that area.

REGULATION 8
(*Article 8 of the Directive*)

Subject to Regulation 9 below, a commercial agent shall be entitled to commission on commercial transactions concluded after the agency contract has terminated if—

(a) the transaction is mainly attributable to his efforts during the period covered by the agency contract and if the transaction was entered into within a reasonable period after the contract terminated; or

(b) in accordance with the conditions mentioned in paragraph 7 above, the order of the third party reached the principal or commercial agent before the agency contract terminated.

INTERPRETATION

This Regulation sets out when the agent is entitled to commission on commercial transactions concluded after the agency contract has come to an end. In particular where the transaction was mainly a result of the agents' efforts during the contract and the transaction was entered into within a reasonable period after the end of the agency contract.

The principal and agent may attempt to define 'reasonable period' in their agreement. However, in the event of a dispute, despite any such definition, the matter would be ultimately for the decision of the Court.

If the order was placed with the principal or agent before the termination of the agency contract, but the contract was not concluded until afterwards, then the principal would still be liable to pay commission.

REGULATION 9

(*Article 9 of the Directive*)

9(1) A commercial agent shall not be entitled to the commission referred to in Regulation 7 above if that commission is payable, by virtue of Regulation 8 above, to the previous commercial agent, unless it is equitable because of the circumstances for

the commission to be shared between the commercial agents.

9(2) The principal shall be liable for any sum due under paragraph (1) above to the person entitled to it in accordance with that paragraph, and any sum which the other commercial agent receives to which he is not entitled shall be refunded to the principal.

INTERPRETATION

This Regulation deals with the apportionment of commission between a new agent and his predecessor for the same transaction.

The new agent is not entitled to commission if it is payable to the previous agent unless it is 'equitable because of the circumstances' for the commission to be shared between them.

It is the principal's duty to pay commission owing to agents and where commission is paid inadvertently to one agent which was in fact owed to the other, the agent must repay it or the principal reclaim it. In either circumstance the agent entitled to the commission should receive it.

REGULATION 10

(*Article 10 of the Directive*)

10(1) Commission shall become due as soon as, and to the extent that, one of the following circumstances occurs:

(a) the principal has executed the transaction; or

(b) the principal should, according to his agreement with the third party, have executed the transaction; or

(c) the third party has executed the transaction.

10(2) Commission shall become due at the latest when the third party has executed his part of the transaction or should have done so if the principal had executed his part of the transaction, as he should have.

10(3) The commission shall be paid not later than on the last day of the month following the quarter in which it became due, and, for the purposes of these Regulations, unless otherwise agreed between the parties, the first quarter period shall run from the date the agency contract takes effect, and subsequent periods shall run from that date in the third month thereafter or the beginning of the fourth month, whichever is the sooner.

10(4) Any agreement to derogate from paragraph (2) and (3) above to the detriment of the commercial agent shall be void.

INTERPRETATION
This Regulation sets out when the commission to be paid to an agent becomes due and when it should be paid.

A transaction may be considered to be 'executed' in any of the following circumstances:

 (i) when the principal has accepted or delivered the goods;

 (ii) when the principal should have accepted or delivered the goods;

 (iii) when the third party accepts or delivers the goods; or

 (iv) when the third party pays for the goods.

It is for the two parties to agree within the terms of the contract which of these circumstances will make the commission become due. Paragraph 2 of the Regulation provides for the latest date that the commission can become due.

It is not unusual for goods to be delivered by instalments. If the agency contract does not make specific provision for the matter, the question as to when commission is due would seem to depend upon the precise nature of the sale or purchase transaction. Where each instalment delivery is the subject of a separate contract, it seems likely that a separate commission payment will be due as each separate delivery is made, or should have been made. Where a single contract applies to a number of instalment deliveries, the position is somewhat less clear. However, in view of the words 'to the extent that' in Regulation 10(1) the agent may be entitled to the commission which is attributable to each particular instalment delivery.

It should be noted that paragraph (4) of Regulation 10 renders void any agreement to derogate to the detriment of the commercial agent from paragraphs (2) and (3) of the Regulation.

REGULATION 11
(*Article 11 of the Directive*)
11(1) The right to commission can be extinguished only if and to the extent that—

 (a) it is established that the contract between the third party and the principal will not be executed; and

 (b) that fact is due to a reason for which the principal is not to blame.

11(2) Any commission which the commercial agent has already received shall be refunded if the right to it is extinguished.

11(3) Any agreement to derogate from paragraph (1) above to the detriment of the commercial agent shall be void.

INTERPRETATION
The Regulation outlines the circumstances when the agent's right to commission is forfeited. Should a contract not be executed the principal must not be at fault for the entitlement to commission to be extinguished. Any commission already paid by the principal under these circumstances would be refunded.

REGULATION 12
(*Article 12 of the Directive*)
12(1) The principal shall supply his commercial agent with a statement of the commission due, not later than the last day of the month following the quarter in which the commission has become due, and such statement shall set out the main com-

ponents used in calculating the amount of commission.

12(2) A commercial agent shall be entitled to demand that he be provided with the information (and in particular an extract from the books) which is available to his principal and which he needs in order to check the amount of commission due to him.

12(3) Any agreement to derogate from paragraphs (1) and (2) above shall be void.

12(4) Nothing in this Regulation shall remove or restrict the effect of, or prevent reliance upon, any enactment or rule of law which recognises the right of an agent to inspect the books of the principal.

INTERPRETATION

The Regulation sets out the principal's obligation to provide the agent with a statement of commission due and must set out the main components in calculating the commission. It also requires the principal to provide the agent with all *necessary* information, including extracts from his (the principal's) books, to check the commission due, should the agent request such information.

N.B. the principal is only required to provide relevant extracts and *not* his full books.

REGULATION 16

(*Article 16 of the Directive*)

16 These Regulations shall not affect the application of any enactment or rule of law which provides for the immediate termination of the agency contract—

(a) because of the failure of one party to carry out all or part of his obligations under that contract; or

(b) where exceptional circumstances arise.

INTERPRETATION

This Regulation preserves the common law and statutory rules of jurisdictions within Great Britain which provide for the immediate termination of an agency contract on

the basis of the two matters set out in sub-paragraphs (a) and (b) of the Regulation. It is thought that the expression 'exceptional circumstances' in paragraph (b) would include matters falling within the doctrine of frustration.

REGULATION 17

(*Article 27 of the Directive*)

17(1) This Regulation has effect for the purpose of ensuring that the commercial agent is, after termination of the agency contract, indemnified in accordance with paragraphs (3) to (5) below or compensated for damage in accordance with paragraphs (6) and (7) below.

17(2) Except where the agency contract otherwise provides, the commercial agent shall be entitled to be compensated rather than indemnified.

17(3) Subject to paragraph (9) below and to Regulation 18 below, the commercial agent shall be entitled to an indemnity if and to the extent that—

(a) he has brought the principal new customers or has significantly increased the volume of business from existing customers and the principal continues to derive substantial benefits from the business with such customers; and

(b) the payment of this indemnity is equitable having regard to all the circumstances and, in particular, the commission lost by the commercial agent on the business transacted with such customers.

17(4) The amount of the indemnity shall not exceed a figure equivalent to an indemnity for one year calculated from the commercial agent's average annual remuneration over the preceding five years and if the contract goes back less than five years the indemnity shall be calculated on the average for the period in question.

17(5) The granting of an indemnity as mentioned above shall not prevent the commercial agent from seeking damages.

17(6) Subject to paragraph (9) and Regulation 18 below, the commercial agent shall be entitled to compensation for the damage he suffers as a result of the termination of his relations with his principal.

17(7) For the purposes of these Regulations such damage shall be deemed to occur particularly when the termination takes place in either or both of the following circumstances, namely circumstances which—

(a) deprive the commercial agent of the commission which proper performance of the agency contract would have procured for him whilst providing his principal with substantial benefits linked to the activities of the commercial agent; or

(b) have not enabled the commercial agent to amortise the costs and expenses that he had incurred in the performance of the agency contract on the advice of his principal.

17(8) Entitlement to the indemnity or compensation for damage as provided for under paragraphs (2) to (7) above shall also arise where the agency contract is terminated as a result of the death of the commercial agent.

17(9) The commercial agent shall lose his entitlement to the indemnity or compensation for damage in the instances provided for in paragraphs (2) to (8) above if within one year following termination of his agency contract he has not notified his principal that he intends pursuing his entitlement.

INTERPRETATION

The Regulation deals with entitlement to indemnity/compensation upon termination of the agency contract. It is for the two parties to choose which of these options they would wish to include in their contract with the backstop of compensation should no choice be indicated. There is however, nothing to preclude the two parties from agreeing to use the compensation provisions in some cases and indemnity ones in others when terminating a particular contract. The indemnity/compensation is only payable where the principal will continue to benefit from the business that the agent has brought to the principal.

It should be noted that although having fixed term contracts or giving correct periods of notice (see Regulation 15) could potentially reduce the level of indemnity compensation it would not necessarily exclude it. The issue of whether compensation is payable on the expiry of a fixed term contract or where the contractual notice period in an indefinite term contract has been given is a matter for the courts to decide.

It is thought that in view of the terms of Regulation 19 it would be possible for the two parties to derogate from this provision *after* the termination of the agency contract.

The word 'indemnity' has a rather more limited meaning than that which it normally bears in English law in that it:

(i) appears to fall short of a complete making good of the loss suffered by the principal; and

(ii) does not necessarily arise in relation to loss caused by the principal.

Its more limited nature may be inferred from Regulation 17(5) which contemplates the possibility of the agent wishing to seek damages. The amount of the indemnity is, in any event, limited by Regulation 17(4). The indemnity might appropriately be reviewed as approximating to a form of liquidated damages.

It remains to be seen how courts in Great Britain would assess amounts of indemnity, and the Department feels unable, at this stage, to offer any guidance as to the approach likely to be adopted.

Article 17.6 of the Directive requires the Commission to submit to the Council, by the end of 1994, a report on the implementation of Article 17 (indemnity/compensation) and, if necessary to submit to the Council proposals for amendments.

As to the meaning of 'substantial' in Regulation 17(3)(a), it is thought that word would be interpreted as meaning 'material 'or 'not insignificant' having regard to the history of dealings between the principal and the agents and other relevant circumstances.

'Equitable' in Regulation 17(3)(b) probably means 'just' or 'fair' rather than necessarily based on the doctrines or principles of equity—the latter, if they exist at all in the law of every member state, being bound to vary from State to State.

REGULATION 20
(Article 20 of the Directive)
20(1) A restraint of trade clause shall be valid only if and to the extent that—
  (a) it is concluded in writing; and
  (b) it relates to the geographical area or the group of customers and the geographical area entrusted to the commercial agent and to the kind of goods covered by his agency under the contract.
20(2) A restraint of trade clause shall be valid for not more than two years after the termination of the agency contract.
20(3) Nothing in this Regulation shall effect any enactment or rule of law which imposes other restrictions on the validity or enforceability of restraint of trade clauses or which enables a court to reduce the obligations on the parties resulting from such clauses.

INTERPRETATION
A 'restraint of trade clause' is any agreement which restricts the business activities of a commercial agent following termination of the agency contract (see the definition in Regulation 2).

The restraint of trade provisions only extend to the kind of goods that were covered in his contract. It is thought that the provisions would not extend to goods of a similar nature aimed at different types of purchasers.

THE SCHEDULE
1. The activities of a person as a commercial agent are to be considered secondary where it may reasonably be taken that the primary purpose of the arrangement with his principal is other than as set out in paragraph 2 below.
2. An arrangement falls within this paragraph if —
  (a) the business of the principal is the sale, or as the case may be purchase, of goods of a particular kind; and
  (b) the goods concerned are such that—
    (i) transactions are normally individually negotiated and concluded on a commercial basis, and
    (ii) procuring a transaction on one occasion is likely to lead to further transactions in those goods with that customer on future occasions, or to transactions in those goods with other customers in the same geographical area or among the same group of customers, and that accordingly it is in the commercial interests of the principal in developing the market in those goods to appoint a representative to such customers with a view to the representative devoting effort, skill and expenditure from its own resources to that end.
3. The following are indications that an arrangement falls within paragraph 2 above, and the absence of any of them is an indication to the contrary—
  (a) the principal is the manufacturer, importer or distributor of the goods;

(b) the goods are specifically identified with the principal in the market in question rather than, or to a greater extent than, with any other person;

(c) the agent devotes substantially the whole of his time to representative activities (whether for one principal or a number of principals whose interests are not conflicting);

(d) the goods are not normally available in the market in question other than by means of the agent;

(e) the arrangement is described as one of commercial agency.

4. The following are indications that an arrangement does not fall within paragraph 2 above—

(a) promotional material is supplied direct to potential customers;

(b) persons are granted agencies without reference to existing agents in a particular area or in relation to a particular group;

(c) customers normally select the goods for themselves and merely place their orders through the agent.

5. The activities of the following categories of persons are presumed, unless the contrary is established, not to fall within paragraph 2 above—

Mail order catalogue agents for consumer goods.

Consumer credit agents.

INTERPRETATION

The Schedule sets out the criteria for determining the persons whose activities as commercial agents are considered secondary under UK law and are excluded from the provisions of the Regulations by virtue of Regulation 2(3).

The first test is to determine whether or not a contract comes under the provisions of the Regulations. The determining factor is whether the agent is required to keep, as his own property, a considerable stock of the product.

The comparison to be made is between the agent's activities as a commercial agent and his other activities and not the relationship with the principal.

It is not possible to say which of the provisions in paragraphs 3 and 4 take priority and this will have to be determined on a case by case basis taking into account the exact nature of the agency contract.

PART II

(a) *Answers to specific questions raised during the consultation exercise*

Q. *Can the principle of set-off continue to apply?*

A. The Regulations do not mention set-off. It is thought that set-off will remain available to the principal, his agent and third parties in accordance with the rules of common law.

Q. *If a principal employs an agent to act for him in a number of different member states, could there be one agency contract governing the relationship?*

A. This would be possible subject to the comments made on page [109] concerning the applicability of English law to contracts outside the UK.

Q. *Regulation 17(8) expressly allows indemnity or compensation where the agency contract is terminated as a result of the commercial agent's death. Is the position the same if the commercial agent (being a company) goes into liquidation?*

A. Where the principal or agent is a company, at common law the actual authority of the principal or agent will be determined by its winding up or dissolution. It should be noted that where the authority is irrevocable it will not be determined by such events.

Q. *Can an age limit be fixed for a commercial agent?*

A. It is thought it can. Fixed contracts are permitted and if, for example, a 40 year old agent is appointed 'until he is 60' this is equivalent to a fixed contract for 20 years or until death.

Q. *To what extent can the Regulations be derogated from?*

A. There are three different types of Regulation within the Regulations: those which cannot be derogated from; those which cannot be derogated from to the detriment of the agent; and those which make no mention of derogation.

It can be argued that where Regulations mean there to be no derogation, they say so. It can also be said that if nothing is said it is to be inferred that it can be derogated from. If this is so then, for example, the agency contract could express the agent's entitlement to commission as arising where the transaction is 'wholly' as a result of his action.

The Department's conclusion on this, although not a firm one, is that the terms of the agency contract can vary the events upon which the agent becomes entitled to commission, although they could not do so to an extent that it excludes the right altogether since this would conflict with Regulation 11(1).

Q. *Are sub-agency agreements covered by the Regulations?*

A. Whilst the position is not clear, the Regulations are, in principle, capable of covering sub-agency agreements.

Q. *Is it possible to include a liquidated damages provision within the contract?*

A. Liquidated damages is a provision within a contract where one party agrees to pay to the other a specified sum of money in the event of a breach of contract.

Such clauses may be permissible provided that they represent a genuine pre-estimate of damage.

The Department's conclusion on this, although not a firm one, is that the terms of the agency contract can vary the events upon which the agent becomes entitled to commission, although they could not do so to an extent that it excludes the right altogether since this would conflict with Regulation 11(1).

Q. *Are sub-agency agreements covered by the Regulations?*

A. Whilst the position is not clear, the Regulations are, in principle, capable of covering sub-agency agreements.

Q. *Is it possible to include a liquidated damages provision within the contract?*

A. Liquidated damages is a provision within a contract where one party agrees to pay to the other a specified sum of money in the event of a breach of contract.

Such clauses may be permissible provided that they represent a genuine pre-estimate of damage.

Although one object of the clause will be to limit the principal's liability, it may not be a pure limitation clause in that it forms a compromise between the parties and is intended to be enforceable whether the actual loss is greater or less than the sum agreed. Nevertheless, as against the principal, such provisions risk attack by the agent as void by virtue of Regulation 19.

Q. *Are the Regulations retrospective?*

A. Only in the sense that they apply to all contracts as from 1 January 1994 and it is inevitable that in some respects account will have to be taken of what occurred before 1994. The Regulations do not, however, apply so as to affect the rights and liabilities of either the principal or agent if they have accrued before 1994.

Q. *Do the Regulations apply to agents who sell Christmas hampers?*

A. It is believed that the activities of such agents would be likely to be held as secondary, thus rendering the agents (by virtue of Regulation 2(4)) outside the scope of the Regulations.

ANNEX

(a) *Examples on the application of Regulation 1*

1 *Principal in Great Britain, agent in France (EU member state)*

The Regulations do *not* apply, since the agent's activities are in France and therefore are not in Great Britain (see Regulation 1(2)). However, if the parties choose English law to govern the contract between them, it is suggested that the contract could provide for the provisions of the Regulations to apply to the relations between them as though the agent's activities were in Great Britain. Although the agent is in France, if the parties choose English law to govern the agency contract, the provisions of French law implementing the Directive would not apply (unless those provisions are held to be 'mandatory rules' (see Article 3 of the Rome Convention on the law applicable to contractual obligations)).

2 *Principal in Great Britain, agent in Australia (non-EU member state)*

The Regulations do not apply, given that the agent's activities are in Australia and therefore not in Great Britain. However, again, it is thought that, as in the first example above, the parties could specifically adopt the provisions of the Regulations by contractual provision to that effect. Any 'mandatory rules' of the relevant Australian State(s) would need to be considered in case they were capable of over-riding any provisions of the contract.

3 *Principal in France, agent in Great Britain*

In the absence of an express choice of French law, the Regulations would apply, given that the agent's activities are in Great Britain. If the parties choose French law, the Regulations would not apply (see Regulation 1(3)), and the agent would have the protection of the Directive as implemented in French law.

4 *Principal in USA, agent in Great Britain*

If the law of a part of Great Britain is chosen by the parties to govern the agency contract, it is concluded that the Regulations will apply.

However, if the law of a state of the US is chosen, no doubt an exclusive jurisdiction clause in favour of the courts of that state would also be included in the agency contract, on the basis of which a Court in Great Britain may well decline jurisdiction. In the absence of such a clause, or if a Court in Great Britain nevertheless accepts jurisdiction, the Court may take the view (perhaps after making an Article 177 reference to the European Court) that the Regulations constitute mandatory rules of the law of a part of Great Britain and that the Regulations should, accordingly, apply, the intention of the Directive being to afford certain protections to commercial agents operating within the European Union (but possibly only where the principal is also established within the European Union (see the recitals to the Directive referred to on page 1 of the notes under the heading 'Preamble to the Directive')). Thus an agent in such circumstances would be unwise to assume that, despite operating in Great Britain, the Regulations would apply.

Appendix 5(a)—Department of Trade and Industry: Implementation of the EC Directive on Self-Employed Commercial Agents

An Explanatory and Consultative Note

CONTENTS

INTRODUCTION

The EC Directive on self-employed commercial agents (Council Directive 86/653/EEC) was adopted on 18 December 1986 after some ten years of discussion. The purpose of the Directive is to harmonise the laws of the Member States on the relationship between commercial agents and their principals and to strengthen the position of the commercial agent. It does this by setting out basic rules regulating the main aspects of the agency contract between them. The United Kingdom and Ireland are required to adapt their laws to give effect to the Directive by 1 January 1994. The remaining Member States must implement the Directive by 1 January 1990 although Italy, exceptionally, has until 1 January 1993 to implement Article 17.

2   The present legal position in the United Kingdom is described at A of this Consultative Document. At B the main features of the individual Articles of the Directive are summarised and explanatory notes given where appropriate. Two Articles of the Directive require Member States to choose one of two specific alternatives. Also, in respect of certain other Articles the Directive allows Member States to take different positions on a few points. These options are discussed in C.

3   The Department would welcome views on the various issues described in this Consultative Document. They should be sent by Friday 30 October 1987 to:

> Chemicals, Textiles, Paper, Timber,
> Miscellaneous Manufacturing and Service
> Industries Division (CTPS)
> Department of Trade and Industry
> Room 804A
> Ashdown House
> 123 Victoria Street
> London SW1E 6RB

4   Further copies of this Consultative Document can be obtained by telephoning (01) 212 0022 or by applying in writing to the address given in the previous paragraph.

A THE LEGAL POSITION

5   There is little United Kingdom statute law in this area: the rights and duties of the principal and commercial agent depend on the express or implied terms of the agency relationship between them. Common law rules exist which apply in the absence of, or may override, express stipulation by the parties. The rules which will apply when the Directive is implemented will be significantly different and will involve changes in the existing law to introduce detailed provisions governing certain aspects of the relationship between principal and agent. It is proposed to make the necessary changes through secondary legislation under Section 2(2) of the European Communities Act 1972. There are further comments in part B when individual Articles refer to the position under Member States national laws.

B SUMMARY OF THE DIRECTIVE

Chapter 1: Scope

6   *Article 1* requires Member States to apply the harmonisation measures outlined in the Directive to their laws governing the relationship between commercial agents and their principals. It defines the term "commercial agent" for the purposes of the Directive as being a self-employed intermediary (individual, company or partnership) who has continuing authority to negotiate the purchase or sale of goods on behalf of another person (the principal) or to negotiate and conclude such transactions on behalf of and in the name of that principal. The Directive applies to both incorporated and unincorporated bodies as well as individuals.

7   Article 1 also lists certain categories of persons the term "commercial agent" is *not* regarded as including. These are:

> —officers of a company or association (as agents of the company or association) and partners (as agents of the partnership);
> —receivers, liquidators and trustees in bankruptcy.

8   The Directive does not apply to commercial agents or distributors who purchase on their own account and in their own name (as principals) for resale nor does it apply

to services. The wide range of service agencies such as travel agents, advertising agents and so on, are not covered.

9   *Article 2* lists categories of commercial agent specifically excluded from the scope of the Directive. These are:

—commercial agents whose activities are unpaid, ie not paid by monetary consideration or in kind;

—commercial agents when they operate on commodity exchanges or in the commodity market. A clearer definition will be required in the United Kingdom's implementing legislation and comments are invited from those with a particular interest or involvement in this area on a definition along the following lines:-

commercial agents operating on a commodity exchange in any part of the world or in the commodity market. For the purposes of this exclusion the term 'commodity market' is defined as a 'a market for any kind of tangible assets (other than assets of a financial nature) which is in fact traded on a commodity exchange in any part of the world'

—the Crown Agents for Overseas Governments.

10   Member States are also given the option of not applying the Directive to people whose activities as commercial agents are considered secondary by the law of that Member State. It is our intention that certain secondary activities be clearly excluded from the scope of the Directive. This is discussed further under C(ii) paragraphs 50 and 51.

11   Whether Member States' commercial agents operating *outside* the European Community would be subject to the Directive would depend on the proper law governing the agency contract, ie if the law governing the agency contract was that of a Member State then the Directive would apply.

Chapter II: Rights and Obligations

12   *Article 3* lists the essential duties of the agent, notably his *general* duty to look after his principal's interests and to act "dutifully and in good faith" and his *specific* duty to make proper efforts to negotiate such business as his principal has entrusted to him to communicate with his principal and to comply with all reasonable instructions from his principal. Under United Kingdom common law the agent already has a number of fiduciary duties which broadly require him to act in good faith.

13   *Article 4* lists the essential duties of the principal. In particular it requires the principal to provide the necessary documentation and information to the agent for the performance of the agency contract to notify the agent as soon as he anticipates the volume of business will be significantly lower than the agent could normally have expected and to inform the agent of his acceptance, refusal and any non-execution of the business the agent has procured for him. In order to comply with the last requirement a principal would need to keep his agent informed of any omissions on his own part in completing his side of the transaction.

14   In addition to the mandatory requirement for the principal to inform the agent of his acceptance, refusal and any non-execution of the business the agent procured for him (Article 4(3)), it is open to Member States to include a provision requiring the

principal to inform the agent within a reasonable period of the *execution* of a commercial transaction the agent procured for the principal. This is discussed more fully at C(ii) paragraph 52.

15   *Article 5* states that the parties may not derogate from the provisions of Articles 3 and 4, ie these provisions are binding on the parties.

Chapter III: Remuneration

16   *Article* 6 records the commercial agent's right to remuneration according to customary practice in the place where he carries on his activities or, where there is no customary practice, to such remuneration as is reasonable, in the absence of prior agreement between the parties and without prejudice to Member States' compulsory provisions on the level of remuneration. There are no compulsory provisions in United Kingdom law covering the level of remuneration for commercial agents although there is generally in any event an implied term for reasonable remuneration. The "place" where the agent "carries on his activities" embraces his operating territory as well as his office base.

17   *Articles 7 to 12* only apply where the agreement or custom is that the agent is to be paid by commission (and not solely by a flat rate fee), or where the reasonable remuneration to which he is entitled in the absence of agreement or any custom is payment by commission.

18   *Article 7* specifies the circumstances under which the agent entitled to commission on commercial transactions concluded during the period of the agency contract. Commission is to be payable on repeat orders from customers *acquired* by the agent even if those orders were not placed through the agent (Article 7(1)).

Additionally, where an agent has an exclusive responsibility for a specific area or group of customers, he is again to be entitled to commission on transactions which were not negotiated by him if they were concluded with customers within that allocated area or clientele, even where those customers had *not* been acquired by him (Article 7(2)). Member States must decide whether to extend this automatic entitlement so that it applies also where the agent's field of responsibility has *not* been given to him to the exclusion of the rights of any other agent (or the principal himself) to operate within it. This is discussed further at C(i), paragraphs 40 and 41.

19   *Article 8* states that the agent is entitled to commission on commercial transactions concluded after the agency contract has come to an end if the transaction was mainly a result of the agents efforts during the period of the agency contract and the transaction was entered into within a reasonable period after the end of the agency contract and/or the order of the third party reached the principal or agent before the agency contract came to an end.

20   *Article 9* deals with the apportionment of commission between a new agent and his predecessor for the same transaction. The new agent is not entitled to commission in accordance with Article 7 if it is payable to the previous agent in accordance with Article 8, unless it is "equitable because of the circumstances" for the commission to be shared between them. The new agent therefore loses his right to commission where his predecessor was mainly responsible for the eventual transaction although this Article allows for apportionment where this would be equitable. However, no

apportionment is available to the Predecessor agent who was partly but not mainly responsible for the transaction concluded by his successor.

21 *Article 10* prescribes

    (i) the point at which commission becomes due, namely when the principal has or should have carried out the transaction or, if earlier, the third party has completed his part of the transaction. (Article 10 goes on to add that the latest date that the commission is due is when the third party has carried out his part of the transaction or should have done so if the principal had completed his part of the transaction as he should have; but it is difficult to see what this adds).

    (ii) the time of payment of commission.

The parties are only permitted to agree on different provisions to those set out in Articles 10(2) and (3) if these are no less favourable to the agent.

22 *Article 11* outlines the circumstances when the agent's right to commission is forfeited. It is intended to *protect* the agent's right to commission by specifying that this right can only be extinguished in the strictly limited circumstance of establishing that the contract between third party and principal will not go ahead for a reason that is not the fault of the principal (ie circumstances outside the principal's control). However, this Article also provides for commission the agent has already received to be refunded if it is established that his right to it had been extinguished. The parties may only derogate from Article 11(1) if this is to the benefit of the agent.

23 In connection with Article 11(1) non-execution of the contract is not regarded as including cases where the principal is paid in another capacity in connection with the transaction. Thus where the principal is indemnified for the non-performance of the contract by receiving payments under an insurance policy, guarantee or contract of indemnity, commission remains payable by the principal.

24 *Article 12* specifies the principal's obligation to provide the agent with a statement of commission due requiring the principal to provide the agent with all necessary information, including extracts from his (the principal's) books, to check the commission due. (However see also the comments under Article 21 which precludes any disclosure from the principal's books which would be contrary to public policy). Article 12 also stipulates that the Directive shall not conflict with Member States' national provisions which recognise the right of the agent to inspect the principal's books. Under United Kingdom law the agent has the eight to inspect the principal's books only in cases of litigation. The parties may not agree on provisions different to Articles 12(1) and (2) if they are less favourable to the agent.

Chapter IV: Conclusion and Termination of the Agency Contract

25 *Article 13* entitles each party to receive from the other on request a signed written contract setting out the terms of the agency contract. They are entitled to require this at any time even if they have previously agreed not to. Member States are also allowed to provide that the agency contract is not valid unless evidenced in writing. This option is discussed further under C(ii) paragraph 53.

26 *Article 14* provides that an agency contract for a fixed period which continues to be performed by both parties after that period has expired shall be deemed to be

converted into an agency contract for an indefinite period. This provision is relevant to the calculation of the periods of notice which must be given to terminate an open ended (not fixed term) agency contract which are laid down in Article 15.

27   *Article 15* prescribes the minimum periods of notice for open ended agency contracts of one month for the first year of the contract, two months for the second, three months for the third and subsequent years. This Article also gives Member States the option of fixing certain minimum periods of notice for the fourth and subsequent years of the agency contract (up to a maximum of six months). This is considered in more detail at C(ii) paragraph 54.

28   Article 15 also applies to collective contracts when, in Member States' legislation, such contracts have legal or contractual force. The term "collective contracts. ordinarily means agreements between organisations of employees and those of employers. The Government is not aware of any collective contracts covering commercial agents' transactions in the United Kingdom. Consequently it is not intended to deal with this in the implementing legislation.

29   *Article 16* provides that the Directive will not affect the laws of Member States relating to immediate termination of the agency contract where (a) one party fails to carry out his obligations and (b) exceptional circumstances arise. "Exceptional circumstances" means circumstances which under the law of the Member State give grounds for immediate termination of the contractual relationship, such as force majeure or unforeseeable, uncontrollable events. Under United Kingdom law, on breach of contract by one party the other party has a right to sue for damages and may also have the right to treat the agency contract as repudiated (and so cancel it). Where exceptional circumstances arise, a frustrating event freezes the agency contract and releases the parties from any further implementation of the contract. Any payments which remain to be made cease to be payable except in so far as the court, in its discretion, decides that payment should be made for benefits already conferred or expenses already incurred.

30   *Article 17* requires Member States to include in their implementing legislation a provision ensuring that the agent is entitled, in certain circumstances, to receive *either* a lump-sum "indemnity" in accordance with the provisions of Article 17(2) *or* compensation for "damage" in accordance with the provisions of Article 17(3), as a result of termination of the agency contract. Such a provision will be new in UK law and is discussed more fully in C(i) paragraphs 42–49. Article 17(2a) Indent 2 allows Member States to take any restraint of trade clause which is included in the agency contract into account when assessing the amount of "indemnity" that is equitable. This is discussed further under C(ii) paragraph 55. Article 17(6) stipulates that the Commission shall report to the Council by 1 January 1995 on the implementation of Article 17 and submit proposals for amendments as necessary. This provision relates to a *review* of the operation of Article 17.

31   *Article 18* specifies the circumstances where the "indemnity"/compensation is not payable. These are when:

—the agent is guilty of a repudiatory breach of the agency contract (the entitlement is unaffected where it is the principal who is in breach);

—the agent has given contractual notice for reasons other than age, infirmity or illness:

—the agent has assigned the benefits and obligations of the agency contract to another person with the principal's consent.

32   *Article 19* renders both Articles 17 and 18 binding to the extent that the parties may not agree on different arrangements, if they are less favourable to the agent, before the agency contract expires.

33   *Article 20* deals with restraint of trade agreements (ie agreements which restrict the agent's business activities after termination of the agency contract). It specifies that such agreements are only valid if they are in writing and relate to the geographical area, or the group of customers as well as the area, entrusted to the agent and the kind of goods covered by the agency contract. The restraint can last for up to two years only of any period for which it is expressed to last as from termination of the agency contract.

34   *Article 20 (4)* states that Article 20 shall not affect national laws that impose other restrictions on the validity or enforceability of restraint of trade agreements or which enable the courts to reduce the obligations on the parties resulting from such an agreement. In the United Kingdom there is a general common law restriction on the enforceability of restraint of trade agreements in that they must be reasonable in ambit.

35   *Article 21* specifies that nothing in the Directive shall require a Member State to provide for the disclosure of information where this would be contrary to public policy. This provision limits the agent's right to have access to extracts from the principal's books (Article 12(2)) in cases where there is information relating to national security to protect.

36   *Article 22* lays down the transitional periods for implementing the Directive. For Member States *other than the United Kingdom and Ireland* the Directive is to be implemented before 1 January 1990. It will apply as from the date of implementation to new agency contracts. Contracts already in existence at the date of implementation must comply before 1 January 1994. Subject to those limits, the date of implementation is left to the choice of individual Member States. By way of exception, Italy has until 1 January 1993 to implement Article 17. The United Kingdom and Ireland must implement the Directive by 1 January 1994 in relation to both future and current agency contracts. The United Kingdom and Ireland have been granted this additional four year transitional period in recognition of the more fundamental changes that will be required to adapt their legal systems to implement the Directive compared to the position in other Member States.

37   The Government is committed to keeping to a minimum the burden placed on business by national and Community measures. An indication from interested parties of any additional costs or delays or other burdens they are likely to face when the Directive is implemented in the United Kingdom would therefore be welcome.

38   The full text of the Directive is provided in the Annex.

C *OPTIONS*

39   The Directive requires Member States to select one of two specific alternatives in respect of two provisions (Articles 7(2) and 17). For certain other Articles the Directive allows Member States to take different positions on some points (Articles 2(2), 4(3), 13(2), 15(3) and 17(2a) Indent 2). These options are discussed below and comments on them are invited.

(i) Articles where choice of a specific alternative is required

40 Article 7(2) deals with an agent's entitlement to commission on transactions other than those initiated by himself when the principal has placed such contracts during the period of the agency contract with third parties within the agent's allocated catchment area or pool of customers. Member States are required to choose whether their legislation should confer this entitlement where the agent is entrusted with a specific geographical area or group of customers (but not necessarily exclusively) (Indent 1), or only where he has an exclusive right (Indent 2) to an area or group of customers.

41 The Government's initial preference is for Indent 2. It finds it difficult to see the justification for the wider-ranging option that Indent 1 would give to the agent. However comments are invited from interested parties on their preferred choice with supporting arguments.

42 *Article 17* introduces a new concept into United Kingdom law. It sets out the agent's right, in certain circumstances on termination of the contract, to an "indemnity" by way of recompense for contribution to the principal's continuing goodwill (Article 17(2)) *or* compensation payment for "damage" (Article 17(3)). Member States are required to include one of these options in their implementing legislation.

43 The "indemnity" or compensation is due when the agency contract is terminated. The Government regards termination as including:

   (i) the principal's breach of the agency contract (and the agent's acceptance of his repudiation), which might include service of a notice shorter than provided for in Article 15 (Article 18(b)). In the case of an "indemnity", entitlement is to be additional to any claim for damages at common law

   (ii) the frustration of the agency contract, including the agent's death (Article 17(4)), retirement or illness (Article 18(b)).

   (iii) the principal giving notice under Article 15 or under an express term for early termination of a fixed-term contract, ie a break-clause:

   (iv) the expiry by passage of time of a fixed term agency contract.

However it is a matter of doubt whether either of the events in (iii) and (iv) could give rise to any deemed "damage" for which compensation under Article 17(3) could be claimed since the termination here would not be premature.

44 No payment arises where the agent:

   (i) is guilty of a repudiatory breach of the agency contract;

   (ii) has given contractual notice for reasons other than age, infirmity or illness

   (iii) has assigned the benefits and obligations of the agency contract to another person.

"Indemnity" Payment

45 *Article 17(2)* lists three conditions for entitlement to an "indemnity" payment:

   (i) contribution by the agent to the principal's goodwill by either:

     (a) a significant increase to business with existing customers, or

     (b) the introduction of new customers:

   (ii) substantial continuing benefits to the principal; and

   (iii) that it is equitable in all the circumstances and in view of the commission the agent has lost.

46   The method of calculation for the indemnity. payment is outlined in Article 17(2b). This sets a maximum size to the payment, namely one year's remuneration, calculated as the average annual remuneration over the preceding five years (total of preceding five years' remuneration divided by five) or the average for any shorter period that the agent has been engaged. It should be noted that this is an upper limit. Since the agent is only entitled to an "indemnity" "to the extent that . . . it is equitable" the amount would be whatever sum is fair and reasonable as determined by agreement (or in default of agreement, by the court), up to that limit.

Compensation for "Damage"

47   *Article 17(3)* specifies the one basic condition for entitlement to compensation, namely "damage" to the agent on termination of the agency contract. Two examples of such "damage" are given:

      (i)   (a)   deprivation of any commission which proper performance of the agency contract would have earned, and

           (b)   substantial benefit (in terms of goodwill) to the principal; or

      (ii)   unrecovered expenses incurred by the agent on the principal's encouragement.

48   If the agent intends to pursue his entitlement to indemnity or compensation for damages he must notify the principal of this intention within one year following termination of the agency contract (Article 17(5)).

49   The Government has an open mind on which option should be chosen and invites comments from interested parties on this important matter.

      (ii)   Articles where Member States may some points take different positions on

50   *Article 2(2)* allows Member States to exclude from the scope of the Directive persons whose activities as commercial agents are deemed by national law to be "secondary". No general definition of "secondary activities" exists under United Kingdom law. It is the Government's intention to define and exclude such activities under United Kingdom implementing legislation.

51   At present the Government has in mind to exclude the following categories of agent from the scope of the Directive:

    —all persons whose activity as a commercial agent is not their primary "business" occupation. Thus, for example, merchants whose primary occupation is the buying and selling of goods on their own behalf but who occasionally act as an agent for another person, would be excluded.

    —all persons for whom the selling of goods from mail order catalogues is a "secondary" activity (although often the sole "business" activity). Thus the many housewives who spend a few hours a week selling from such catalogues would be excluded.

Comments on the above and suggestions of other categories of agent for exclusion under this Article are invited.

52   *Article 4(3)* Under this provision the principal is required to inform the agent within a reasonable period of his acceptance, refusal and any non-execution of a commercial transaction which the agent has brought his way. The Government does not, therefore, intend to stipulate in its implementing legislation that the principal must also inform the agent of his execution of the commercial transaction the agent procured for him. It does not regard this as a matter for legislation bearing in mind that commission becomes due when, under the agreement negotiated by the agent, the

principal ought to have carried out the transaction, even if he has not actually done so (Article 10(1b)). Also when the transaction falls through for reasons for which the principal is not to blame so that the agent is deprived of his commission (Article 11(1)), the principal is obliged to inform the agent that the contract has not been performed (Article 4(3)).

53   *Article 13(2)* allows Member States to provide that the agency contract is not valid unless evidenced in writing. Current United Kingdom law does not require commercial contracts to be evidenced in writing. It may be sensible to retain the degree of flexibility provided by Article 13(1) to cover exceptional cases where the agent prefers not to have a written contract and those minor transactions where written contracts are not worthwhile. In any event Article 13(1), from which the parties to the agency contract may not derogate, clearly stipulates that the renunciation of the right to a signed written document setting out the terms of the agency contract will not be effective. Written agency contracts would be expected to be the normal practice following implementation of the Directive. Comments from interested parties on this matter are invited.

54   *Article 15(3)* gives Member States the option of fixing minimum periods of notice (stipulated in this provision) for the fourth and subsequent years for indefinite period agency contracts. The Government does not propose to take up this option. It feels the three months notice provided for in Article 15(2) is sufficient. If the parties want to fix longer periods of notice this is a matter for agreement between them.

55   *Article 17(2a) Indent 2* An earlier draft of the Directive included a provision by which, except on the agent's death, the maximum amount of "indemnity" under Article 17(2b) was to be halved if the agency contract did not include any restraint of trade clause. This provision has now been deleted from the Directive. However Member States now have the option of legislating to the effect that the inclusion of a restraint of trade clause in the agency contract should be taken into account in assessing the amount of "indemnity" that is equitable. Views on whether such a provision should be included in the United Kingdom's implementing legislation are invited.

Appendix 6—1996 Commission Report on the Application of Article 17 of Council Directive 86/653

This Report is made under Article 17(6) of Council Directive on the co- ordination of the laws of the Member States relating to Self-Employed Commercial Agents 86/653/EEC.[1] Article 17 of Directive requires Member States to take the measures necessary to ensure that the commercial agent is, after termination of the agency contract, indemnified or compensated.

Article 17 represents a compromise between the Member States. It was therefore agreed that Member States should have the choice between the indemnity system and the compensation system and that the Commission would undertake a report to the Council on the practical consequences of the different solutions.

This report is made on the basis of responses to a questionnaire which was sent out, inter alia, to organisations representing agents and principals, chambers of commerce and federations of industry and legal practitioners specialising in agency law. The authorities of Member States were also invited to contribute with their views and experience.

THE TWO SYSTEMS

1. The Indemnity System

Under the indemnity system, the agent is entitled, after cessation of the contract, to payment of an indemnity if and to the extent that he has brought new customers to the principal or has significantly increased the volume of business with existing customers and the principal continues to derive substantial benefits from such customers after the cessation of the contract. The payment of the indemnity must be equitable having regard to all the circumstances and, in particular, the commission lost by the commercial agent on the business transacted with such customers. Finally, the Directive provides a ceiling on the level of indemnity of one year calculated from the agent's average annual remuneration over the preceding five years and if the contract goes back less than five years the maximum is to be calculated on the average for the period in question.

The indemnity represents the continuing benefits to the principal due to the efforts of the agent. The agent, however, will only have received commission during the duration of the contract, which will not typically reflect the value of the goodwill generated for the principal. It is for this reason that the payment of a goodwill indemnity is commercially justified. An indemnity will only be payable if the agent has brought to the principal new customers or increased business with existing customers. If no goodwill has been generated

[1] OJL 382 p 17 of 31.12.1986

or there is a group of customers whom the principal can derive no benefit from, no indemnity need be paid. Therefore, a principal should not be forced to pay an unreasonable amount of indemnity.

The indemnity system was modelled on Article 89b of the German Commercial Code which had provided for the payment of a goodwill indemnity since 1953 and concerning which a large body of case-law has developed regarding its calculation. This case-law and practice should provide invaluable assistance to the Courts of other Member States when seeking to interpret the provisions of Article 17(2) of the Directive.

First it is necessary to ascertain whether an agent has a right to an indemnity having regard to the circumstances in which the agency contract was terminated An indemnity is payable on termination of the contract except where one of the circumstances in Article 18 of the Directive applies. Clearly, the indemnity is payable on the end of a fixed term contract and in principle, an indemnity or limited indemnity is payable on the bankruptcy of the principal.

Secondly, the conditions set out in Article 17(2)(a) of the Directive have to be met, namely that either the agent has brought new customers or has substantially increased the volume of business with existing customers. As regards the volume of business with old customers, the German courts look to see if the increase in volume is such that it can be considered to be economically equivalent to the acquisition of a new customer. In relation to new customers, the addition of one new customer is sufficient. However, new customers from outside his territory for which the agent is not entitled to commission are excluded as there is no loss of commission for which the agent needs to be compensated. The agent must have acquired the new client and in this respect the instrumentality of the agent is crucial. A small level of involvement is sufficient and it is enough that the agent has merely contributed to bringing the new customer. However, the agent must have played an active role and therefore the existence of a new customer who falls within the territorial scope of an exclusive agency agreement will not automatically suffice

Thirdly, the principal must continue after the end of the agency contract to derive substantial benefits with such customers. This is presumed to be the case even if the principal sells his business or client list if it can be shown that the purchaser will use the client base.[2] If the agent continues to meet the needs of the same clients for the same products, but for a different principal, the agent is prevented from seeking an indemnity.[3] It is also possible for the court to consider a fall in the turnover of the principal's business. Fourthly, the payment of an indemnity must 'be equitable.

As to the actual calculation of the indemnity, it is undertaken in the following way:

Stage 1

(a) The first stage in line with the second indent of Article 17(2)(a) is to ascertain the number of new customers and the increased volume of business with existing customers. Having identified such customers the gross commission on them is calculated for the last 12 months of the agency contract. Fixed remuneration can be included if it can be considered to be remuneration for new customers.[4] Special circumstances may justify departing from this, for example, where is a long start up period.

---

[2] Case 18 U 162/76 Oberlandesgeticht Hamm of 14.3.1977
[3] Case BB 605/60 Bundesgerichtshof of 25.4.1960
[4] Case VII ZR 194/63 Bundesgerichtshof of 15.2.1965

(b) An estimate is then made as to the likely future duration of the advantages to the principal deriving from business with the new customers and such old customers with whom the business has been significantly increased (intensified customers) which is calculated in terms of years. The aim is to predict the likely length of time the business with the new and intensified customers will last. This will involve considering the market situation at time of termination and the sector concerned The fact that sales drop after termination of the contract does not automatically lead to a corresponding reduction in the level of indemnity as sales may decline due to lowering s in quality of goods or competition.[5] The usual period is 2–3 years, but can be as much as 5 years.

(c) The next factor to consider is the rate of migration. It is acknowledged that over time customers will be lost as customers naturally move away. The rate of migration is calculated as a percentage of commission on a per annum basis and is taken from the particular experience of the agency in question. This clearly varies, but in one case the Bundesgerichtshof held that the rate of migration was 38%.[6]

(d) The figure is then reduced in order to calculate the present value taking into account that there is an accelerated receipt of income. Such a calculation based on average interest rates is a concept found in other jurisdictions

Stage 2

It is at this stage that the question of equity is considered as set out in Article 17(2)(a) second indent of the Directive. The figure is rarely adjusted for reasons of equity in practice. The following factors are taken into account:

—Whether the agent is retained by other principals;

—The fault of the agent;

—The level of remuneration of the agent. For example, did the principal recently reduce the rate of commission e.g. because he felt that agent's earnings were becoming too high or pay to the agent a large amount of commission on contracts with customers which the agent did not introduce or had little to do with? Also, did the agent receive special compensation for keeping a consignment inventory, special bonuses for new clients, del credere commission, any special allowance for trade fairs or extra payments for sub-agents? Did he incur costs regarding loss of sub-agents?

—Decrease in turnover of the principal;

—Extent of the advantage to the principal;

—Payment of pension contributions by the principal;

—The existence of restraint of trade clauses. Clearly, a principal will be required to pay a higher indemnity for this.

Stage 3

The amount calculated under Stages 1 and 2 is then compared with the maximum under Article 19(2)(b) of the Directive. This provision provides that the amount of the indemnity may not exceed a figure equivalent to remuneration for one year calculated from the

---

[5] BB 227/70 Celle of 13.1 1.69
[6] Case VIII ZR 94/93 Bundesgerichtshof of 23.2.1994

commercial agent's average annual remuneration over the preceding five years and if the contract goes back less than five years the indemnity shall be calculated on the average for the period in question. The maximum is in fact therefore a final corrective, rather than as a method of calculating the indemnity.[7]

In calculating the maximum, remuneration includes all forms of payment not just commission and is based on all customers, not only new or intensified customers.[8] If the sum under stages 1 and 2 is less than the maximum then this sum is awarded. If however, the sum exceeds the maximum, it is the maximum which is awarded. It is unusual for the maximum to be reached unless the agent has procured all or most of the customers

An example of stages 1 to 3 is set out:

Commission on new customers and/or intensified customers over last 12 months of agency			50,000 ECUs
Anticipated duration of benefits is 3 years with 20% migration rate			
Year 1	50,000–1,000	=	40,000 ECUs
Year 2	40,000–8,000	=	32,000 ECUs
Year 3	32,000–6,400	=	25,600 ECUs
Total lost commission			97,600 ECUs
Correction to present value say 10%. This figure being equal to the actual indemnity			87,840 ECUs

This figure might be adjusted
for reasons of equity (stage 2 above)

A final correction must be made should
the amount exceed the maximum
under Article 17(2)(b) of the Directive.

Article 17(2)(c) states that the grant of an indemnity shall not prevent the commercial agent from seeking damages. This provision governs the situation where the agent under national law is entitled to seek damages for breach of contract or failure to respect the notice period provided for under the Directive. Annex B attempts to identify these provisions.

It can thus be seen that the method of calculation of the indemnity is extremely precise and should lead to a predictable outcome. Principals should therefore be able to ascertain their risks in advance and to be able to enter into agency contracts with some degree of assurance. From the agent's perspective, clearer rights make it easier for the claim to be made and established.

---

[7] Case VII ZR 47/69 Bundesgerichtshof of 19.11.1970
[8] Case VII ZR 23/70 Bundesgerichtshof of 3.6.1971

2. The Compensation System

Under Article 17(3) of the Directive the agent is entitled to compensation for the damage he suffers as a result of the termination of his relations with his principal. Such damage is deemed to occur particularly when the termination takes place in circumstances:
—depriving the agent of the commission which proper performance of the agency contract would have procured him whilst providing the principal with substantial benefits linked to the agent's activities.
—and/or which have not enabled the agent to amortize the costs and expenses he had incurred for the performance of the agency contract on the principal's advice.
There is no maximum level of compensation.

The compensation system was based on French law, which dated from 1958 and whose aim was to compensate the agent for the loss he suffered as a result of the termination of the agency contract. As for the indemnity system in Germany, a body of case-law has developed in France concerning the right and level of compensation. Various judgments of the French courts have justified the payment of compensation on the ground that it represents the cost of purchasing the agency to the agent's successor or on the ground that it represents the time it takes for the agent to re-constitute the client base which he has been forcefully deprived of.

By judicial custom the level of compensation is fixed as the global sum of the last two years commission or the sum of 2 years commission calculated over the average of last three years of the agency contract which conforms with commercial practice. However, the courts retain a discretion to award a different level of compensation where the principal brings evidence that the agent's loss was in fact less, for example, because of the short duration of the contract or where, for example, the agent's loss is greater because of the agent's age or his length of service.

The indemnity is calculated on all remuneration, not just commission. It is based on the gross figure. No distinction is made between old and new customers and it includes special commission. There is no practice to reduce for professional costs. Finally, outstanding commissions must also be included in the calculation.

The indemnity represents that part of the market lost to the agent and his loss is fixed at that moment. Accordingly, future occurences are not taken into account, such as the principal ceasing to trade, the agent continuing to work with the same client or developments in the market place. Similarly, the agent is not required to mitigate his loss.

The Directive has brought about a greater interest in claiming damages for failure to respect the proper notice period. The amount awarded is the highest of the period not respected calculated on commission received for the last two years or the commission received during the identical period the previous year.

Further, more specific comments on the system in France can be found in Annex B.

POSITION IN MEMBER STATES

All Member States have implemented the Directive and a list of the laws is annexed to this Report as Annex A. With the exception of France, the UK and Ireland, Member States have incorporated the indemnity option into their national law. The UK has permitted the parties to choose the indemnity option, but if they fail to do so, the agent will be entitled to compensation. Ireland has failed to make any choice at all in its legislation and accordingly the Commission has opened Article 169 proceedings. The Commission has also opened infraction proceedings against Italy for failure to implement Article 17 of the Directive correctly. Further details can be found in Annex B concerning Irish and Italian law.

In most Member States there has yet to be any reported court decision, whilst in other Member States there are only a small number of cases. This is explained by the fact that the laws in most Member States are still very new and that these laws have only applied to all contracts in operation as from 1 January 1994. In addition, in France and Germany where there are cases, many agencies are not international in nature and the law follows long established traditions.

The second reason for the lack of reported cases is the tendency for the parties to settle cases before the court hearing. Agents are not always in the financial position to pursue their claims through the courts and therefore are forced to accept settlements. In addition, the uncertainty linked to court proceedings, invariably in a different jurisdiction deters agents from pursuing their claims through the courts.

The cases in Germany and France show a continuity with the existing jurisprudence in these countries. In Portugal, where the Directive represents a change to the previous situation the case-law shows an approach which is different to that of the German courts with an attempt by the judge to apply directly the principle of equity. In Italy, where there has only been one judgment under the new Article 1751 of the Civil Code, the Viterbo Magistrate Court has ruled, that having regard to the lack of criteria for calculation of the indemnity in Article 1751 of the Civil Code, it would apply the collective agreement. The collective agreement follows a system of calculation based on the duration of the agency and is not related to the number of new customers brought. Thus, it also takes a different approach to the German courts. However, this is a single judgment of the Italian courts and has yet to be confirmed. In Denmark, only three judgments have been reported. A fourth judgment is now subject to appeal. The reported cases reveal a tendency to take over and follow German jurisprudence.

Having regard to the relative lack of jurisprudence and the nature of the subject matter, the Commission in its preparation for this Report sought to ascertain the practical as well as the legal situation. An outline of the legal and practical position is set out in more detail in Annex B.

There are no statistics available in any of the Member States. The International Union of Commercial Agents and Brokers have now started to collect data. This is a helpful development, as IUCAB should be able to collect a good level of data through its member organisations in Member States and IUCAB has offered to present these statistics periodically to the Commission. The Portuguese authorities have also established a centralised method of collecting information from all courts on the nature and outcome of cases which involve EC law or the Lugano Convention, which of course, includes the Directive on Commercial Agents.

BUSINESS PRACTICE

The Commission sought to ascertain whether, as a result of the Directive and in particular the right to an indemnity or compensation, there had been any change in business practice. The Commission also wanted to establish whether, as a result of the different options, distortions in competition had arisen. The lack of statistics makes it more difficult to reach conclusions in this regard.

Overall, the Commission found that there had not been any change in business practice. There was some evidence that principals were moving to distributorship contracts in France, Germany, Luxembourg and Belgium. This can be partially explained by the fact that on lawful termination of distributorship contracts no indemnity or compensation is payable or a reduced level. In the UK, Ireland and Sweden it was reported that principals were now considering much more carefully whether agency contracts were the most appropriate business arrangements and were therefore taking a much more cautious approach. However, principals were not always actually moving away from agency contracts.

In the UK there appears to have been a specific reaction. First prior to the coming into force of the UK Regulations implementing the Directive, principals terminated their agency contracts and on the whole re-negotiated new contracts. There were, however, occasions where new agency contracts were not entered into or the agents were taken on as employees. This reflects the fundamental change brought about by the Directive to UK law and the fear of principals of the unknown. It is too soon to determine whether there will be a permanent shift away from agency contracts in the UK.

Under French law and practice, compensation awarded in the vast majority of cases amounts to 2 years commission which is twice the legal maximum provided for under the indemnity option. This clearly makes the appointment of an agent in France under French law a much more costly enterprise. This has led some principals seeking when appointing an agent in France to seek to apply a law other than French law or to avoid entering into agency contracts altogether. There is no evidence of any widespread problems or distortions in trade as regards those Member States who have opted for the indemnity system and those who have opted for the compensation option.

REACTIONS OF PRINCIPALS AND AGENTS

It can generally be said that agents have given a positive considered to have increased their rights. This would be the case in Austria, Denmark, Finland, Ireland, Luxembourg, Sweden and the UK. French agents continue to feel positively about the system of compensation in France and do not wish for change.

The reaction of principals has been mixed. To some extent, principals are bound to feel negative about change as they now have to grant greater rights to agents. For other principals it is not that they are against paying an indemnity on termination, but rather there is a degree of discontent in that the system lacks clarity. French principals appear to support the compensation system and have not raised any objections regarding it.

There is no tendency amongst either agents or principals in the Member States who have implemented the indemnity option to favour anything other than the indemnity system. In the UK, where the parties are able to opt in favour of payment of an indemnity, no clear preference emerges although most contracts do not contain an indemnity provision. Principals are still unclear about what the differences between the two systems are. There is a certain level of interest in the indemnity amongst some principals because of the maximum limit, but other principals prefer the compensation option as agents must prove actual loss.

A number of difficulties have arisen in relation to Article 17 of the Directive.

(1) Interpretation difficulties

Many commentators and lawyers have pointed to the imprecise and uncertain nature of Article 17, which causes difficulty ill trying to advise clients on the extent of an agent's rights on termination. This was reported in particular in Denmark, Ireland, Italy, Spain, Sweden and the UK.

(a) Indemnity

As regards the indemnity option, there has been a tendency in some Member States to seek reliance on the maximum figure whereas under the German system, which influenced the Directive, the maximum has no bearing on the actual method of calculation of the indemnity. It is merely used at the end of the process as a final adjuster. In some Member States attempts are made to try and establish an equitable amount taking into account various different factors, which again is not the approach taken by the German courts. Denmark and Austria appear to follow the German model but in the case of Austria, the maximum limit is often reached, whereas in Germany it is very rarely reached except when all the customers have been brought by the commercial agent.

In Italy, it appears, at the moment, that the previous system continues to apply even though a new law was introduced. This has been re-enforced in the ruling in the Pretura Viterbo case in which the court held that the provision of Article 1751 of the Italian Civil Code, which implements Article 17(2) of the Directive, was so uncertain as to the method of calculation of the indemnity it would apply the collective agreement. The method of calculation under the collective agreement does not correspond with the German model, but is based on the length of the contract, the level of commission and the percentages set out in the collective agreement.

It therefore appears there is a divergence of approaches. However, there is of course still only a very limited jurisprudence of the courts of Member States concerning Article 17 outside Germany.

(b) Compensation

As regards the compensation option, clearly this has not presented problems of interpretation in France where pre-existing jurisprudence has continued to be applied. However, as regards the UK which applies the compensation option in default of the choice of the parties, there is a fundamental difference in approach. At this stage, there is no UK case-law but the parties in practice are attempting to apply common law principles. These common law principles are directly opposed to the well-established method of calculation of compensation in France. For example, the English system will take account of future developments after termination of the contract and this results in the need to for the injured person to mitigate his loss. Whereas, under French law, events after the termination of the agency contract have no bearing on the compensation to be awarded. Under French Law, the standrd award is two years commission which represents the value of the purchase of an agency or the period it will take the agent to re-establish his client base. It is difficult to see how the UK courts will reach this figure. This, no doubt, derives from the previous legal position in the UK, that agency contracts could be terminated on notice without any payment being due. This naturally has had consequences for business practices. There was no real concept of goodwill attaching to an agency to which the agent had a right to a share in. It is not possible to predict how the UK courts will interpret the Directive, but it seems likely that they will have regard to existing common law principles.

The same difficulties are likely to arise in Ireland if Ireland opts for the compensation option.

(c) Consequences of uncertainty

The difficulties in interpretation have had an effect on the reactions of agents and principals to the Directive. For both it has entailed increased time being spent on negotiation since rights and levels of rights are not clearly established. This benefits neither party. It has also led to different amounts being awarded. Uncertainty and divergence also lead to a reluctance to create agencies and act as a barrier to principals to take on agents in other Member States. It is important that the Directive is uniformly interpreted and leads to predictable and clear results.

(2) Position of Agents

The Directive has led to an improvement in the position of agents vis-à-vis their principals. Nevertheless it appears that agents are not always able to enforce their rights to the full because they lack the resources to take court action. This is a problem of a general nature and not specific to the Directive Possible remedies lie outside the remit of this Report. However, it is the view of the Commission that clarification of the provisions of the Directive and methods of calculation will be of assistance to agents and make the enforcement of rights easier.

(3) Choice of Law

Finally, certain problems have been encountered with regard to choice of law clauses in contracts and attempts have been made to avoid the application of certain laws by choice of law clauses or jurisdiction clauses. The Directive does not lay down any rules concerning private international law. The parties are therefore free to choose the law which is to govern the agency contract, subject to the rules contained in the Rome Convention 1980 on the law applicable to contractual obligations. In the Commission's opinion Articles 17 and 18 of the Directive are mandatory rules and accordingly, the courts of the Member States can apply the law of the forum in accordance with the 1980 Rome Convention and thereby ensue the application of the Directive. The 1968 Brussels Convention on jurisdiction and enforcement of judgments in civil and commercial matters will also assist in ensuring, that in so far as Community cases are concerned and the agent is carrying on his activities in the

EC, that a court of a Member State will have jurisdiction.[9] Accordingly, there does not appear to be any need to amend the Directive in this regard.

CONCLUSION

The Commission notes that the indemnity option has been chosen by the vast majority of Member States and that this has received the support of agents and principals in those Member States. The Directive provides for a ceiling on the level of indemnity, but does not give precise guidance for its method of calculation. A clear and precise method of calculation would lead to greater legal certainty, which would be of advantage to both parties. As regards the compensation option, which has been maintained by France, it does not appear to have caused problems for agents and principals in France. The level of compensation in France is generally much higher than the level of indemnity. The implementation in the UK whereby the parties have the choice of the system has led to uncertainty, particularly as neither of the two options is known to the British legal system.

At this stage, there is very little jurisprudence concerning the Directive. Having regard to the information received, it appears that there is a need for clarification of Article 17. Any more further far-reaching conclusions are premature. The Commission considers that this Report, which gives detailed information, particularly concerning the method of calculation of the indemnity as it is carried out in Germany, provides further clarification of Article 17 of the Directive and secondly, by so-doing should facilitate a more uniform interpretation of Article 17 of the Directive.

---

[9] *Arcado Sprl v Haviland SA* Case No 9/87 [1988] ECR 1539 the court held that right to compensation was contractual in nature and therefore Article 5(1) of the 1968 Brussels Convention applied thus opening the possibility of an additional basis of jurisdiction

ANNEX A

LIST OF MEMBER STATES LAWS IMPLEMENTING THE DIRECTIVE
ON COMMERCIAL AGENTS (86/653/EEC)

Expiry of implementation period: 31.12.89
(United Kingdom and Ireland: 31.12.93)
(Italy, concerning article 17: 31.12.92)

1. *Belgium*	Law of 13.4.1995 published in Moniteur Belge of 2.6.1995, pg. 15621 entry into force: 12.6.1995
2. Denmark	Law no 272 of 2.5.90 publication: Lovtidende A. 1990 p. 922 entry into force: 4.5.90 application to contracts in operation: 1.1.92
3. *Germany*	Law of 23.10.89 publication: Bundesgesetzblatt 1989 I 1910 entry into force: 1.1.90 application to contracts in operation: 1. 1.94
4. *Greece*	Presidential Decree no 219 of 18.5.1991 publication: OJ of the Greek government no 81 of 30.5.1991 and no 136 of 11.9.1991 as amended by Decrees no 249/93, 88/94 and 312/95. entry into force: 30.5.1991 application to contracts in operation: 1.1.94
5. *Spain*	Law 12/1992 of 27.5.1992 publication: BOE no 129 of 29.5.1992 entry into force: 19.6.1992 application to contracts in operation: 1.1.94
6. *France*	Law no 91–593 of 25.6.1991 publication: OJ of the French Republic 17.6.1991 p. 8271 entry into force: 28.6.1992 Decree 92–506 of 10.6.1992 Publication: OJ of the French Republic 12.6.1992 p. 7720 entry into force: 1.1.1994 application to contracts in operation: 1.1.94
7. *Ireland*	Statutory Instrument: SI No 33 of 1994 of 21.2.1994 Entry into force: 1.1.1994 application to contracts in operation: 1.1.94

8. Italy   Legislative Decree no 303 of 10.9.1991
                    publication: Gazetta ufficiale no 57 of
                    20.9.1991.
                    entry into force: 1.1.1993
                    application to contracts in operation: 1.1.94

9. Luxembourg   Law of 3 June 1994
                    publication: Memorial A-No 58 of 6.7.1994, p. 1088
                    application to contracts in operation: 1.1.94

10. Netherlands Law of 5.7.89
                    publication: Staatsblad 1989 no 312
                    entry into force: 1.11.89
                    application to contracts in operation: 1.1.94
                    Re-enacted by Law no 374 of 1993 as Articles 400–445 of Title 7 of the
                    Burgerlijk Wetboek

11. Austria   Federal Act of 11.2.1993
                    published in Federal Gazette 88
                    entry into force: 1.3.1993
                    application to contracts in operation: 1.1.1994

12. Portugal   Decree no 178/86 of 3.7.86
                    publication: Diário da República, I série, 1986, p. 1575
                    entry into force: 2.8.86
                    application to contracts in operation: 2.8.86
                    amended by law No 118/93 of 13.4.93 published Diario da
                    República No 86 p.1818 of 13.4.93
                    application to contracts in operation: 1.1 94

13. Finland   Law no 417 of 8.5.1992
                    published in Gesetzblatt of 14.5.1992
                    entry into force: 1.11.1992
                    application to contracts in force: 1.1.1994

14. Sweden   Law no 351 of 2.5.1991
                    entry into force: 1.1.1992
                    application to contracts in force: 1.1.1994.

15. UK   Statutory Instrument SI 1993 no 3053 of 7.12.93
                    and SI 1993 no 3173 of 16.12.1993
                    entry into force: 1.1.94
                    application to contracts in operation: 1.1.1 994
                    Northern Ireland:
                    Statutory Rules of Northern Ireland 1993 no 483 of 17.12.1993
                    entry into force: 13.1.1994
                    application to contracts in operation: 13.1.1994

ANNEX B

BELGIUM

The law on Commercial Agent Contract only came into force on 12 June 1995. Accordingly, there are no cases decided by the courts on the new law.

Article 20 of the law introduced the right to a goodwill indemnity. Prior to the new law, the right to a goodwill indemnity had been rejected by the main decisions of the Belgian courts as goodwill was considered to attach to the principal more than to the agent. Accordingly, the new law has brought about an important change to the law.

The law contains no guidance as to how the indemnity is to be calculated, but it is argued by most commentators that is for judge to determine the amount taking into account various factors such as level of commission in last years of the contract, level of development of customers, extent to which principal will continue to derive benefits, duration of contractual relations, level of involvement of the principal, existence of a pension financed by the principal or whether the agent's contract with the principal is his sole agency. One author has specifically drawn on the German method of calculation.

Practising Belgian lawyers considered that regard would be had to the law on commercial representatives and to the German experience. Under the Law on Commercial Representatives of 3 July 1978, however, the indemnity is calculated on the basis of 3 months wages for a commercial representative who has acted for the same principal for a period of one to five years. This period is increased by one month for each further five years.

Under Article 18(3) of the Belgian law, it is possible to claim damages for lack of notice, which amounts to lost commission in accordance with method of calculation set out in this Article.

Finally, under Article 21 of the Belgian law, an agent who has a right to an indemnity can claim in addition damages for the harm actually suffered. It is not clear in what circumstances is this payable and whether entitlement to an indemnity gives automatically a right to seek damages. In the view of the Commission this latter interpretation would be contrary to Article 17(1) of the Directive as the effect of such an interpretation would be that the two options would apply cumulatively.

DENMARK

With the implementation of the Directive in Denmark and the introduction of the right to an indemnity under Section 25 of Law No 272 of 2 May 1990, a new right was granted which had not existed under the previous law.

To date, only three judgments have been reported.[10] In *Lope Handel* the principal was ordered to pay losses for the failure to respect the contractual period of notice and to pay an indemnity of 1 years commission on the new customers acquired for the principal by the

---

[10] *Lope Handel v GE Lighting* (Commercial Court of Copenhagen of 25.9.1995); *S&L Eskimo* (High Court, Western Division of 14.11.1995); *Cramer v B&B* (Commercial Court of Copenhagen of 15.12.1995)

agent. It was proved that the new customers were lost one year after termination of the agency contract. In *S&L*, the principal was ordered to pay an indemnity equivalent to the maximum. It was proved that practically all the customers were brought by the agent. In *Cramer*, the court found that a substantial number of customers were once-only customers with whom the principal could expect no further business. The principal was ordered to pay an indemnity amounting to DKK 150,000. For comparison the maximum would have been 400,000.

In practice it appears that agents seek the maximum amount and principals try to argue the figure down. At present, although there is no set picture, there is no tendency to pay the maximum figure. Calculations appear to follow the German model.

As for other Member States, no useful statistics are available.

Section 6 of the law implements Article 17(2)(c) of the Directive and provides that if an agent or principal is in breach of his obligations to the other, the other is entitled to compensation for any damage caused thereby.

GERMANY

Article 89b of the Handelsgesetzbuch sets out the agents right to an indemnity. The method of calculation is set out in the Report itself.

In practice it appears that there has been no change in Germany as to the method of calculation of the indemnity following the implementation of the Directive in Germany as the indemnity provision of the Directive did not require change to German law. The change noted by industry was in relation to contracts with other EU countries, which prior to the Directive did not provide for an indemnity.

GREECE

The implementation of Article 17 of the Directive by Article 9 of Presidential Decree 219 of 18 May 1991 did not conform with the Directive, in particular, in that it did not implement the second indent of Article 17(2)(a) which requires that the indemnity be equitable. Greece has following correspondence with the Commission introduced a new law in 1995 which implements Articles 17(2)(a).

Article 9(1)(c) states that the right to seek an indemnity does not prevent an agent from seeking damages under the Civil Code. Damages are payable and awarded according to whether the contract was fixed term or of indefinite duration.

An agent may also seek damages for lack of proper notice.

SPAIN

Article 28 of law No 12/1992 of 27 June 1995 provides for the payment of an indemnity Article 29 of the law provides for the award of damages if the principal unilaterally breaks an agency contract which is for an indefinite period. The Directive has filled a legal gap in Spanish law in that prior to the law implementing the Directive there was no specific law covering commercial agents or commercial agency contracts. However, Article 29 is not restricted merely to breach of contract and by virtue of this Spain has seemingly implemented both options contained in Article 17 of the Directive unless the Court interprets the scope of Article 29 narrowly.

Owing to the recent coming into force of the law there is a lack of jurisprudence in this area. The case-law prior to the new law may be of relevance for the future since some of the principles may act as guidance for future judgment by the Spanish courts.

Under the old law, it was also possible to claim both damages and a goodwill indemnity and agents used to cumulate both claims. The difference between both remedies was sometimes blurred in practice. The Supreme Court has repeatedly recognised the possibility of obtaining an indemnity for goodwill. The judge is given a wide discretion to fix the level of the indemnity and in general it is calculated depending on the agent's earnings.[11] As regards damages, the courts considered a number of different matters in arriving at the award, including the level of the last commission, the nature of the activity, loss of prestige and whether the contract was exclusive or not.[12]

Finally, damages are payable for failure to respect the correct notice period which is the amount of commission the agent would have received if the notice period had been respected.[13]

However, despite these judgments it is still difficult to reach general conclusions, particularly as in Spain the level of indemnity is fixed after the hearing and the decision is not published.

FRANCE

Unlike for many other Member States, the Directive has not brought about radical change to the pre-existing law in France. Under Article 12 of Law No 91/593 of 25 June 1991, French law continues to give a right to compensation on termination of the agency contract. The change brought about relates to the circumstances in which compensation is payable and not in its calculation. The right to compensation now exists for the non-renewal of the contract and termination by the agent for reasons of old age, sickness or infirmity and on death.

Compensation is calculated as before according to the jurisprudence as neither the old law or the present law sets out the method of calculation. In the vast majority of cases it amounts to two years gross commission which is calculated from the agent's average remuneration over the preceding three years or the global sum of the last two years commission. This sum has become the customary award and is confirmed with court decisions applying the new law.[14]

The indemnity is calculated on all remuneration, not just commission. It is based on the gross figure. No distinction is made between old and new customers and it includes special commission. There is no practice to reduce for professional costs. Finally, outstanding commissions must also be included in the calculation.

[11] Supreme Court judgments of 22 March 1988 and 19 September 1989

[12] Judgment of Court of Appeal of Lugo of 4.6.1994; Court of Appeal Valence of 14.7.1993 and Court of Appeal Barcelona of 30.1.1995

[13] Judgment of Supreme Court of 19.9.1989

[14] See for example: Court of Appeal Toulouse 20.12.1994 Les Annonces de la Seine, No 39 1.6.1995 p 28; Court of Appeal Dijon, 16.6.1994 Les Annonces de la Seine, No 39, p 26; Court of Appeal Paris, 17.1.1995, Les Annonces de la Seine 1.6.1995; No 39. p 8.

The indemnity represents that part of the market lost to the agent and his loss is fixed at that moment. Accordingly, future occurrences are not taken into account, such as the principal ceasing to trade, the agent continuing to work with the same clients or developments in the market place. Similarly, the agent is not required to mitigate his loss.

The French courts do not order the payment of two years gross commission as compensation where it can be shown that the loss suffered by the agent is less, for example, because of the short duration of the contract. Similarly, the level may be increased, where, for example, an agent's loss is greater because of his age or length of the agency contract.

The Directive has brought about a greater interest in claiming damages for failure to respect the proper notice period. The amount taken is the highest of the period not respected calculated on commission received for the last two years or the commission received during the identical period the previous year.

IRELAND

Ireland has not implemented this provision and therefore agents do not have either a right to compensation or an indemnity. Under the common law, an agent can seek damages for breach of contract. In a fixed term contract, this will allow the agent to claim the commission he would have received until the end of the contract, subject to the agent's duty to mitigate his loss. However, this is not sufficient for the purposes of implementing the Directive. In cases of contracts of indefinite period the claim is usually for remuneration during the notice period to be respected. In addition, in both cases, he may claim for the economic loss suffered as a result of the breach of contract.

To date there are no reported cases.

ITALY

Italy amended Article 1751 of the Civil Code by Article 4 of legislative Decree No 303 of 10 September 1991 to introduce the indemnity system set out in the Directive. However, in the view of the Commission the implementation by Italy is incorrect in that Italy has treated the two indents in Article 17(2)(a) of the Directive as alternative conditions whereas they are in fact cumulative. Accordingly the Commission has opened infraction proceedings.

It appears that the old system of collective agreements continues to apply. The Enasarco agreement of 30.10.1992 was agreed to by both principals and organisations representing agents. By doing so they have de facto re-introduced the criteria which were applicable under the previous text of Article 1751.

In its judgment of 1 December 1994, the Viterbo Magistrate Court applied the collective agreement. The court held that Article 1751 of the Civil Code could not be applied in practice as it does not fix any criteria for calculating the indemnity except the maximum. Accordingly, the court considered it appropriate to apply the collective agreement. The Court also stated that the circumstances in Article 1751 were not intended for calculating the amount of indemnity, but for determining whether an indemnity was justified if at least one of the circumstances applied. Further, the court considered that wisely the social partners, in order to avoid practically insoluble problems, had replaced the old collective agreement thereby enabling Article 1751 of the Civil Code to be applied in practice. It is not clear at this stage whether this judgment will be followed.

The system of the collective agreement is based on level of commissions and duration of the agency contract and the set percentages laid down in the agreement.

Under the collective agreement, the agent in most cases receives an amount which is much less than the maximum envisaged under the Directive.

LUXEMBOURG

Luxembourg's law implementing the Directive of 3 June 1994 applies to all contracts existing before 1 January 1994 as well as to contracts entered into force after that date. Article 19 provides for an indemnity to be paid on termination. The new law introduced a right which did not exist under the pre-existing law. Those consulted thought it was too soon to develop a theory about how the law would be interpreted.

Article 23(1) sets out the right to damages for unjustified failure to give due notice and Article 23(2) provides for damages to be paid for a serious breach of contract. Article 24 states that this amounts to a sum equal to the remuneration that would have been received in the period between the breach and the normal end of the contract. To calculate this sum regard is to be had to the previous level of commissions and to other relevant matters. This sum can be reduced if the judge considers it too high in the circumstances of the case.

THE NETHERLANDS

Article 7:442 of the Civil Code provides for an indemnity to be paid on termination of the agency contract. Under Article 7:439 damages are payable for unjustified failure to respect the correct notice period and Articles 7:440 and 7:441 provide for damages to be paid for breach of contract. This covers the period from actual termination to the date on which the agency would have been terminated had proper notice been given. This amount is the amount of remuneration which would have been received and is based on the commission received prior to termination and other relevant circumstances. The judge can reduce the amount if he considers that it is too high having regard to the facts of the particular case. Under Article 7:441.3, the party can seek in place of the sum under Article 7:441.1 and 2., compensation for the actual damage suffered and he bears the burden of proving his loss.

There is not any reported case to date concerning the new law and nor are there any statistics.

AUSTRIA

The Austrian law of 11 February 1993 came into force on 1 March 1993. Under Article 24, the agent has a right to an indemnity. To date there are no reported cases concerning the amount of indemnity or damages payable on termination of an agency contract under the 1993 law. The Directive has lead to a change in the previous law and in particular to a doubling of the maximum limit. Therefore, previous case-law is not useful guidance. Under the old law, there was a digressive reduction in the upper limit of compensation of aggregate amount of one year's commission calculated as a yearly average over the previous three years according to the length of the relationship.

In practice, it appears that commercial agents calculate the indemnity on the basis of the average income of the last five years taking into account the fluctuation of customers by computing a digression of income on the basis of 5 years. In most cases, this exceeds the upper limit set by law. On this basis, the parties negotiate in order to find a reasonable settlement. The method of calculation is based on German experiences.

It was considered too soon to make any judgment about the average level of indemnity paid. A claim for damages or performance of the contract can be made if a party terminates the contract prematurely without just cause under Article 23. Article 23 also applies to a breach of Article 21 which is concerned with notice periods. Any other claims for damages are dealt with in accordance with the provisions of the General Civil Code and the Commercial Code.

PORTUGAL

Portugal adopted its law in 1986 which followed to a large extent the proposal for the Directive and included at Article 33 the right to an indemnity. The law came into force on 2 August 1986. It has been amended by Articles 33 and 34 of Decree No. 118/93 to bring Portugese law in conformity with Article 17 of the Directive.

In Portugal there have been a number of court judgements.[15] The courts have calculated the level of indemnity taking into account the importance of new clients, the increased development of existing customers, the advantages to the principal after the termination of the contract and the loss of commission by the agent. The courts consider the indemnity as a measure of compensation for the agent for the benefits to the principal existing at the end of the contract with the clients developed by the agent.

Under Article 32 of the law and under Articles 562–572 of the Civil Code, there is also a right to be indemnified for the damages suffered for breach of contract. Article 29 specifically provides for damages for failure to respect the notice period or alternatively to damages for lack of due notice. The agent can seek, as an alternative to damages, a sum calculated on the basis of the average monthly remuneration over the previous year multiplied by the time remaining if the contract had continued to run. If the contract is of less than one years duration then the whole contract period is to be used.

FINLAND

Under section 28 of Act No 417 of 8 May 1992, the right to indemnity on termination of an agency contract was introduced. The Directive has brought about a change in the pre-

---

[15] Accórdão da Relação de Coimbra of 14.12.1993 Court of Appeal in Colectãnea de Jurisprudéncia, Year XVIII, 1993, Volume V, P 46; Accórdão do Supremo Tribunal de Justiça of 4.5.1993 in colectãnea de Jurisprudéncia—Accordrãos do Supremo Tribunal de Justiça, Year I, Volume II, 1993, p 78 and also same court, judgment of 27.10.1994 in Year II, Volume III, 1994, p 101; Acórdão da Relação do Porto of 18.10.1994 in Colectãnea de Jurisprudência, Year XIX, Volume IV, 1994, p 212.

existing law. The law came into force on 1 November 1992 and there has been no court decision to date.

In practice, it appears that agents seek the maximum amount and the principal makes a counter-offer. The negotiations result in an amount which is not based on any specific calculation, rather it is the outcome of bargaining. Generally, the indemnity is in the region of 3–6 months average commission. It was felt by the agents federation that the amount of indemnity period was slightly higher under the new law than under the old law, but no statistics are available to support this.

Under Section 9 of the law, the right to damages for harm caused by a violation of the agency contract is laid down or for when a party has neglected one of his obligations. Further, Sections 26 and 27 of the Act provide for damages where notice periods are not respected

SWEDEN

Article 28 of Law No 351 of 2 May 1991 introduced a right to receive an indemnity which did not exist under the previous law, which only sought to ensure that an agent received commission on orders concluded after the withdrawal of the agents authority provided that the orders were brought about through the acts of the agent during the currency of the agreement.

As for other Member States, there has yet to be any court decision. In practice agents seek the maximum amount permitted under the law and the parties negotiate on this basis to reach an equitable sum. In doing so, the parties take into account, inter alia, the duration of the contract, the agent's promotional activities, the number of new customers, orders given after termination, the possibility of a new contract for the agent and the costs incurred and investments made by the agent.

There are no statistics but the Swedish authorities estimated that awards were typically between 6 months and 1 year commission calculated as an average over the last years of the contract. This would represent an increase in the amount of compensation.

Article 34 of the law provides for damages for breach of contract.

UNITED KINGDOM

The UK has a opted its own particular system in that under Regulation 17 of Statutory Instrument No 3053 of 1993 the parties may choose whether an agent will have the right to an indemnity or compensation.[16] It is only in default of a contractual provision that the law requires compensation to be paid. This method of implementation has of itself produced uncertainty, particularly since neither of the two options are familiar to the UK legal systems.

The law has only recently come into force in the UK and has caused a certain amount of confusion as parties and lawyers attempt to apply concepts with which they are unfamiliar and which are a certain degree alien to UK traditions. Various different approaches have developed.

---

[16] Regulation 17 of SI No 483 of 1993 for Northern Ireland

In relation to compensation, lawyers try to apply traditional common law principles which does not work well since under the common law, termination of a contract in accordance with its terms or at the natural end of a fixed term contract does not give rise to a damages claim. Under the common law, the court tries to put the agent in the position he would have been in if the contract had been properly performed, but the injured party is expected to mitigate his loss and the court will have regard to future events. Typically for a fixed term contract, this would give the agent the right to claim commission for the duration of the contract. In the case of a contract for an indefinite period, the agent could seek damages for the notice period amounting to the remuneration he would have received in this period. The agent could also seek compensation for costs incurred in pursuance of the agency. Lawyers therefore have difficulties in reaching a view as to the level of compensation where the agent has died, become ill or retired. Typical compensation payments are between 3–6 months with some payments of 15 months depending on the level of service.

Some lawyers have therefore tried to apply by analogy the law relating to unfair dismissal or redundancy which is determined by age, length of service and the weekly wage.

As regards the indemnity provision, agents claim the maximum amount and then through negotiations a smaller sum is agreed. Typical payments appear to be between 3–6 months commission based on what would have been earned rather than the average of the last 5 years.

Most contracts do not contain a provision providing for an indemnity, but this does not necessarily reflect a preference for the compensation option rather than the indemnity option.

To date, there have been no cases and parties are reluctant to litigate since lawyers are unconfident in advising what their clients' rights are and consequently what the courts will award. However, there are likely to be cases in the near future.

Index